Grade **5**

FINISH LINE
New York
ELA
THIRD EDITION

Continental

CREDITS

Illustrations: Pages 8, 13, 15, 20, 27, 28, 33, 43, 56, 70, 73, 89, 130, 131, 192, 210, 212, 215, 217, 220, 233: Laurie Conley; Page 10, 39, 60, 154: Margaret Lindmark; Page 24: Denny Bond; Page 41: Sally Springer; Page 53: James McConnell; Page 82: Matt LeBarre; Page 267: Estella Hickman; Page 271: Joe Veno

Photos: Pages 22, 89: © Royalty-Free/Corbis; Page 79: www.istockphoto.com/Soubrette; Page 84: www.istockphoto.com/PattieS; Page 93: Image used under Creative Commons from Waugsberg; Page 101: InterNetwork Media, Inc.; Page 103: *Independence Rock,* Image used under Creative Commons from Thunderbrand, *graffiti,* Image used under Creative Commons from Matthew Trump; Page 106: www.istockphoto.com/Escaflowne; Page 109: Library of Congress, Prints and Photographs Division, LC-DIG-ggbain-06861; Page 111: www.photos.com; Page 113: Image used under Creative Commons from Julien Harneis; Page 181: Image used under Creative Commons from Beyond My Ken; Page 184: Library of Congress, Prints and Photographs Division, LC-USZ62-45683; Page 185: Winsor McCay; Page 200: United States coin images from the United States Mint; Page 203: www.istockphoto.com/the broker; Page 241: Image used under Creative Commons from Kmusser; Page 259: Library of Congress, Prints and Photographs Division, LC-B201-5202-13; Page 263: Image used under Creative Commons from Swampyank; Page 269: www.istockphoto.com/rainbow-7; Page 272: U.S. Fish and Wildlife Service, Bob Hines; Page 280: Image used under Creative Commons from Ranveig; Page 291: Tony Weller

ISBN 978-0-8454-7919-3

Copyright © 2015 The Continental Press, Inc.

TABLE OF CONTENTS

About Finish Line New York ELA

Finish Line New York ELA, Third Edition will give you practice in the reading and writing skills necessary to be an effective communicator in the 21st century. It will also help you to prepare for tests that assess your skills and knowledge.

The material in this book is written to the Common Core Learning Standards (CCLS) developed by your state. The book is divided into units of related lessons. The reading passages in a unit center around a common theme related to content taught at the grade level. Each reading lesson concentrates on one main standard and is broken into four parts:

 ## Introduction

The Introduction of each lesson reviews the standard you are going to study and explains what it is and how you use it. You may work with example text, pictures, or graphic organizers to help you better understand the skill.

 ## Focused Instruction

The Focused Instruction guides you through reading a passage. In this section, you will work with a partner, in small groups, or as a class to practice the skill. You will read a story, poem, play, or nonfiction piece and work through a series of questions to help you organize your thoughts. There are hints and reminders along the sides of the pages to help you remember what you have learned.

 ## Guided Practice

The third part is Guided Practice, where you will work alone to answer questions. The format of these items is similar to many test questions—multiple choice and short answer. Again, there will be hints and reminders to help you answer the questions.

4 Independent Practice

Finally, you will complete the Independent Practice by yourself. These questions will be a variety of types—one- and two-part multiple choice, short response, and extended response or essay. The Independent Practice does not have hints or reminders. You must use everything you learned in the first three parts to complete this section.

At the end of each unit is a unit review. You will review all the skills you worked on in that unit to answer questions. You will see different item types, just like the Independent Practice section. There will not be any hints or reminders.

A glossary of key terms from the book appears at the end of the book for reference.

Now you are ready to begin. Good Luck!

Key Ideas and Details in Literary Text

When your friend asks you what a story is about, what do you say? You may not know it, but when you describe the events of a story, you are summarizing it! In this unit, you will practice writing summaries of stories and poems. You will also think about the topic and tone as you read, looking for clues and key details to help you. When you make inferences, or logical guesses, and when you compare and contrast, you also look for key details to help you.

LESSON 1 Supporting Inferences in Literary Text will help you make inferences to discover ideas and details that the author does not state directly. You will analyze details and use your knowledge to make these inferences.

LESSON 2 Determining the Theme of a Poem is about identifying tone and topic in a poem to help you find the theme. You will look closely at the language in the poem to see what it is about and what the poet's attitude is.

LESSON 3 Determining the Theme of a Story or Play focuses on finding the theme in stories and plays. You will make inferences and analyze details to help you find the theme.

LESSON 4 Summarizing a Literary Text tells how to write summaries of stories and poems that give the main points without telling all the details. Writing summaries will help you better understand the stories and poems that you read.

LESSON 5 Comparing and Contrasting Characters looks closely at how characters are the same and different in the stories, poems, and plays that you read. You will look closely at details about characters' actions and use Venn diagrams to help you compare and contrast characters.

LESSON 6 Comparing and Contrasting Settings examines where and when the events take place in a story, play, or poem. You will look for clues that tell you about the setting. You will think about how the setting can change over time in the story and compare and contrast different settings.

CCLS RL.5.1: Quote accurately from a text when explaining what the text says explicitly and when drawing inferences from the text.

Supporting Inferences in Literary Text

 **Introduction**

THEME: ≫ Memorable Moments

Authors don't always tell you everything about the characters, setting, plot, or theme of a story. Instead, you must sometimes make an **inference,** or an educated guess, about ideas that are not stated directly. You make an inference by combining details in the text with what you already know.

Look at the illustration. Then look at the details in the chart. What inference can you make based on these details?

Details from the Illustration	What You Already Know	Inference
Girl is wearing flip flops and carrying a beach ball and tote with a towel in it. She is going to a car. The girls in the car are excited to see her.	People take a beach ball and towel with them when they are going to a beach or swimming pool.	

Making inferences when you read helps you understand ideas that the author doesn't state directly. Instead, authors use details about characters, including what they say and do, to convey meaning. They also use details about setting and plot. As a reader, your job is to note those details, and then combine them with what you already know to make an inference.

Read the first part of the poem. Then answer the questions.

Casey at the Bat
by Ernest Lawrence Thayer

The outlook wasn't brilliant for the Mudville nine that day:
The score stood four to two, with but one inning more to play.
And so when Cooney died at first, and Burrows did the same,
A sickly silence fell upon the patrons of the game.

5   A straggling few got up to go in deep despair. The rest
Clung to that hope which springs eternal in the human breast:
They thought, if only Casey could but get a whack at that—
We'd put up even money, now, with Casey at the bat.

But Flynn preceded Casey, as did also Jimmy Blake,
10 And the former was a lulu and the latter was a cake;
So upon that stricken multitude grim melancholy[1] sat,
For there seemed but little chance of Casey's getting to the bat.

_____

[1]**melancholy:** feeling of depression

Think About It

What can you infer about Casey's skill as a batter? The question asks you to make a logical guess about Casey's batting skills.

What are the Mudville nine? _____

How well is the Mudville nine doing in the game? The Mudville nine _____

_____.

What does the crowd think about Casey as a batter? The crowd thinks _____

_____.

What can you infer about Casey? I can infer that Casey is a _____

batter because _____.

Which lines from the poem support your inference? _____

_____

_____

Continue reading the poem. Then answer the question.

But Flynn let drive a single, to the wonderment of all,
And Blake, the much despised, tore the cover off the ball;
15 And when the dust had lifted, and they saw what had occurred,
There was Jimmy safe at second and Flynn a-hugging third.

Then from 5,000 throats and more there rose a lusty yell;
It rumbled on the mountaintops; it rattled in the dell;
It struck upon the hillside and recoiled upon the flat,
20 For Casey, mighty Casey, was advancing to the bat.

There was ease in Casey's manner as he stepped into his place;
There was pride in Casey's bearing and a smile on Casey's face.
And when, responding to the cheers, he lightly doffed his hat,
No stranger in the crowd could doubt 'twas Casey at the bat.

25 Ten thousand eyes were on him as he rubbed his hands with dirt;
Five thousand tongues applauded when he wiped them on his shirt.
Then while the writhing pitcher ground the ball into his hip,
Defiance gleamed in Casey's eye, a sneer curled Casey's lip.

And now the leather-covered sphere came hurtling through the air,
30 And Casey stood a-watching it in haughty grandeur there.
Close by the sturdy batsman the ball unheeded sped—
"That ain't my style," said Casey. "Strike one," the umpire said.

From the benches, black with people, there went up a muffled roar,
Like the beating of the storm-waves on a stern and distant shore.
35 "Kill him! Kill the umpire!" shouted someone in the stand;
And it's likely they'd a-killed him had not Casey raised his hand.

A CLOSER LOOK

What happens when Casey comes to bat? Underline words in the last stanza that tell what happens in the game.

With a smile of Christian charity great Casey's visage² shone;
He stilled the rising tumult; he bade the game go on.
He signaled to the pitcher, and once more the spheroid flew;
40 But Casey still ignored it, and the umpire said, "Strike two."

"Fraud!" cried the maddened thousands, and echo answered fraud;
But one scornful look from Casey and the audience was awed.
They saw his face grow stern and cold, they saw his muscles strain,
And they knew that Casey wouldn't let that ball go by again.

45 The sneer is gone from Casey's lip; his teeth are clenched in hate;
He pounds with cruel violence his bat upon the plate.
And now the pitcher holds the ball, and now he lets it go,
And now the air is shattered by the force of Casey's blow.

Oh, somewhere in this favored land the sun is shining bright;
50 The band is playing somewhere, and somewhere hearts are light;
And somewhere men are laughing, and somewhere children shout;
But there is no joy in Mudville—mighty Casey has struck out.

_____

²**visage:** face

Think about the last stanza. Why might there be no joy in Mudville that night?

What inference can you make about the baseball game?

A   The Mudville team played a great game.

B   The crowd did not want Casey to come to bat.

C   The Mudville team lost the baseball game.

D   The opposing team did not play fairly.

DISCUSS IT

Think about the crowd's reaction to Casey and Casey's behavior on the pitch. What inference can you make about Casey's status as a batter on the team? Turn to another student and talk about the crowd's feelings for Casey.

Read the passage. Then answer the questions.

One for the Team

A CLOSER LOOK

How is Aisha feeling before the game starts? Underline words that show how she feels.

How does Aisha feel when she sees her cousin Jasmine? Underline words that show Aisha's feelings when she sees Jasmine.

1   Aisha's heart raced as she flew into the gym and dropped her gym bag on the floor. It all came down to this day, this game—the regional playoffs. As point guard, Aisha ran the offense. She was not the best scorer, but she was fast and could run the team's plays smoothly and with precision.

2   Aisha bent down and reached into her bag for her water bottle.

3   "Aisha!" a voice screeched.

4   Aisha looked up to see her cousin Jasmine, point guard for the opposing team. Aisha's stomach clenched.

5   "Hey, Jasmine, how's it going?" Aisha asked quietly.

6   "Awesome! I'm psyched for this game," Jasmine said, pulling her left foot up behind her to stretch. "I've learned some stretches that keep me from getting leg cramps while I'm playing."

7   Aisha watched her cousin demonstrate a few more stretches. Then she shifted her weight from one foot to the other and checked her watch. "Yeah, we're pretty psyched for this game, too," she said in a louder voice than she had meant to use. "Coach drew up an awesome game plan that really uses everyone's skills."

8   But Jasmine had her back to Aisha as she walked off toward her team. "That's great, Aisha" Jasmine said over her shoulder. "Oh, and good luck today!"

9   Minutes later, ten players stood facing each other in the middle of the court as the buzzer sounded. Jasmine's team won the tip-off, and Jasmine took the ball down the court.

10   Aisha's heart plunged—she saw that the opposing team's center was wide open near the hoop. But before she could block what she thought would certainly be a straight pass for a perfect shot, Jasmine tried for a three-pointer. Aisha easily blocked the shot.

11   Now in control of the ball, Aisha dribbled down the court and waited for the offense to get set. They'd done it a million times in practice—everyone knew exactly where they were supposed to be, and they moved smoothly and quickly. Aisha waited for her center to get into position and then she passed. The center made an easy layup. The crowd whooped, and Aisha's stomach began to relax, but just a little.

12 Jasmine, in possession of the ball after Aisha scored, dribbled down the court. Her center moved back and forth, trying to signal that she was open. Aisha's defense got into position. But once again behind the three-point line, Jasmine hurled the ball toward the basket. The ball bounced hard off the backboard, and Aisha's teammate made an easy rebound and passed the ball to Aisha.

13 Again and again, the same scene played out. Aisha took the ball down the court, and unless she had a straight shot, she passed to an open player who took a shot or made a layup. And again and again, Jasmine opted for a difficult shot, rarely passing to another player.

14 Then the final buzzer sounded. Aisha's teammates were ecstatic—the players on the court high fived each other and were immediately joined by the players on the bench. *This is what it's all about,* Aisha thought. But then she looked over at Jasmine, who was sitting on the bench, her head in her hands. Aisha went over to her cousin.

15 "Hey, Jasmine, great game you played," she said, patting her cousin on the back.

16 Jasmine looked up and smiled, "Nah, Aisha, I didn't play so well. But *you* did. You guys really have a lot of chemistry on the court," she said. "Nice work out there," Jasmine added as she picked up her gym bag, smiled, and left the gym.

How do people usually behave when they are nervous? What details about Aisha's actions help you know how she is feeling?

1 Which sentence from the passage *most* supports the inference that Aisha is nervous about the game?

A "Then she shifted her weight from one foot to the other and checked her watch."

B "Now in control of the ball, Aisha dribbled down the court and waited for the offense to get set."

C *"This is what it's all about,* Aisha thought."

D "Aisha bent down and reached into her bag for her water bottle."

When your stomach clenches, how are you usually feeling?

2 The author writes that Aisha's "stomach clenched" when she saw her cousin Jasmine. What is the *most* logical inference based on this detail from the text?

A Aisha feels sick and may not be well enough to play basketball.

B Aisha knows that Jasmine is not a good player and feels sorry for her.

C Aisha gets annoyed by Jasmine and is anticipating Jasmine's boasts.

D Aisha loves her cousin Jasmine and is excited to play against her.

Which sentences show teamwork? Which sentences show a lack of teamwork?

3 List two details from the story that support the inference that Aisha's team won because they played well together.

_____

_____

_____

_____

_____

_____

Read the passage. Then answer the questions.

excerpt from A Little Princess

by Frances Hodgson Burnett

1   "Here we are, Sara," said Captain Crewe, making his voice sound as cheerful as possible. Then he lifted her out of the cab and they mounted the steps and rang the bell. Sara often thought afterward that the house was somehow exactly like Miss Minchin. It was respectable and well furnished, but everything in it was ugly; and the very armchairs seemed to have hard bones in them. In the hall everything was hard and polished—even the red cheeks of the moon face on the tall clock in the corner had a severe varnished look. The drawing room into which they were ushered was covered by a carpet with a square pattern upon it, the chairs were square, and a heavy marble timepiece stood upon the heavy marble mantel.

2   As she sat down in one of the stiff mahogany chairs, Sara cast one of her quick looks about her.

3   "I don't like it, Papa," she said. "But then I dare say soldiers—even brave ones—don't really LIKE going into battle."

4   Captain Crewe laughed outright at this. He was young and full of fun, and he never tired of hearing Sara's queer speeches.

5   "Oh, little Sara," he said. "What shall I do when I have no one to say solemn things to me? No one else is as solemn as you are."

6   "But why do solemn things make you laugh so?" inquired Sara.

7   "Because you are such fun when you say them," he answered, laughing still more. And then suddenly he swept her into his arms and kissed her very hard, stopping laughing all at once and looking almost as if tears had come into his eyes.

8   It was just then that Miss Minchin entered the room. She was very like her house, Sara felt: tall and dull, and respectable and ugly. She had large, cold, fishy eyes, and a large, cold, fishy smile. It spread itself into a very large smile when she saw Sara and Captain Crewe.

9   "It will be a great privilege to have charge of such a beautiful and promising child, Captain Crewe," she said, taking Sara's hand and stroking it. "Lady Meredith has told me of her unusual cleverness. A clever child is a great treasure in an establishment like mine."

1 Which sentence from the passage *most* supports the inference that Sara expects to have a difficult time in this new place?

    A   "'But why do solemn things make you laugh so?' inquired Sara."

    B   "As she sat down in one of the stiff mahogany chairs, Sara cast one of her quick looks about her."

    C   "'But then I dare say soldiers—even brave ones—don't really LIKE going into battle.'"

    D   "'Here we are, Sara,' said Captain Crewe, making his voice sound as cheerful as possible."

2 Read these sentences from the passage.

> "Oh, little Sara," he said. "What shall I do when I have no one to say solemn things to me? No one else is as solemn as you are."
>
> "Because you are such fun when you say them," he answered, laughing still more. And then suddenly he swept her into his arms and kissed her very hard, stopping laughing all at once and looking almost as if tears had come into his eyes.

What inference can you make based on these details from the passage?

    A   Sara is getting older and her father thinks she will soon be getting married.

    B   Sara is unhappy because she has come to live with her father.

    C   Sara's father gets angry at her for being such a serious child.

    D   Sara and her father will soon be separated.

3 Read the information in the boxes. Then complete the table.

Details from the Text	What You Already Know	Inference
"It was respectable and well furnished, but everything in it was ugly; and the very armchairs seemed to have hard bones in them."	A place that has ugly, hard furniture is not a pleasant place.	

Which of the following can you infer about Sara's feelings?

A   Sara is eager to explore her new surroundings.

B   Sara does not like new and different places.

C   Sara is not comfortable in her new surroundings.

D   Sara feels as if she's been to this place before.

4 What inference can you make about Miss Minchin's character? Use at least two details from the story to support your answer.

_____

_____

_____

_____

_____

_____

_____

_____

Determining the Theme of a Poem

 **Introduction**   THEME: ⟫⟫ **Memorable Moments**

Every poem has a **theme,** or a lesson about life that the poet wants to share. The theme may be the poet's opinion or observation about nature, people, or life in general. The poet reveals the theme through the details, descriptions, and events in the poem.

You can determine the theme of a poem by first identifying the **topic,** or what the poem is about. Once you know the topic of a poem, you can identify how the poet feels about the topic. This is called the **tone** of a poem. The tone of a poem may be funny, angry, hopeful, happy, or something else. Look for words, phrases, or images that the poet uses to describe the topic. For example, if a poet describes the rain as "clean" and "life-giving," the tone is positive, grateful. If, however, a poet describes the rain as "gray, relentless, a cold wall of water," the tone is negative and depressing.

Read the poem.

Stopping by Woods on a Snowy Evening
by Robert Frost

Whose woods these are I think I know.
His house is in the village though;
He will not see me stopping here
To watch his woods fill up with snow.

5   My little horse must think it queer
To stop without a farmhouse near
Between the woods and frozen lake
The darkest evening of the year.

He gives his harness bells a shake
10 To ask if there is some mistake.
The only other sound's the sweep
Of easy wind and downy flake.

The woods are lovely, dark and deep,
But I have promises to keep,
15 And miles to go before I sleep,
And miles to go before I sleep.

Look at the graphic organizer below which has information about the poem's topic and the tone of the poem filled in for you. Use these details to help you write the poem's theme in the graphic organizer.

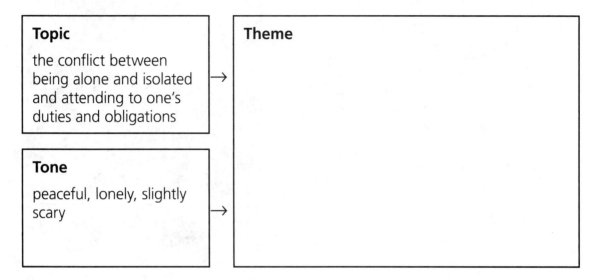

Topic

the conflict between being alone and isolated and attending to one's duties and obligations

→

Theme

Tone

peaceful, lonely, slightly scary

→

Remember, the topic is what the poem is about. This poem is about someone who stops in a wooded area on a dark, cold evening. The topic becomes clear in the last stanza ("But I have promises to keep"). The narrator can't stay in the woods, though he would like to. The tone of the poem is peaceful ("The only other sound's the sweep/Of easy wind and downy flake"). But it is also lonely and a little scary ("The darkest evening of the year/The woods are lovely, dark and deep,").

When you read poetry, it is important to identify the theme. The theme holds the poem together and gives it meaning. Understanding the theme will help you make sense of the poem and give it a deeper meaning.

Read the first part of the poem. Then answer the questions.

A Day

by Emily Dickinson

I'll tell you how the sun rose,
A ribbon at a time.
The steeples swam in amethyst[1],
The news like squirrels ran.
5   The hills untied their bonnets,
The bobolinks[2] begun.
Then I said softly to myself,
"That must have been the sun!"

———————————————

[1]**amethyst:** purple
[2]**bobolinks:** a kind of bird

Think About It

What is the topic of the first part of the poem? The question asks what this part of the poem is mostly about.

What does the poet describe? _____

What lines in the poem tell the subject of the poem? _____

_____

How does the poet feel about the sunrise? Use details from the poem to support

your answer. _____

_____

_____

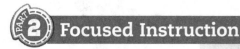

A CLOSER LOOK

The topic of the first part of the poem is sunrise. What is the topic of the second part of the poem? Underline the line that tells you.

Continue reading the poem. Then answer the question.

But how he set, I know not.
10 There seemed a purple stile³
Which little yellow boys and girls
Were climbing all the while
Till when they reached the other side,
A dominie⁴ in gray
15 Put gently up the evening bars,
And led the flock away.

---

³**stile:** step or set of steps for climbing over a wall or fence
⁴**dominie:** church minister or teacher

The title of the poem is "A Day." Think about the author's attitude toward the beginning and the ending of the day.

What *best* describes the theme of this poem?

A   Purple colors are visible during both sunrise and sunset.

B   Bobolinks tell the time of day by singing.

C   A day begins at sunrise with activity, and ends at sunset with quiet.

D   The news that it is morning spreads as fast as squirrels can run.

DISCUSS IT

Think about the theme of the poem. Why do you think the poet wanted to share this message? Turn to another student and talk about the importance of this theme.

Read the poem. Then answer the questions.

My Heart Leaps Up
by William Wordsworth

My heart leaps up when I behold
   A rainbow in the sky:
So was it when my life began;
So is it now I am a man;
5 So be it when I shall grow old,
   Or let me die!
The Child is father of the Man;
And I could wish my days to be
Bound each to each by natural piety¹.

¹**piety:** a strong, passionate feeling toward something; religious feelings; a regard for one's parents

A CLOSER LOOK

What does the poet think is important in life? Underline the lines that tell what he hopes his life will be like.

How does the poet describe his life so far?

1 What does the poet's reaction to a rainbow reveal about him?

A   Because he enjoyed rainbows when he was a child, he enjoys them now that he is a man.

B   He is thrilled every time he sees a rainbow.

C   He appreciates being a child of his father.

D   He has deep and powerful feelings about what he experiences in life.

What is the speaker's reaction to what he sees?

2 Part A

How does the tone of the poem contribute to the theme?

A   It is upbeat and conveys a sense of hope.

B   It is sad and conveys a sense of regret.

C   It is angry and conveys a sense of bitterness.

D   It is sarcastic and conveys a sense of humor.

Part B

Which lines from the poem *best* support the answer to Part A?

A   "So was it when my life began;"

B   "So is it now I am a man;"

C   "So be it when I shall grow old,"

D   "Or let me die!"

Think about the poet's message, and include details or lines that support what the poem is about.

3 The theme of the poem is that the poet hopes he always has the strong, passionate feelings he had as a child. List at least two details from the poem that support this theme.

_____

_____

_____

_____

_____

_____

Read the poem. Then answer the questions.

The Moon
by Robert Louis Stevenson

The moon has a face like the clock in the hall;
She shines on thieves on the garden wall,
On streets and fields and harbor quays,
And birdies asleep in the forks of the trees.

5 The squalling cat and the squeaking mouse,
The howling dog by the door of the house,
The bat that lies in bed at noon,
All love to be out by the light of the moon.

But all of the things that belong to the day
10 Cuddle to sleep to be out of her way;
And flowers and children close their eyes
Till up in the morning the sun shall rise.

1 Which *best* states the topic of the poem?

 A Children sleep when the moon comes up.

 B The moon reveals thieves at night.

 C There are both night creatures and day creatures.

 D Animals that come out at night are dangerous.

2 Complete the chart.

Tone	Words and Phrases that Develop Tone
	"birdies" (line 4) "All love to be out" (line 8) "Cuddle to sleep" (line 10) "And flowers and children close their eyes" (line 11)

Which description of the tone belongs in the chart?

A   worried and sympathetic

B   afraid and warning

C   happiness and gentleness

D   funny and silly

3 Part A

How does the second stanza contribute to the theme of the poem?

A   It notes the animals that come out at night.

B   It notes the animals that make the most noise.

C   It notes the kinds of things that people fear at night.

D   It notes the sense of danger invoked by a full moon.

Part B

How does the third stanza support the theme of the poem?

A   It suggests that most animals don't like the night.

B   It implies that people don't need to fear the night.

C   It points out creatures that are awake with the sun.

D   It describes animals that are quiet and gentle.

4 The theme of the poem is that some creatures come alive by the light of
the moon, while others rest when the moon is out. Write a paragraph that
describes how the poet supports this theme.

_____

_____

_____

_____

_____

_____

_____

LESSON 3

Determining the Theme of a Story or Play

 **Introduction**   THEME: ➤➤➤ Memorable Moments

The **theme** is the big idea of a story or play. It is a lesson or messages about life that the author wants to share. To understand the theme of a story, you must make an inference, or a logical guess, based on the events in a story or play and how the main character responds to those events. You must also identify the main conflict in the story, and then ask how the conflict is resolved. For example, if a character overcomes a big problem by working hard, the theme might be that hard work pays off. The author establishes theme through the characters' responses to events, and through description and dialogue.

Look at the illustration. Think about how the girl feels in each illustration, Then complete the chart.

What challenge does the character face?	She is trying to shape a bowl on the potter's wheel.
How does she respond to the challenge at first?	
What happens in the end?	
What is the theme or lesson?	

Remember, the theme of a story is the lesson or message. To identify the theme, you should look at how characters respond to challenges.

Read the first part of the story. Then answer the questions.

Detectives with Backpacks
by Shandra White

1   It was Jason's fault that she was late. Her brother seemed to take longer in the bathroom every day. That was something to take up at a family meeting.

2   Katrina was glad for her soccer training as she ran the last block to school, although she never played soccer while wearing a backpack full of books. The five-minute bell had rung, and kids were filing into the building. Katrina hated being late for anything, even school. You never know what you might miss, and she was proud of her perfect attendance record.

3   A knot of kids was talking excitedly in front of Room 114. The classroom door was ajar, but here were Monica and Henry and the Hazewood twins and two or three others all jabbering at once. Katrina heard the words "police" and "stolen" before Emma Hazewood half-turned and saw her.

4   "Katrina, have you heard?"

5   "Heard what?"

6   Six kids started talking, but it was Monica Peters, a head taller than anyone else, who broke in and said, "Quiet, all of you. Let me tell it." She was excited and out of breath. "The police were just here, and they took Mr. Dabney away."

7   "Mr. Dabney the custodian?" Katrina wasn't sure she had heard Monica correctly. "Mr. Dabney" and "police" hardly belonged in the same sentence together.

8   "You know any other Mr. Dabney?" Monica said. "You know the money the PTA raised to pay for new band instruments? Well, Mr. Dabney stole it."

9   "Oh, come on, Monica! You don't know that!" Henry Campbell said. "'Innocent until proven guilty.'"

10   "Oh, right, Henry," Monica said. "They found the envelope in his broom closet and a big wad of cash in his wallet. And maybe you don't know this," she added importantly to Katrina, "but my mom told me that Mr. Dabney has been in trouble with the police before!"

11 "That still isn't proof of anything," Henry objected, but just then the door opened fully and Ms. Vetzner stood there with her stern face on.

12 "Class it's nine o'clock. And maybe you don't know *this*," she said, with a look at Monica, "but a wise man once called gossip 'the evil tongue.'" The teacher made sure she made eye contact with everyone.

13 "Now, let's get started on our work for today, and we'll let the police do theirs."

Think About It

What challenge does the main character Katrina face? To answer the question, think about what Katrina does and thinks.

What has happened to Mr. Dabney? _____

_____

Read these lines from the story

"'Mr. Dabney the custodian?' Katrina wasn't sure she had heard Monica correctly. 'Mr. Dabney' and 'police' hardly belonged in the same sentence together."

What can you infer about Katrina's opinion of Mr. Dabney? _____

_____

What does the teacher tell Monica about gossip? _____

_____

What is the main problem Katrina has? _____

_____

Continue reading the passage. Then answer the questions.

A CLOSER LOOK

How does Katrina feel about the story she's just heard? Circle words the author uses to describe Katrina's actions after hearing about Mr. Dabney.

14 Still talking, the kids filed into class. Katrina hung back, last in line. She was thinking of the first grade, when she was always leaving her jacket or a book or something behind in class. Mr. Dabney had seemed like a giant from a fairy tale to her then, monstrous and slow-moving and a little scary. When he frowned and said, "Oh, Katrina, not again!" he might as well have been saying "fee-fie-fo-fum." But he was really very kind. He would joke and chat with her dad as he unlocked the classroom door for her, and he would always leave her with a smile. Everyone liked Mr. Dabney. Katrina couldn't imagine him being a thief.

15 "That's impossible!" she murmured aloud, entering the classroom just before Ms. Vetzner shut the door behind her.

What did Katrina learn about Mr. Dabney as she came to know him?

Part A

How does Katrina's memory of Mr. Dabney contribute to the theme of the story?

A It shows that Mr. Dabney has worked at the school for a long time.

B It shows that Mr. Dabney is very sneaky and cannot be trusted.

C It shows that things are not always as they seem at first.

D It shows that Katrina doesn't have a very good memory.

Part B

Which detail from the story *best* supports the answer to Part A?

A "She was thinking of the first grade, when she was always leaving her jacket or a book or something behind in class."

B "When he frowned and said, 'Oh, Katrina, not again!'"

C "Mr. Dabney always seemed like a giant from a fairy tale to her then, monstrous and slow-moving and a little scary."

D "Everyone liked Mr. Dabney. Katrina couldn't imagine him being a thief."

DISCUSS IT

Think about the story's theme. Do you know of other stories that share this theme? Turn to another student and talk about other stories that share the theme that things or events are not always as they first seem.

A CLOSER LOOK

What has Pocahontas done for Captain John Smith and the settlers before? Underline the lines that tell you.

Read the play. Then answer the questions.

Jamestown

CAST:

POCAHONTAS, *the daughter of Chief Powhatan*

CAPTAIN JOHN SMITH, *an English colonist*

Scene 2

It is midnight in Jamestown in the colony of Virginia. POCAHONTAS *enters, running. She knocks at the door of* CAPTAIN SMITH'S *cabin.*

SMITH: *(within)* Who knocks?

POCAHONTAS: Pocahontas!

CAPTAIN JOHN SMITH *comes from the cabin.*

POCAHONTAS: Powhatan is coming! He is coming with his braves! They come creeping while you sleep!

SMITH: What is this?

POCAHONTAS: They come to take you prisoner!

SMITH: What? Now? *(runs hands through hair)* It is brave of you to warn us, Pocahontas.

POCAHONTAS: I could not bear it if bad things happened. I love my father, but I hate the fighting.

SMITH: You have saved us, Pocahontas. This is the second time you have saved me.

POCAHONTAS *starts to go.*

POCAHONTAS: Good-bye, Captain. I go now.

SMITH: Girl! Girl! You must not go! They will know you warned us!

POCAHONTAS: They will not know, Captain. At midnight they were to leave the camp. I will get back by that time.

SMITH: It is midnight now. They have missed you by this time, Pocahontas.

POCAHONTAS: *(fearfully)* What shall I do? What shall I do?

SMITH: You must stay with us.

POCAHONTAS: I cannot leave my father, Captain. *(She starts to go.)*

SMITH: You must not go! I fear not even your father can save you now!

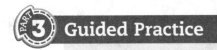

POCAHONTAS: I do not know what to do.

SMITH: You are so brave, Pocahontas! Stay with us. Do not go back.

Why does Pocahontas say she came to the cabin?

1 What challenge does Pocahontas face?

  A She must go against her people to help the settlers.

  B She is not allowed to visit the settlement.

  C She does not like the settlers.

  D She is afraid of Powhatan.

What does Captain Smith say about her?

2 What can you infer about Pocahontas?

  A She is disobedient.

  B She is brave.

  C She is angry.

  D She is friendly.

What is the message the play is trying to convey?

3 What is the theme of the play?

  A Disobeying your parents is wrong.

  B You should always help strangers.

  C You should think carefully about your actions.

  D Courage is doing the right thing even when you are afraid.

How do Pocahontas's actions and words support the theme?

4 What details from the play support the theme?

  _____

  _____

  _____

  _____

  _____

Read the story. Then answer the questions.

The Guitar

1 "I can't believe we had cereal again," Josh complained as he and his friend Steven walked from the cafeteria to their morning activity.

2 "Hey, what do you expect? This is summer camp, man!" Steven said, elbowing Josh in the ribs.

3 As the boys passed the office, they noticed a familiar face through the window.

4 "I wonder what Gary's doing in there," Josh said. "He looks worried." Josh paused and turned back toward the office window.

5 "I'm sure it's nothing. Come on, we're going to be late for music," Steven said, walking faster toward a structure in the middle of the camp.

6 The boys walked into the building, their eyes slowly adjusting to the dim lights. A group of kids were huddled together, talking quietly.

7 Josh pulled on his friend Aidan's shirt. "Hey, what's going on?" he asked quietly.

8 Aidan looked around and lowered his voice. "You won't believe this, Josh, but Gary stole the electric guitar. He must have taken it from the music room last night. He's in the camp's office now! Jennifer says she saw him coming in here late yesterday," Aidan said. And then, as if to prove his point, he added, "She said Gary looked really suspicious."

9 Josh sank down into a chair. Josh thought about the events of the day before. Ms. Ramos had said that everyone would be performing for their families at the end of camp by playing a musical instrument. Gary *had* said how much he wanted to play the electric guitar. But then again, *everyone* wanted to play the electric guitar. Josh remembered something else, something far more troubling. After dinner, Gary had left early, saying something about finding the baseball cap he'd lost.

10 As much as Josh didn't want to admit it, he couldn't deny the facts. His best friend Gary was a thief—the evidence was right there, for everyone to see. Josh sighed and looked around. The rest of the kids were still huddled, talking quietly. Then suddenly, the door opened and Gary walked in; the room grew quiet. Josh looked away, and the other kids turned their backs.

11 "What's up?" Gary asked, looking first to the group of kids and then to Josh. "Did something happen?"

12 Josh paused, and then began to speak. But then he noticed Gary's baseball cap. "Hey, I thought you said you lost that?" he asked.

13 "Ah, yeah," Gary replied. "I did, but the camp counselor found it and gave it back to me. Pretty lucky, huh?" he said, smiling.

14 Josh hesitated. He wanted to ask about the electric guitar, but he didn't know exactly what to say. Just then, Ms. Ramos opened the door. In her right hand was a guitar case. She paused, unsure why all eyes in the room were on her and why the room had gone silent.

15 Steven spoke up first. "Where'd you find the guitar, Ms. Ramos?" he asked, glancing over at Gary as he spoke.

16 Ms. Ramos walked into the room and set the guitar case down. "I took it with me last night to replace the strings," she explained, taking the guitar out. She strummed the strings, and looked up cheerfully. "See, good as new!"

17 Josh relaxed, grinning. "Yeah. Good as new," he repeated, smiling at Gary.

1 What is the problem that Josh faces?

  A He does not like summer camp.

  B He is sick of cereal for breakfast.

  C He believes his best friend is a thief.

  D He does not like to face the truth.

2 Josh is clearly bothered by the evidence against Gary that seems to be piling up. Choose two details from the story that show that Josh is upset by the idea that Gary stole the guitar.

  A Josh sank down into a chair.

  B Josh pulled on his friend Aidan's shirt.

  C But then again, *everyone* wanted to play the electric guitar.

  D Josh looked away, and the other kids turned their backs.

  E Gary *had* said how much he wanted to play the electric guitar.

  F Josh relaxed, grinning. "Yeah. Good as new," he repeated, smiling at Gary.

3 Part A

How does Ms. Ramos's appearance at the end of the story *best* contribute to the theme?

   A   It shows that people were right about their assumptions.

   B   It shows that people are sensitive to body language.

   C   It shows that people should not jump to conclusions without all the facts.

   D   It shows that people usually want to think the worst about others.

Part B

Which detail from the story *best* supports the answer to Part A?

   A   "'I took it with me last night to replace the strings,' she explained, taking the guitar out."

   B   "She strummed the strings, and looked up cheerfully."

   C   "'See, good as new!' she sang out."

   D   "Josh relaxed, grinning. 'Yeah. Good as new,' he repeated, smiling at Gary."

4 The theme of the story is that appearances can be deceiving. How do Josh's and the other kids' reactions to the missing guitar help develop the theme? Use at least two details from the story to support your answer.

_____

_____

_____

_____

_____

_____

_____

_____

LESSON 4

Summarizing a Literary Text

 **Introduction**

THEME: >>> **Memorable Moments**

A **summary** is a short retelling of the main ideas in a passage. Often, you are asked to retell the main events in your own words. To do this, pay attention to the important details of a text and how they build on each other to create a complete literary work with a definite theme and meaning. Summarizing the details of a text can help you determine the theme of a story, poem, or play and understand how the author develops the theme. A summary answers the questions: Who? What? When? Why? and How?

> **Read the story. Then use important details in the text to answer the questions in the chart.**
>
> Once there was a lonely boy named José who had no friends. He had just moved to a new city with his parents. José liked to play soccer, but he didn't have any friends to play with, and you can't play soccer alone.
>
> One day, José took his soccer ball to the park to practice and was kicking it around by himself. The sun was shining and it was a beautiful summer day, but he was all by himself. "This isn't much fun," he thought. "Guess I'll go home and watch some TV." So, picking up his ball, he walked toward the park gate.
>
> Just then a girl about his age was coming into the park. "Hi," she said. "Is that a soccer ball? Want to play with me?"
>
> "Sure," said José. And just like that, he had made a friend thanks to his soccer ball. Before long, several more boys and girls joined the game. Suddenly, José wasn't a lonely boy anymore.

What is José's problem at the beginning of the story?	He has just moved to a new city and has no friends there.
What does José do first in the story?	
What does José do next?	
What happens after that?	
How does the story end?	

Now use your answers to the questions to summarize the story. Fill in the blanks to write your summary.

_____ has just moved to a new city and has no friends. When he takes

_____,

he meets some girls and boys who want to play soccer with him. José _____

_____ and isn't lonely anymore.

Summarizing the details of the text helps readers see how the theme develops.

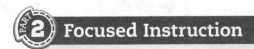

Read the first part of the poem. Then answer the questions.

excerpt from The Rime of the Ancient Mariner
by Samuel Taylor Coleridge

And now the STORM-BLAST came, and he
Was tyrannous and strong:
He struck with his o'ertaking wings,
And chased south along.

5 With sloping masts and dipping prow,
As who pursued with yell and blow
Still treads the shadow of his foe
And forward bends his head,
The ship drove fast, loud roared the blast,
10 And southward aye we fled.

Think About It

What is happening in the poem so far? To answer the question, ask yourself,
"What one thing is the poet describing in each stanza?"

What is happening in the first stanza of the poem? _____

_____

What is described in the second stanza? _____

_____

**Use your answers to the questions to summarize the first part of this
poem.**

A storm moving _____ is blasting _____

_____. The ship _____

_____.

Continue reading the poem. Then answer the questions.

A CLOSER LOOK

What problem is described in this part of the poem? Underline words that tell what is causing trouble now for the ship.

And now there came both mist and snow,
And it grew wondrous cold:
And ice, mast-high, came floating by,
As green as emerald.

15 And through the drifts the snowy clifts
Did send a dismal sheen:
Nor shapes of men nor beasts we ken—
The ice was all between.

The ice was here, the ice was there,
20 The ice was all around:
It cracked and growled, and roared and howled,
Like noises in a swound!

At length did cross an Albatross[1]:
Through the fog it came;
25 As if it had been a Christian soul,
We hailed it in God's name.

It ate the food it ne'er had eat,
And round and round it flew.
The ice did split with a thunder-fit;
30 The helmsman steered us through!

And a good south wind sprung up behind;
The Albatross did follow,
And every day, for food or play,
Came to the mariners' hollo!

---
[1]albatross: a large seabird with webbed feet and a beak

> What is happening in lines 11 through 20? What happens when an albatross appears?

Which of the following is the *best* summary of this part of the poem?

A The storm was over and the weather got warmer, so the ship was able to sail southward.

B A seabird came out of the fog, and then the fog broke up the ice.

C The cold caused the ship to be surrounded by ice, but at the time a seabird appeared, the ice broke up and the ship sailed on.

D Mist and snow and ice made everything so cold that no men or beasts could be seen.

> What happened every day?

Write a summary of the last stanza.

_____

_____

_____

_____

 DISCUSS IT

Discuss with a partner what should be included in a summary of the whole poem.

Read the passage. Then answer the questions.

The Washerwoman's Donkey
a fable from India

1   There once was a poor woman who earned her living by taking in laundry. She had a donkey that would carry the dirty laundry down to the river and the clean laundry back to town. The donkey became weak and broken-down from carrying the heavy loads. Finally, one day he refused to carry anymore. The woman wanted him to get well, but she was too cheap to buy him hay. She covered him with a tiger's skin to keep him warm and, during the night, brought him to a neighbor's pasture where he could graze.

2   The donkey soon discovered that the other animals kept their distance from him. He realized that they all thought he was a tiger. So he ate as much as he wanted and soon began feeling strong again.

3   The farmer who owned the pasture came by. He was alarmed when he saw a tiger among his animals. He wrapped his gray cloak around himself and began to sneak away.

4   Just then the donkey looked up and saw the gray figure. He thought it was a female donkey. It was love at first sight. Happily, he began hurrying after her. Seeing the tiger bounding toward him, the terrified farmer began to run faster. The donkey was dismayed to see his love flee from him. But he quickly realized that she was only running because she thought he was a tiger. So he gave out a loud bray.

5   Now the farmer understood that it was no tiger that was after him. He picked up a stick and drove the donkey from his pasture.

What does the washerwoman make him do?

1 What challenge does the donkey face at the beginning of the story?

   A He wishes to find a mate.

   B Other animals make fun of him.

   C He is beaten by the washerwoman.

   D He is weak and tired from his work.

How does the donkey respond to the other animals?

2 How does the donkey respond to the challenge?

   A He disguises himself as a tiger.

   B He runs away to a farmer's pasture.

   C He refuses to carry any more loads.

   D He lets other animals think he is a tiger.

Which is the main idea of the paragraph?

3 Which sentence is the *best* summary of paragraph 4?

   A The donkey falls in love.

   B The farmer runs from the donkey.

   C The tiger skin causes comical confusion.

   D The donkey shows that he is not a tiger.

What are the main events in the story?

4 Write a summary of the story.

_____

_____

_____

_____

_____

_____

Read the poem. Then answer the questions.

To the Thawing Wind
by Robert Frost

Come with rain, O loud Southwester!
Bring the singer, bring the nester;
Give the buried flower a dream;
Make the settled snowbank steam;
5 Find the brown beneath the white;
But whate'er you do tonight,
Bathe my window, make it flow,
Melt it as the ice will go;
Melt the glass and leave the sticks
10 Like a hermit's crucifix;
Burst into my narrow stall;
Swing the picture on the wall;
Run the rattling pages o'er;
Scatter poems on the floor;
15 Turn the poet out of door.

1 What is this poem about?

  A a window

  B a poet

  C poems

  D the wind

2 Which is the *most* important idea to include in a summary of this poem?

  A The wind will melt the ice and snow.

  B The wind will scatter poems in the poet's house.

  C The wind will burst in and swing a picture on the wall.

  D The wind will leave sticks around.

3 Which *best* describes the time of year?

  A It is spring, and soon even glass will melt.

  B It is winter, and the snow banks will turn into streams.

  C It is winter, but warmer spring weather will come.

  D It is spring, and the time for flowers to dream.

4 Circle five lines in the poem that you think contain the most important information. Then write a summary of the poem.

_____

_____

_____

_____

_____

_____

LESSON 5

Comparing and Contrasting Characters

Introduction

THEME: >>> Memorable Moments

A story or a play is about the people, or **characters.** The author includes details that tell about the characters, such as what they like, what they say, how they act, and how they interact with others. You can use these details to **compare and contrast** characters, or see how they are alike and different. You can compare and contrast two characters or more than two characters. Analyzing how characters are alike and different can help you understand each one better.

Read the story. Look for ways the characters in this story are alike. Then look for ways they are different.

Jacob and Anthony

Jacob and Anthony were best friends. They rode the same school bus and always sat together. They had been happy when they found out they would both be in Mr. Smith's fifth-grade class. Everyone liked Mr. Smith because his class got to do the best science projects, and both boys loved science.

Jacob was very interested in biology. He enjoyed identifying plants, insects, and animals when he was hiking with his troop. He had an aquarium in his room where he kept tropical fish.

Anthony was interested in geology. He spent a lot of time searching around the cliffs near his home for rocks. He had a huge collection of rocks that he had carefully identified and labeled.

When Mr. Smith announced it was time to plan projects for the fall science fair, Jacob and Anthony gave each other a thumbs-up.

To show how two characters are alike and different, you can use a Venn diagram. This graphic organizer shows the qualities that are unique to each character and the qualities they share.

Fill in the missing information from the story in this Venn diagram.

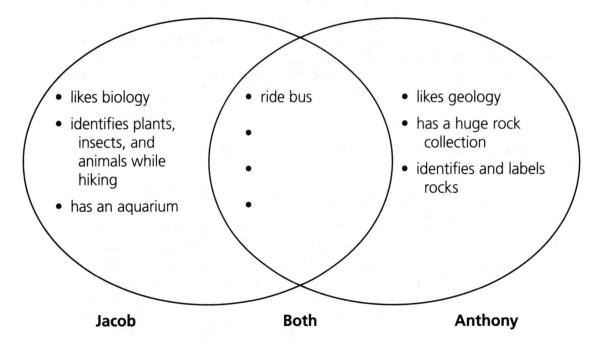

- likes biology
- identifies plants, insects, and animals while hiking
- has an aquarium

- ride bus
-
-
-

- likes geology
- has a huge rock collection
- identifies and labels rocks

Jacob **Both** **Anthony**

Whenever you read a story or a play, pay attention to details about the characters' feelings, words, and actions. Also, pay attention to what the other characters say about the characters. They often reveal important details about the character. Comparing and contrasting the characters will help you understand the story better.

Read the first part of the passage. Then answer the questions.

Jasmine's Hidden Talent

1 "Mom and Dad," exclaimed Yolanda, "Thank you so much!" Jasmine's older sister danced around the room as workers moved the piano into place. "I can't believe you actually bought me a piano!"

2 "Well, it's not just for you; it's for the whole family," said Mom. "But knowing how much you wanted one, I've been keeping my eye out for a used piano in good shape. This one was a bargain, but it still wasn't cheap, so I'll expect you to practice and entertain us with some wonderful music."

3 "Oh, I will," laughed Yolanda. "When can I start taking lessons?"

4 "I talked to Mrs. Perry who plays piano for the school, and she's willing to give you and Jasmine lessons. All you have to do is help her with her yard work because her arthritis is making it difficult for her to keep up her place."

5 "Did you say I was taking piano lessons, too?" asked Jasmine. "I never asked for piano lessons."

6 "Well, Dad and I thought both of you could take lessons since we have a piano," replied Mom. Jasmine sighed.

Think About It

How are Yolanda and Jasmine alike and how are they different? To answer the question, look for details in the text about what each girl says and does.

Complete this Venn diagram to list details about Yolanda, about Jasmine, and about both girls.

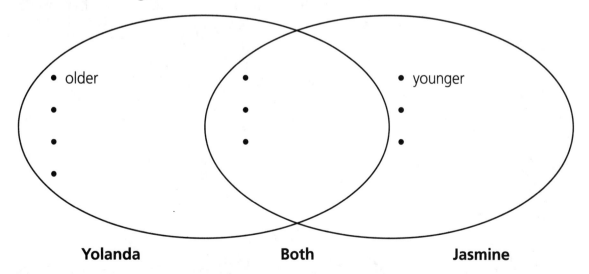

Yolanda: • older • • • •
Both: • • •
Jasmine: • younger • •

Yolanda   Both   Jasmine

Continue reading the story. Then answer the questions.

7   Every Thursday after school, the girls went to Mrs. Perry's house for lessons. Jasmine dreaded the lessons, and she dreaded practicing even more. The sour notes she produced made her frustrated and embarrassed. Yolanda, however, was progressing exceptionally well and was soon playing melodies with both hands.

8   One Saturday morning, Jasmine and Yolanda raked leaves in Mrs. Perry's yard. After the leaves were raked to the curb, Mrs. Perry appeared on the porch with two bottles of water and a brown bag. "Come sit on the steps for a minute," she called.

9   "I'd like you to plant these tulip bulbs by the porch," she said. "You need to dig a hole about six inches deep for each bulb and place the bulbs about 12 inches apart. They will be beautiful next April," she explained.

10   "These bulbs are buried treasure," smiled Jasmine. "We'll see the treasure in the spring!" Jasmine got to work, carefully estimating how deep and far apart to plant the bulbs. But Yolanda said, "You do it, Jasmine. You like digging in the dirt, but I have to keep my hands nice for playing piano." Jasmine lifted her eyebrows, but she happily finished planting the tulips.

11   That night Mom said, "Mrs. Perry called to thank you girls for doing such a nice job in her yard. However, she doesn't think Jasmine is making much progress at piano and suggests she stop lessons. But you can keep trying if you want to, Jasmine."

12   Jasmine just smiled and shook her head. "No, Mom, that's fine with me. But can I keep helping in Mrs. Perry's yard? That's what I really like to do!"

13   "I think that would be wonderful," replied her mom as she gave her a hug. "We all have different talents."

A CLOSER LOOK

One way to compare and contrast characters is to look at how they interact with others. Underline how Jasmine responds to Mrs. Perry's request that the girls plant tulip bulbs. Circle Yolanda's response.

> Look for details that describe the girls or things that they do.

Which tells something that *only* Jasmine did?

A Jasmine practiced piano.

B Jasmine planted tulip bulbs.

C Jasmine raked leaves.

D Jasmine took piano lessons.

> What happens at Mrs. Perry's?

What does Jasmine discover about herself?

_____

_____

_____

_____

 DISCUSS IT

Compare your Venn diagram with a partner's. Are there other things you can add to your diagram? Are there things you should move?

Read the play. Then answer the questions.

A CLOSER LOOK

Props are items used in a play. Circle the props used in this play.

In the Castle

from King Alfred
by Florence Holbrook

CAST:

> **QUEEN**
>
> **JOHN**
>
> **HENRY**
>
> **REED**
>
> **ALFRED**

Scene 1

A large, airy room in the castle. The room includes several comfortable couches and a single, locked cabinet. The queen and her four boys are seated. A fire roars merrily in the fireplace. Outside the wind howls and the rain blows.

JOHN: Tell us a story, lady mother.

HENRY: Yes, tell us a story.

REED: I wish it would stop raining, so that we might take our hawks for a hunt!

QUEEN: *(unlocks the cabinet and removes a large, velvet-covered volume)* I have something to show you, my princes. Is this not beautiful?

ALFRED: *(fingers the book lovingly)* How lovely the red velvet, and see, the clasp is of gold!

REED: And there are jewels in the clasp! What is it, mother?

QUEEN: It is a book, darlings, a very precious volume. The jewels, however, are the least valuable part of it. Shall we look within?

JOHN: *(looking over his mother's shoulder)* Pray show us, lady mother!

QUEEN: Observe the forms! Mighty warriors, fair ladies, and royal chiefs of the olden times, all in bright and glowing colors.

HENRY: *(yawns and looks bored)* I guess they seem to be brave. Who are they?

QUEEN: *(slowly opens the book)* These pictures are beautiful and appeal to the eye, but neither they nor the velvet and gold of the binding give the joy which is greatest.

ALFRED: *(looks confused)* What do you mean, dear lady mother?

QUEEN: This is a book I greatly enjoy, for it is full of the tales of the mighty King Arthur and his knights. You will like to hear me read these brave stories when you are tired with your day's work, or on rainy days when you can neither hunt nor ride. That is because you do not know how to amuse yourselves when time is heavy on your hands, since you can neither read nor play upon the musical instruments that give us so much pleasure.

REED: *(reaches out to the book)* The book is so lovely. Let me take it, lady mother!

QUEEN: *(looks at him for a moment)* I would that the children of my royal husband could read the book.

ALFRED: *(thinks for a minute)* Our father does not think much of books and music. He likes to hunt and fight, and so do I.

HENRY: Our father is usually in the right.

REED: While I love to hunt, I also love to hear the stories of great kings and warriors.

HENRY: *(looks over at Queen)* To which of us will you give the book, lady mother?

QUEEN: *(thinks for a few minutes)* I will bestow it on he who first learns how to read it.

ALFRED: *(looks happy)* Will you really, dear mother?

QUEEN: Yes, upon the faith of a queen, I will. I will not give it to one who cannot read it. Books are meant for the learned and not the ignorant.

ALFRED: *(timidly)* May I… may I take the book a little while?

QUEEN: Yes, you may take the precious volume, Alfred, for I know you will not injure it, and I hope you will soon learn how to make its wisdom your own.

ALFRED: *(holds the book tightly to his chest)* Thank you, lady mother.

1 Part A

How does Henry's reaction to the book differ from Alfred's reaction?

A Henry thinks the book is puzzling, while Alfred thinks it is shocking.

B Henry thinks the book is unexciting, while Alfred thinks it is troubling.

C Henry thinks the book is delightful, while Alfred thinks it is frightening.

D Henry thinks the book is uninteresting, while Alfred thinks it is exciting.

What are the boys most interested in doing?

Part B

Which sentence *best* supports the answer to Part A?

A **HENRY:** *(yawns and looks bored)* I guess they seem to be brave. Who are they?

B **ALFRED:** *(looks confused)* What do you mean, dear lady mother?

C **ALFRED:** *(thinks for a minute)* Our father does not think much of books and music.

D **HENRY:** *(looks over at Queen)* To which of us will you give the book, lady mother?

Why do they want the Queen to tell them a story?

2 What do you learn about the boys from what the Queen says?

A They love to hunt.

B They like to play musical instruments.

C They do not know how to read.

D They do not know how to ride horses.

What does the King like to do?

3 How are the King's interests different from the Queen's? Support your answer with details from the play.

_____

_____

_____

_____

Read the passage. Then answer the questions.

from Around the World in 80 Days

by Jules Verne

Phileas Fogg, an Englishman, has made a bet that he can circle the globe in 80 days. In this passage, Fogg is traveling across India.

1 Toward evening the train entered the passes of the Sutpour Mountains, which separate the Khandeish from Bundelcund. The next day Sir Francis Cromarty asked Passepartout what time it was; to which, on consulting his watch, he replied that it was three in the morning. This great timepiece, always set on the Greenwich meridian, which was now some 77 degrees west, was at least four hours slow. Sir Francis corrected Passepartout's time…. He tried to have him understand that the watch should be regulated in each new meridian, since he was constantly going east, toward the sun, and therefore the days were shorter by four minutes for each degree gone over. Passepartout obstinately refused to alter his watch, which he kept on London time. It was an innocent habit that could harm no one.

2 The train stopped, at eight o'clock, in the midst of a glade some 15 miles beyond Rothal, where there were several bungalows and workmen's cabins. The conductor, passing beside the cars, shouted, "Passengers will get out here!"

3 Phileas Fogg looked at Sir Francis Cromarty for an explanation, but the general could not tell what a halt meant in the midst of this forest of dates and acacias.

4 Passepartout, not less surprised, rushed out and speedily returned, crying, "Sir, no more railway!"

5 "What do you mean?" asked Sir Francis.

6 "I mean to say that the train isn't going on."

7 The general at once stepped out, while Phileas Fogg calmly followed him, and they proceeded together to the conductor.

8 "Where are we?" asked Sir Francis.

9 "At the hamlet of Kholby."

10 "Do we stop here?"

11 "Certainly. The railway isn't finished."

12 "What! Not finished?"

13 "No. There's still a matter of 50 miles to be laid from here to Allahbad, where the line begins again."

14 "But the papers announced the opening of the railway throughout."

15 "What can I say, officer? The papers were mistaken."

16 "Yet you sell tickets from Bombay to Calcutta," retorted Sir Francis, who was getting angry.

17 "No doubt," replied the conductor, "but the passengers know they must provide means of transportation for themselves from Kholby to Allahbad."

18 Sir Francis was furious. Passepartout would willingly have knocked the conductor down, and did not dare to look at his master.

19 "Sir Francis," said Mr. Fogg, quietly, "we will, if you please, look about for some means to reach Allahbad."

20 "Mr. Fogg, is this a delay greatly to your disadvantage?"

21 "No, Sir Francis, it was foreseen."

22 "What! You knew that the way—"

23 "Not at all; but I knew that some obstacle or other would sooner or later arise on my route. Nothing, therefore, is lost…. A ship leaves Calcutta for Hong Kong at noon on the 25th. This is the 22nd, and we shall reach Calcutta in time."

24 There was nothing to say to so confident a response.

25 It was but too true that the railway works stopped at this point. The papers were like some watches, which have a way of getting too fast, and had been premature in their announcement of the completion of the line. Most of the travelers were aware of the interruption, and leaving the train, they began to engage such vehicles as the village could provide—four wheeled palkigharis, wagons drawn by zebus, carriages that looked like traveling pagodas, palanquins, ponies, and whatnot.

26 Mr. Fogg and Sir Francis Cromarty, after searching the village from end to end, came back without having found anything.

27 "I shall go on foot," said Phileas Fogg.

28 Passepartout, who had now joined his master, made a wry grimace, as he thought of his magnificent but too frail babouches. Happily he too had been looking about him, and, after a moment's hesitation, said, "Sir, I think I have found a means of conveyance."

29 "What?"

30 "An elephant! An elephant that belongs to an Indian who lives but a hundred steps from here."

31 "Let us go and see the elephant," replied Mr. Fogg.

1 Which of these sentences *best* describes Phileas Fogg?

   A He is a lazy man concerned about his ease and comfort.

   B He is a careful man who thinks twice before taking risks.

   C He is a composed man, not easily disturbed by bad news.

   D He is a man of action, impatient with thought or reflection.

2 What is the relationship between Fogg and Passepartout? Use details from the story to support your answer.

_____

_____

_____

_____

3 Which sentence *best* explains why Sir Francis Cromarty becomes angry?

   A His friend Fogg is in danger of losing his bet.

   B The newspapers printed incorrect information.

   C He is an easily excitable man who enjoys a fight.

   D Railway officials failed to tell him that the line wasn't complete.

4 In this passage, how are Cromarty's and Fogg's responses to the situation the same or different?

_____

_____

_____

_____

LESSON 6

Comparing and Contrasting Settings

 **Introduction**

THEME: >>> Memorable Moments

Every story has a **setting.** The setting is the place where the story happens and the time when it takes place. Many stories contain more than one setting. The author describes the setting to help the reader make a picture in his or her mind of the place and time. The setting may also affect the characters' experiences. For instance, if characters walked through a dark forest, they might feel scared. If they walked into a party, they might feel happy. The setting helps set the **mood,** or feeling about a place.

When a story has more than one setting, it is important to compare and contrast the settings to understand the backdrops for the actions and mood of the characters in each setting.

Look at the illustrations.

56 UNIT 1 Key Ideas and Details in Literary Text

Think about how each setting affects the girls' attitudes. Answer the questions.

How does the setting contribute to the girls mood in the first illustration?

_____

Why? _____

How do the girls feel in the second illustration? _____

_____

Why? _____

What is the setting in the third illustration? _____

_____

How do the girls feel? _____

Whenever you read a story or a play, pay attention to details about the settings. Comparing and contrasting the settings will help you understand the characters' feelings and actions.

Read the first part of the story. Then answer the questions.

A New Home for Gabriella

1   "I'm sorry, Gabby," said Gabriella's dad. "I know you love Austin and Texas, but when my company offered me a better job in Columbus, Ohio, Mom and I knew we had to go. It's going to be better for all of us. We'll have a nicer house, and you and Luis will make new friends." Dad's expression let Gabby know he felt sorry to tell her about moving, but he expected her to act more grown up. Tears wouldn't change anything.

2   The next morning, Gabby walked slowly around her neighborhood. She entered the sunny park and pushed herself gently in a swing for a while, just thinking about everything she was going to have to leave behind. Then, jumping from the swing with a sigh, she wandered on toward her school building. She circled around it and peeked in the dark window of what would have been her fifth-grade classroom in the fall. Finally, she knocked on Elena's door. They'd been friends since preschool. How could she leave Elena behind? "I'll text you every day," she promised Elena as she left an hour later. "I've got to go home now and finish packing." The friends hugged one last time.

Think About It

How is one setting similar to or different from another? The setting refers to the times and places in which the story takes place.

Underline clues about where the characters are and what time it is.

What places does Gabby visit in the story so far? _____

_____

In what ways are the park and the school different? _____

_____

The author doesn't say it is summertime. How can you figure out the season?

_____

_____

A CLOSER LOOK
Gabby's house in Columbus, Ohio, is new to her and different from the house she left behind. Underline details that describe the setting of Gabby's new home.

Continue reading the passage. Then answer the question.

3 Several days later, Gabby climbed stiffly out of the back seat of the family car. It had been a 1,200-mile trip, and even though she had been reluctant to leave Austin, she was glad to be out of the car. The new house loomed high above as Gabby stared up to the second floor. It appeared huge compared to their smaller one-floor house in Austin. The trees were tall and skinny, and the grass felt different under Gabby's feet. She pulled her phone from her pocket and began to text Elena. *In Columbus…house too big… trees skinny…grass weird. Wish I were in Austin.*

4 The house was a disaster zone after the moving van brought in the furniture and what seemed like thousands of boxes. Gabby felt as though she had dropped into a strange world, but she had to admit it was nice to have a large bedroom with a gigantic closet.

5 "Hey, Gabby," Dad called up the stairs. "Luis and I are going to the park down the street to play catch. Take a break from unpacking and come with us."

6 The park was bigger than the one in Austin and had a baseball field, soccer field, and lots of playground equipment. While Dad and Luis practiced pitching and catching, Gabby settled into a swing. She pushed herself higher and higher. As she closed her eyes, she imagined herself back in Austin. When she opened her eyes, she was surprised to see another girl swinging beside her. "What's your name?" the girl asked.

7 "I'm Gabby, and I just moved here from Texas."

8 The girl smiled as she said, "I'm Emma, and I've lived here all my life. If you're going to be in fifth grade, we might be in the same class at school this fall."

Who lives in each city?

Which tells something that was *only* in the Austin setting?

A   a park

B   Elena's house

C   a school

D   summertime

DISCUSS IT
With a partner, choose setting details that appear in the first and second parts of the story. Compare and contrast them.

Read the passage. Then answer the questions.

Black Beauty
by Anna Sewell

1   The first place that I can well remember was a pleasant meadow with a pond of clear water in it. Over the hedge on one side we looked into a plowed field, and on the other we looked over a gate at our master's house, which stood by the roadside. While I was young I lived upon my mother's milk, as I could not eat grass. In the daytime I ran by her side, and at night I lay down close by her. When it was hot we used to stand by the pond in the shade of the trees, and when it was cold we had a warm shed near the grove.

2   There were six young colts in the meadow beside me. They were older than I was. I used to run with them, and had great fun. We used to gallop all together round the field as hard as we could go. Sometimes, we had rather rough play, for they would frequently bite and kick as well as gallop.

3   One day, when there was a good deal of kicking, my mother whinnied to me to come to her, and then she said, "I wish you to pay attention to what I am going to say. The colts who live here are very good colts, but they are cart-horse colts, and of course they have not learned manners. You have been well-bred and well-born. Your father has a great name in these parts, and your grandfather won the cup at the Newmarket races. Your grandmother had the sweetest temper of any horse I ever knew, and I think you have never seen me kick or bite. I hope you will grow up gentle and good, and never learn bad ways; do your work with a good will, lift your feet up well when you trot, and never bite or kick even in play."

4   I have never forgotten my mother's advice; I knew she was a wise old horse, and our master thought a great deal of her. Her name was Duchess, but he often called her Pet.

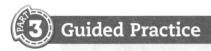

5 Our master was a good, kind man. He gave us good food, good lodging and kind words; he spoke as kindly to us as he did to his little children. We were all fond of him, and my mother loved him very much. When she saw him at the gate she would neigh with joy, and trot up to him. He would pat and stroke her and say, "Well, old Pet, and how is your little [colt]?" Then he would give me a piece of bread, which was very good, and sometimes he brought a carrot for my mother. All the horses would come to him, but I think we were his favorites. My mother always took him to town on a market-day in a light gig.

> Where did the young colts gallop?

1 The story tells that Black Beauty lived on his mother's milk when he was young because he could not eat grass. This means that the horses _____.

  A lived in a field of grass

  B ate food inside the shed

  C ate carrots and bread from the master

  D played in the plowed field

> Why do the horses move from one place to another when the temperature changes?

2 How are the settings of the pond and the shed different?

  A The pond has grassy fields. The shed is near town.

  B The pond has shade. The shed is warm.

  C The pond is hot. The shed is warm.

  D The pond is near the grove. The shed is near the master's house.

> Look for words that describe Black Beauty's home and the gate.

3 Write a paragraph describing how the setting of the field is right for certain activities while the setting at the gate is right for different activities. Use details from the story in your description.

_____

_____

_____

_____

_____

_____

Read the passage. Then answer the questions.

excerpt from Kidnapped
by Robert Louis Stevenson

The following is from the book Kidnapped *by Robert Louis Stevenson. The story takes place about 250 years ago in Scotland. In this excerpt, the main character's parents have recently died. Now he is walking to find his Uncle Ebenezer, who lives at the House of Shaws.*

1   In the forenoon of the second day, coming to the top of a hill, I saw all the country fall away before me down to the sea; and in the midst of this descent, on a long ridge, the city of Edinburgh smoking like a kiln. There was a flag upon the castle, and ships moving or lying anchored in the firth; both of which, for as far away as they were, I could distinguish clearly; and both brought my country heart into my mouth.

2   Presently after, I came by a house where a shepherd lived, and got a rough direction for the neighborhood of Cramond; and so, from one to another, worked my way to the westward of the capital by Colinton, till I came out upon the Glasgow road. And there, to my great pleasure and wonder, I beheld a regiment marching to the fifes, every foot in time; an old red-faced general on a grey horse at the one end, and at the other the company of Grenadiers, with their Pope's-hats. The pride of life seemed to mount into my brain at the sight of the red coats and the hearing of that merry music.

3   A little farther on, and I was told I was in Cramond parish, and began to substitute in my inquiries the name of the house of Shaws. It was a word that seemed to surprise those of whom I sought my way. At first I thought the plainness of my appearance, in my country habit, and that all dusty from the road, consorted ill with the greatness of the place to which I was bound. But after two, or maybe three, had given me the same look and the same answer, I began to take it in my head there was something strange about the Shaws itself.

4   The better to set this fear at rest, I changed the form of my inquiries; and spying an honest fellow coming along a lane on the shaft of his cart, I asked him if he had ever heard tell of a house they called the house of Shaws. He stopped his cart and looked at me, like the others.

5   "Ay" said he. "What for?"

6   "It's a great house?" I asked.

7   "Doubtless," says he. "The house is a big, muckle house."

8   "Ay," said I, "but the folk that are in it?"

9   "Folk?" cried he. "Are ye daft? There's nae folk there—to call folk."

10   "What?" say I; "not Mr. Ebenezer?"

11 "Ou, ay" says the man; "there's the laird, to be sure, if it's him you're wanting. What'll like be your business, mannie?"

12 "I was led to think that I would get a situation," I said, looking as modest as I could.

1 One thing the settings in paragraph 1 and paragraph 2 of *Kidnapped* have in common is that _____.

   A   the narrator is close to the sea

   B   the narrator is near a shepherd's house

   C   the narrator is traveling to the house of Shaws

   D   the narrator is in the capital by Colinton

2 What is unique about the Glasgow road?

   A   It has soldiers marching.

   B   It has ships in the harbor.

   C   It has a shepherd.

   D   It has a man with a cart.

3 The narrator is walking, and the setting changes as he walks. Which part of the setting brings him pleasure?

   A   the firth, because he sees the ships

   B   the city of Edinburgh, because it is smoking like a kiln

   C   the Glasgow Road, because he sees soldiers marching

   D   the castle, because of the flag

4 Compare and contrast the setting at the beginning of *Kidnapped* with the setting at the end. Tell details from each part of the story to show how and why the setting changes.

_____

_____

_____

_____

_____

_____

_____

_____

_____

_____

Read the poem. Then answer the questions.

The First Red-Bird
by Evaleen Stein

I heard a song at daybreak,
So honey-sweet and clear,
The essence of all joyous things
Seemed mingling in its cheer.

5   The frosty world about me
I searched with eager gaze,
But all was slumber-bound and wrapped
In violet-tinted haze.

Then suddenly a sunbeam
10   Shot slanting o'er the hill,
And once again from out the sky
I heard that honied trill.

And there upon a poplar,
Poised at its topmost height,
15   I saw a little singer clad
In scarlet plumage bright.

The poplar branches quivered,
By dawn winds lightly blown,
And like a breeze-swept poppy-flower
20   The red-bird rocked and shone.

The blue sky, and his feathers
Flashed o'er by golden light,
Oh, all my heart with rapture thrilled,
It was so sweet a sight!

1 From the poem's title and details, you can infer that the season is _____.

    A spring

    B fall

    C winter

    D summer

2 Which *best* tells the theme of the poem?

    A Red birds are the prettiest.

    B The most joyous thing is a bird's song.

    C A sunbeam makes a bird want to sing.

    D Look for small, lovely things to make you happy.

3 Write a paragraph that summarizes the poet's thoughts in this poem.

_____

_____

_____

_____

_____

Read the story. Then answer the questions.

The One That Didn't Get Away

1 Isaac and Ari sat on their backpacks and waited impatiently in the driveway for Uncle Zack to arrive. He was taking them camping and fishing in the mountains for the first time, and they could hardly wait to get going!

2 An hour later, the boys climbed out of their uncle's truck at the foot of the trail. "Isaac and Ari, grab your backpacks. I'll unload the other stuff," their uncle called.

3 Isaac let out a whistle when he saw the huge backpack his uncle was shouldering. "Well, it takes a lot of gear to go camping with three guys," said his uncle. Isaac liked the way he said "three guys."

4 The trail proved to be steeper than it looked from the parking lot. There were plenty of rough stones to watch for. Eventually it leveled off, and when it forked, Uncle Zack directed them to the left. A few minutes later, they entered a campground next to a small mountain lake surrounded by tall pine trees.

5 Ari ran down to the lake to look around while Uncle Zack unzipped his backpack and started unloading supplies. Isaac was so tired that he sat down, leaned against his backpack, and heaved a sigh. Then he felt something kick his foot. Uncle Zack ordered, "Get a move on, we have to set up camp while we still have plenty of daylight. I need help putting up the tent, and you need to get your gear unpacked."

6 Wearily, Isaac stretched his tired muscles. "Yeah, I know you're sore," laughed Uncle Zack. "But remember, it will be a lot easier carrying all this gear down the trail than it was carrying it up."

7 As night fell over the campsite, a fire crackled and snapped in the ring they had made of stones from the edge of the water. Their hot dogs were toasting nicely on the pointed green sticks Uncle Zack had whittled with a pocketknife. A can of beans was heating in the hot coals, and the boys felt like they had never been so hungry in their lives.

8 The next morning, just as the sky was beginning to brighten, Uncle Zack called, "Get your poles and the tackle box, guys! There are fish in this lake, and we're going to be eating some of them for breakfast."

9 Uncle Zack demonstrated casting a lure and slowly reeling it in. It wasn't long before Ari yelled, "I've got one!" and landed a beautiful bass. Then a fish grabbed Uncle Zack's lure, and he grinned as his pole bent. He struggled to reel in another bass that weighed several pounds. Isaac tried not to show his disappointment about not catching anything as they headed back to camp.

10 Ari yawned after his fish breakfast and crawled into the tent. And Uncle Zack sat down to untangle some fishing line. "I think I'll go try again," said Isaac as he picked up his pole and walked back to the edge of the water. On his third cast, he felt a hard tug. Yelling in excitement, he felt the fish pull the lure back and forth while the tip of his pole was bent almost to the water!

11 Uncle Zack and Ari heard him yelling and came running. "You've got a big one!" exclaimed his uncle. Ari was hopping from one foot to the other. At last, the big fish tired, and Isaac landed a bass twice as large as Uncle Zack's!

12 "Let me get a picture," said his uncle as he pulled his phone from his pocket and began snapping. "You're going to have one great fish story to tell, and these pictures will prove it isn't just a story!"

4 What is one difference between the settings of the campsite and the nearby lake?

A   The campsite has a tent, and the lake has a backpack nearby.

B   The campsite has a fire ring, and the lake is surrounded by pine trees.

C   The campsite has a steep, forked trail, and the lake has a big fish.

D   It is night time at the lake, and daytime at the campsite.

5 How does the campsite setting affect how Uncle Zack behaves toward Isaac?

A   Uncle Zack unzips his backpack and starts unloading supplies.

B   Uncle Zack understands that Isaac needs to rest after the hike up the trail.

C   Uncle Zack realizes they need to set up camp right away, so he tells Isaac to help.

D   Uncle Zack ignores Ari, who has run down to the lake.

6 Which sentence is the *best* theme of this story?

A   Camping can be fun.

B   If at first you don't succeed, try again.

C   Hiking with a backpack is hard work.

D   Fishing can be disappointing.

7 Write a summary of this story. Before you begin, underline parts of the story that contain important information.

_____

_____

_____

_____

_____

Read the story. Then answer the questions.

excerpt from The Glass Dog

from American Fairy Tales *by L. Frank Baum*

1   An accomplished wizard once lived on the top floor of a tenement house and passed his time in thoughtful study and studious thought. What he didn't know about wizardry was hardly worth knowing, for he possessed all the books and recipes of all the wizards who had lived before him; and, moreover, he had invented several wizardments himself.

2   This admirable person would have been completely happy but for the numerous interruptions to his studies caused by folk who came to consult him about their troubles (in which he was not interested), and by the loud knocks of the iceman, the milkman, the baker's boy, the laundryman and the peanut woman. He never dealt with any of these people, but they rapped at his door every day to see him about this or that or to try to sell him their wares. Just when he was most deeply interested in his books or engaged in watching the bubbling of a cauldron there would come a knock at his door. And after sending the intruder away he always found he had lost his train of thought or ruined his compound.

3   At length these interruptions made him angry, and he decided he must have a dog to keep people away from his door. He didn't know where to find a dog, but in the next room lived a poor glassblower with whom he had a slight acquaintance; so he went into the man's apartment and asked:

4   "Where can I find a dog?"

5   "What sort of a dog?" asked the glassblower.

6   "A good dog. One that will bark at people and drive them away. One that will be no trouble to keep and won't expect to be fed. One that has no fleas and is neat in his habits. One that will obey me when I speak to him. In short, a good dog," said the wizard.

7   "Such a dog is hard to find," returned the glass-blower, who was busy making a blue glass flowerpot with a pink glass rosebush in it, having green glass leaves and yellow glass roses.

8   The wizard watched him thoughtfully.

9   "Why can't you blow me a dog out of glass?" he asked, presently.

10   "I can," declared the glassblower; "but it would not bark at people, you know."

11   "Oh, I'll fix that easily enough," replied the other. "If I could not make a glass dog bark, I would be a mighty poor wizard."

12   "Very well. If you can use a glass dog, I'll be pleased to blow one for you. Only, you must pay for my work."

13 "Certainly," agreed the wizard. "But I have none of that horrid stuff you call money. You must take some of my wares in exchange."

14 The glassblower considered the matter for a moment.

15 "Could you give me something to cure my rheumatism?" he asked.

16 "Oh, yes, easily."

17 "Then it's a bargain. I'll start the dog at once. What color of glass shall I use?"

18 "Pink is a pretty color," said the wizard, "and it's unusual for a dog, isn't it?"

19 "Very," answered the glassblower; "but it shall be pink."

20 So the wizard went back to his studies and the glassblower began to make the dog.

8 Part A

Complete the table by comparing and contrasting the two characters in this story.

Wizard	Glassblower
•	•
•	•
•	•
•	•
•	•

Part B

Which description *best* supports a contrast in Part A?

A They both like and want a dog.

B One man has plenty of money, and one is poor.

C One is a wizard and one is an artist.

D They are both annoyed by salespeople.

9 A possible theme for this story is _____.

    A a barking dog can keep salespeople away

    B a glass artist can be a friend

    C people can help each other meet their needs

    D a wizard can't magically solve all of his problems

10 What can you infer about the relationship between the wizard and the glass artist? Use details from the story to support your answer.

_____

_____

_____

_____

_____

_____

Key Ideas and Details in Informational Text

Good articles don't just list facts. Instead, they have a main idea that is supported with important details about people and events. You can often learn more from active reading when you make inferences, ask questions, and practice writing summaries. When you reread the title, the topic sentence, and look for clues in the text, you can really learn a lot! In this unit, you will make inferences, determine the main ideas and how they are supported, summarize texts, and explain relationships in texts.

LESSON 7 Supporting Inferences in Informational Text is about making inferences in informational texts by combining what you know with evidence from what you read. You will look for details in the text that help support your idea.

LESSON 8 Determining Main Ideas and Details helps you analyze the main ideas of a text by figuring out the topic, rereading the topic sentence and title, and looking for clues in the details and examples.

LESSON 9 Summarizing Informational Text focuses on retelling informational texts by answering *who, what, when, where, why,* and *how* questions. You will practice summarizing paragraphs and identifying the best summaries.

LESSON 10 Explaining Relationships in Text is about the connections between important concepts in articles, and why the author included information about certain people or events. You will practice understanding the important relationships between people and events.

LESSON 7

Supporting Inferences in Informational Text

Introduction

THEME: >>> The Power of Nature

When you read informational texts, you must sometimes make **inferences,** or evidence-based guesses, about what the author means. To make an inference, you combine what you read with what you already know. But remember, an inference isn't simply a wild guess. You must support your inference with specific **details** that are stated **explicitly,** or directly, in the text.

Look at the illustration below. Read the caption. Then complete the chart on the next page.

Palm trees can withstand hurricane conditions.

Readers make an inference by combining details in the text with what they already know.

Look at the chart. Details about the illustration have been filled in for you. What inference can you make based on these details?

Details from the Text	What You Already Know	Inference
The illustration shows trees bending. The caption explains that palm trees can withstand hurricane conditions.	When a tree bends, it is because of high winds. If the tree bends and doesn't break, its trunk is flexible.	

Look outside. What details can you note about the weather that leads you to determine if it is a good day for a bike ride? For example, is the wind blowing? Are there clouds? Do you see rain falling? You may not realize it, but you note and recall all of these details about the weather and then combine those details with what you already know to make an inference about what you want to do outdoors today.

Similarly, you read details in an informational text and make inferences about ideas that the author doesn't directly state. It is your job to note and remember these details and to connect them to each other so that you understand important concepts. Doing so will help you understand informational texts.

Read the first part of the passage. Then answer the questions.

When Lightning Strikes

1   Dark storm clouds have gathered in the west, and the air feels heavy and still. A low, persistent rumble grows louder with each minute. Does this sound familiar?

2   If you've ever been tempted to stay outside to watch a thunderstorm roll in, don't take the risk. The fact that you can hear the thunder means that lightning is close enough to strike. How close? To figure out the distance between you and a flash of lightning, count the number of seconds from the time you see the lightning until the time you hear the thunder. Then divide that number by five to determine how many miles the lightning is from you. Even if the lightning seems far, if you can hear the thunder, it's close enough to pose a danger. What should you do? Go inside!

Think About It

How can thunder help you stay safe from lightning? The question asks how hearing thunder can help protect you from lightning. To answer the question, look for details in the text that explain the relationship of thunder to lightning and how to determine how far away lightning is from you.

How can you calculate the distance that lightning is away from you? _____

_____

_____

What does the author say about being able to hear thunder? _____

_____

What do you already know about the dangers of lightning striking a person?

_____

_____

What can you infer about using thunder as a way to stay safe in a storm?

_____

_____

Continue reading the passage. Then answer the question.

A CLOSER LOOK
Why should you avoid water or a tree standing alone? Underline words and phrases that answer this question.

3 There may be times when a thunderstorm moves in and you find yourself far away from a building or other enclosed structure. In this dangerous situation, there are a few things you can do to protect yourself from lightning. First, try to find a car and get inside with the windows rolled up. If you are too far away from a car, seek a low area like a valley. Avoid hilltops and elevated areas where lightning is more likely to strike. Do not seek shelter under an isolated tree or in a tent or open-sided structure. Do not stand under cliffs or overhangs, and stay far away from bodies of water. Remember, water conducts electricity, which magnifies the danger. Barbed wire fences, power lines, and windmills also conduct electricity and should be avoided during a thunderstorm. Additionally, do not lie flat on the ground. Instead, roll your body into a ball. If you can find a forested area with many trees, that's the place to be. However, avoid lone or isolated trees, as they are more likely to be struck.

4 If you are indoors, there are a few precautions you must still take. First, stay away from faucets, sinks, and bathtubs, as the metal pipes can transmit electricity. Likewise, do not use corded phones, computers, or other devices that are electrical. Don't lie on concrete floors or lean on concrete walls, as the metal wires or bars in concrete transmit electricity. Lightning can also strike through windows and doors if there is wire or metal providing a path along which the lightning can travel. Your best bet? Find an interior room and stay off electrical devices to wait out the storm.

Why does the author explain which places to avoid if you are outside?

Which inference is *best* supported by the text?

A   During a storm, you should avoid contact with water and metal, both indoors and outdoors.

B   Many people are struck by lightning because they do not run indoors.

C   It is not possible for lightning to hurt you inside your home.

D   You should avoid standing under isolated trees because they may blow down on you.

DISCUSS IT
Think about the author's advice. What information was new to you? What information did you already know? Turn to another student and talk about what you each learned about the dangers of lightning, both indoors and outdoors.

Read the passage. Then answer the questions.

A CLOSER LOOK

Underline the pathway that Dr. Franklin expected the electrical current to take.

adapted from More About Electricity
by Dr. Worthington Hooker

1   Electricity passes through some things more easily than it does through others. Those that it passes through easily are said to be good conductors of electricity. There are some things, such as glass and silk, that let so very little electricity pass through or over them that they are called nonconductors.

2   Dr. Benjamin Franklin made use of silk in the experiment by which he discovered that lightning and electricity are the same thing. He managed in this way: He made his kite of a large silk handkerchief instead of paper. He had on it a pointed iron wire, and the string of the kite was fastened to this wire. This kite he sent up in a thunderstorm, when there was plenty of electricity in the clouds. The iron wire would, of course, receive some of the electricity, and it would not go from the wire to the kite, because that was made of silk, which, you know, is a nonconductor.

3   It would go down the string, this being tied to the wire. Passing down the string, it would go to Dr. Franklin's hand, and down his body into the earth. It would do this silently, because it would keep going a little at a time all the while.

4   But Dr. Franklin managed to prevent the electricity from coming to his hand. He stopped it on the way. He did this by tying a silk ribbon to the hemp string, and holding the kite by this ribbon. The electricity could not go through this silk, and so it stayed in the hemp string.

> Why is the silk in the kite important to Dr. Franklin's plan?

1 What inference can you make about hemp string from reading the passage?

   A It was not easy to get in Dr. Franklin's time.

   B It is a good conductor of electricity.

   C It was difficult for Dr. Franklin to work with it.

   D It is a good alternative to using only wire.

> What did Dr. Franklin expect would happen when the lightning hit the wire?

2 Which sentence from the text supports the inference that "lightning seeks a pathway to the ground?"

   A "Electricity passes through some things more easily than it does through others."

   B "It would do this silently, because it would keep going a little at a time all the while."

   C "This kite he sent up in a thunderstorm, when there was plenty of electricity in the clouds."

   D "Passing down the string, it would go to Dr. Franklin's hand, and down his body into the earth."

> How do you know that electricity did not go through Dr. Franklin?

3 List two details from the text that help support the inference that Dr. Franklin was concerned with his own safety during his experiment.

_____

_____

_____

_____

_____

_____

Read the passage. Then answer the questions.

Lightning Science

1 Have you ever rubbed a balloon on your head to get a static charge in your hair? Or, maybe you shuffled across a carpet and then touched a doorknob? The hair that stood on end and the spark you received are both examples of static electricity. Lightning works in a similar way.

2 In a thundercloud, particles of ice and water are constantly being pushed around by the wind and the atmosphere, causing the particles to bump into each other. As a result, the cloud builds up a static charge, usually a negative charge near the bottom of the cloud and a positive charge near the top of the cloud. As the cloud moves over the ground, it attracts positive charges in the ground that move up tall objects, such as trees, flagpoles, houses, and steeples. Negative charges come down from the cloud, seeking the best path to the ground. That's when you get lightning.

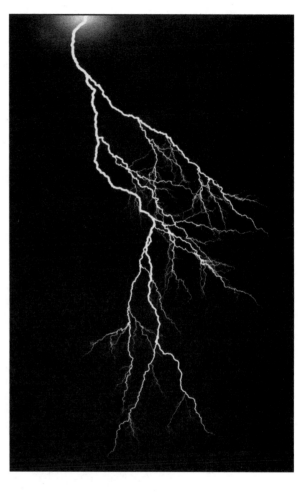

3 But what causes thunder? In a split second, lightning heats the air around it to extremely high temperatures, as much as five times hotter than the surface of the sun. The heated air expands very quickly, creating a shockwave and compressing the air that surrounds it. Then the air cools, causing it to contract, or draw together, rapidly. This contracting creates that first CRACK you hear, followed by rumbles as the air vibrates.

4 There are actually several different kinds of lightning. The forked lightning that you are familiar with is cloud-to-ground lightning. But cloud-to-ground lightning is not the most common. Intra-cloud lightning happens most frequently. This form of lightning occurs between oppositely charged parts of the same cloud, usually between the negatively charged bottom part of the cloud and the positively charged top of the cloud. An observer on the ground would likely see nothing more than a flash or something like a sheet of white light from intra-cloud lightning. For this reason, it is also called sheet lightning. Inter-cloud lightning is similar, but instead of occurring inside one cloud, this kind of lightning occurs between oppositely charged clouds. St. Elmo's Fire is a type of lightning that occurs during thunderstorms, but instead of appearing as a bolt of lightning, it appears as a glow around a tall object, such as a church steeple. The glow can last for several minutes. Chain, or bead, lightning appears in glowing segments, like beads, instead of one continuous bolt. Lightning can even occur in balls that glow, spin, and float. Scientists are still puzzled about what exactly causes this ball lightning. However, they are certain that it exists, as many people around the world have reported seeing it. These lightning balls can be anywhere from the size of a tennis ball to the size of a beach ball, and the ball glows with an electrical charge. Ball lightning looks amazing, but it can be dangerous, burning objects and injuring people.

1 How does a static charge build up inside a storm cloud?

    A The top of the cloud sends static to the bottom of the cloud.

    B Wind pushes electricity from one cloud to another.

    C Ice and water particles bump into each other.

    D Ice particles melt, causing a charge to build up.

2 Which information from the text supports the inference that not much is known about ball lightning?

    A Scientists are puzzled by its causes, but are certain it exists.

    B The size of ball lightning can vary anywhere from the size of a tennis ball to a beach ball.

    C Many people around the world have reported seeing ball lightning.

    D Ball lightning looks amazing, but it can burn objects and injure people.

3 Part A

What *best* explains how lightning happens?

A Lightning appears as a glow around a tall object, such as a church steeple.

B A static charge builds up when you shuffle across a carpet.

C Negative charges at the bottom of clouds move down and meet positive charges moving up from the ground.

D Clouds build up a negative charge near the bottom and a positive charge near the top.

Part B

Which sentence from the text *best* supports the answer in Part A?

A "Then the air cools, causing it to contract, or draw together, rapidly."

B "As the cloud moves over the ground, it attracts positive charges in the ground that move up tall objects, such as trees, flagpoles, houses, and steeples."

C "These lightning balls can be anywhere from the size of a tennis ball to the size of a beach ball, and the ball glows with an electrical charge."

D "This contracting creates that first CRACK you hear, followed by rumbles as the air vibrates."

4 How does the author support the idea that negatively charged particles and positively charged particles are attracted to each other? Use two details from the text to support your answer.

_____

_____

_____

_____

_____

_____

_____

_____

LESSON 8

CCLS RI.5.2: Determine two or more main ideas of a text and explain how they are supported by key details; summarize the text.

Determining Main Ideas and Details

 **Introduction**

THEME: ⟫ The Power of Nature

In writing an informational text, an author first develops a **topic.** A topic is simply what the article is about. To support this topic, the author develops several important points, or **main ideas.** The main idea of a paragraph is the most important thought in the paragraph. The main idea or ideas of an article are the most important thoughts of the article.

Sometimes, an author states the main idea of a paragraph directly, often in the first or last sentence. This is called a **topic sentence.** Other times, readers have to infer a main idea based on **key details** and **examples,** or bits of information about the main idea. Readers can sometimes get clues to the main ideas of an article by reading the title of the article. The title often tells the topic and sometimes provides one of the author's main ideas.

Read the poster below.

Determining the main ideas of a text is a way to check your understanding of it. Look at the poster again. Ask yourself what two things does the author want you to know. How do the details support these ideas? Then look at the graphic organizer. Read the first main idea and the details that support it.

Fill in the second main idea and its key details.

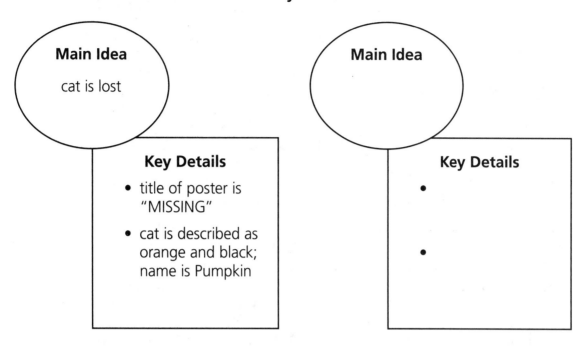

Main Idea

cat is lost

Key Details

- title of poster is "MISSING"
- cat is described as orange and black; name is Pumpkin

Main Idea

Key Details

-
-

Determining main ideas is an important skill that helps you understand what you are reading, whether it is a school textbook, an online article, or an article from a magazine.

Read the first part of the passage. Then answer the questions.

Helping Victims of Natural Disasters

1   When waters rose in New Orleans after Hurricane Katrina struck and a killer tornado tore through Moore, Oklahoma, many people were killed, and thousands were left homeless. When Hurricane Sandy stormed up the East Coast in 2012, 776,000 people had to leave their homes. Natural disasters are a fact of life. In the United States, most government and private organizations are prepared for such disasters. They provide temporary shelters, food, and clothing to the victims. But the story is different in other parts of the world.

2   In 2012, more than 30 million people around the world were forced out of their homes by natural disasters. Many of these people were in poor and underdeveloped countries. There, government response is often slow. The resources to help people in need are not always available right away. As a result, many people will be left homeless for years. For example, in Haiti, where a devastating earthquake destroyed homes and communities in 2010, hundreds of thousands of people were still living in tents as of 2013. Haiti is a very poor country. It has not been able to address the needs of the earthquake victims. In fact, even international help has lagged in relieving the suffering of Haitians.

Think About It

What are the most important points the author wants you to understand in these two paragraphs? Look for details in each paragraph that tell you the most important idea the author wants you to know.

What is the topic of the passage? _____

Underline details in each paragraph that relate to the topic.

How is the topic in the second paragraph slightly different than the topic in the first

paragraph? _____

_____

Now describe the main ideas in the first two paragraphs using details from the text as evidence.

The main idea of the first paragraph is _____

_____

_____.

Some details that support the main idea include _____

_____

_____.

The main idea of the second paragraph is _____

_____

_____.

Some details that support the main idea include _____

_____

_____.

Continue reading the passage. Then answer the question.

A CLOSER LOOK
Underline two ways you can help people in need.

3   What can we do to help address all this need? One of the best actions is to donate to a charity that aids people in disaster situations. Look for reliable charities as well as charities that help people around the world. When you make a donation to a helpful organization, you can feel sure that your dollars are going to help those in need. You also know that you are doing what you can to help those in faraway places where the need is often great.

4   But what about helping people closer to home who are affected by natural disasters? Donating money is not the only way to help. Many relief organizations depend on volunteers when disaster hits. Volunteers respond to almost 70,000 disasters a year in their local communities. Volunteers are able to experience the satisfaction of helping their neighbors.

Paragraphs 3 and 4 each begin with a question that acts as a kind of topic sentence. Which details answer those questions?

How are the main ideas of the third and fourth paragraphs different?

A   The third paragraph is about how to contribute money. The fourth paragraph is about how to sign up with a relief organization.

B   The third paragraph is about finding charities in faraway places. The fourth paragraph is about finding charities close to home.

C   The third paragraph is about helping by donating to charities. The fourth paragraph is about helping by volunteering.

D   The third paragraph is about how to find charities. The fourth paragraph is about 70,000 disasters close to home.

DISCUSS IT
Think about the points the author makes about helping victims of natural disasters. What other ways are there to help? Turn and talk with a classmate about other ways that people can help disaster victims, both in the United States and around the world.

Read the passage. Then answer the questions.

A Wall of Water

1   A tsunami is one of the most destructive natural forces, unleashing a wall of water on coastal areas. It all begins with an earthquake, volcanic eruption, or landslide. Any of these events could cause a displacement of ocean water. The result is a series of waves that move through the deeper parts of the ocean quickly, as fast as a jet plane flies. At this point, the waves are merely a ripple, but the energy of the waves extends deep into the water. As the waves approach shore, they slow down, and the water behind them builds up. This is what produces that wall of water. The tsunami can be several feet high, so that when it hits land it destroys sea walls, homes, and even entire towns.

2   *Tsunami* is a Japanese word that means "harbor wave." That the Japanese coined the term is not surprising—some of the worst tsunamis have hit Japan. In March 2011, one particularly destructive tsunami hit the northeastern part of Japan. Villages were destroyed, and many people were killed. In a number of places, the water surged over 14-foot-high sea walls, leveling everything in its path. But Japan isn't the only country to suffer the effects of powerful tsunamis. Indonesia suffered a devastating tsunami in December 2004 when an earthquake struck off the coast. The resulting tsunami generated 50-foot-high waves that killed thousands of people and swept away homes and entire towns.

3   Many countries and regions of the world where tsunamis frequently hit are equipped with warning systems to alert people to the danger. The warning systems use equipment that monitors earthquake and volcanic activity. If an earthquake or volcano occurs in the area, a computer model calculates whether or not a tsunami could occur. Then officials have just a short time to warn people by sending out alerts over radio, television, and the Internet. People in affected areas are told to move to higher ground, and are usually given an evacuation route to follow. Safe areas are set up so that people have a place to gather. Sometimes, though, the warnings are not heeded or do not come quickly enough. In those instances, the loss of life and property can be devastating.

A CLOSER LOOK

What is the main idea in paragraph 3? Circle a sentence that tells what the paragraph is mostly about. What details help support the main ideas? Underline words and phrases that help explain the main ideas.

Picture a wall of water. Which answer choice could account for this description?

1 Which statement *best* explains why a tsunami is sometimes referred to as a "wall of water"?

A   A tsunami can be very destructive.

B   A tsunami is actually a series of waves.

C   A tsunami can travel as fast as a jet plane.

D   A tsunami can be several feet high.

What idea do most of the examples and details in the paragraph support?

2 **Part A**

What is the *most* important point the author makes in the second paragraph?

A   Both Japan and Indonesia have suffered recent devastating tsunamis.

B   The term *tsunami* is actually a Japanese word.

C   A tsunami is one of the most damaging forces of nature.

D   Building sea walls does not always protect an area from a tsunami.

Part B

Write two sentences that *best* support the answer to Part A.

_____

_____

_____

_____

What do tsunami warning systems do, and what happens when they are not heeded?

3 Use at least three details to support the main idea that tsunami warning systems can save lives.

_____

_____

_____

_____

_____

_____

Read the passage. Then answer the questions.

Tornado!

by Einar F. Klamst

1 It's a hot, humid afternoon on the Great Plains. Thunderstorms are forecast. The gray sky turns a darker, almost greenish shade. The mass of clouds looks like a wall. Large hail begins to fall. Residents of the region know that sky well. It's time to take shelter. It's tornado weather.

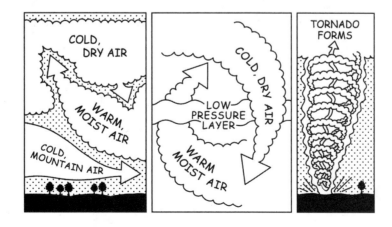

2 A tornado is a violently rotating column of air in contact with the earth. Tornados occur in many parts of the world but most frequently in the central United States in spring and summer. A tornado forms when a layer of warm, moist air is trapped under a layer of cold, dry air. In the early spring, cold air rushing in from the Rocky Mountains causes the warm air layer to be pushed up. As it meets the cold air above it, clouds form and thunderstorms develop in a layer of low pressure. Water vapor in the rapidly rising air condenses[1] in the colder air. Under the right (or wrong) conditions, it begins to rotate around the low-pressure layer. The rising air within the storm tilts the rotating air from horizontal to vertical, forming the well-known funnel-shaped cloud. If it touches the ground—tornado!

3 In late spring and summer, tornados can start in a different way, along what meteorologists call a "dryline." This is an invisible line with warm, moist air to the east and hot, dry air to the west. During the afternoon, the hot air moves in and pushes the warm, moist air upward. Something similar can happen when the moving hot air flows "uphill," toward higher ground. When the rising moist air meets the cold air above it, thunderstorms develop, and under the right conditions, a tornado.

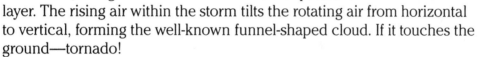

---

[1]**condense:** to make denser or more compact

4 Many funnel clouds form without anyone seeing them. They're transparent, because they consist of water vapor. When they touch down, they pick up dust and dirt and become visible. An ordinary tornado has wind speeds of "only" 112 miles per hour and is about 250 feet wide. It travels about a mile before changes in pressure cause it to break up. Only about one tornado in 50 is classified as violent. These can whirl around at speeds greater than 250 miles per hour and exceed two miles in width. They can last more than an hour and carve a path of destruction dozens of miles long.

5 Most deaths from tornados result from flying debris. When you see the warning signs, take shelter! If no underground shelter is available, stay in an inner room under a sturdy piece of furniture. Stay away from windows. Do you hear a loud roaring sound, like a freight train? A tornado is on its way.

1 Where do tornados most often occur?

 A   the Rocky Mountains

 B   the Great Plains

 C   the western United States

 D   everywhere in the world

2 Which detail from the text supports the main idea that tornados can be dangerous?

 A   "When you see the warning signs, take shelter."

 B   "Many funnel clouds form without anyone seeing them."

 C   "Do you hear a loud roaring sound, like a freight train?"

 D   "When they touch down, they pick up dust and dirt and become visible."

3 **Part A**

What details support the main idea that two different sets of conditions can produce tornados?

A Some tornados are transparent and can pick up debris that makes them visible.

B Tornados can occur both in the spring and in the summer.

C Tornados form when cold air rushes in from the Rocky Mountains and when a dryline forms.

D Some tornados are dangerous, but many are not.

Part B

What two details support your answer to Part A?

_____

_____

_____

_____

4 Explain the *most* important idea in the fourth paragraph and provide two details to support your answer.

_____

_____

_____

_____

_____

_____

_____

_____

LESSON 9

Summarizing Informational Text

 **Introduction**

THEME: >>> **The Power of Nature**

When you **summarize** an informational text, you write only the most important information. A **summary** is a shortened version of a text, covering the **main ideas** and most important **key details.** These details usually include such information as *who, what, when, where, why,* and *how.*

Read the paragraph. Then finish filling in the chart to help you identify the details that should be included in a summary.

For the last decade or so, honeybees have not been returning to the hive. They simply fly away and don't come back. There are no dead bees to be found, but farmers think that they are certainly dying. And no one is really sure why. Scientists have a name for the problem—colony collapse disorder—but they don't know what causes it. They do have a few suspicions, though, starting with the use of pesticides. Scientists think that some pesticides may be to blame for the honeybees' plight. Others think that the pesticides may be making the bees weaker and unable to fight off disease and parasites. Still others point to the shrinking food supply for bees that results from fewer wild areas.

Main Idea	Most Important Details
Honeybees are disappearing.	• • •

Now write a brief summary of one to two sentences, using the information in the chart.

_____

_____

_____

_____

Read the first part of the passage. Then answer the questions.

Hives Are Alive

1   Have you ever seen the inside of a factory? Did you notice how everyone has a job to do and how the work is completed quickly and efficiently? Well, beehives work in much the same way. Each bee has a job to do, and the jobs are carried out quickly and efficiently. It all seems pretty complex for a simple insect, but the honeybee is no simple insect. Honeybees are social insects that live in highly organized colonies. In fact, a single bee without a colony would not survive for long. Honeybees in a colony depend on one another, and the colony or hive depends on each bee.

2   There are three different kinds of honeybees in a colony. The queen is the largest and is the only bee that can lay eggs. In fact, that is her primary job, and she can lay up to 1,500 eggs in a single day. Her other job is to produce chemicals that help maintain order in the hive. The chemicals act like orders from a boss, telling bees what they should be doing and when they should do it.

The queen bee in the center of a hive.

Think About It

How would you summarize the first two paragraphs of the passage? The question asks you to write a brief summary of the information you have read so far. To answer the question, identify the main ideas and the details that you think are most important in understanding the text.

Use this chart to list the main ideas and the most important details.

Main Ideas	Most Important Details
1. Honeybees are social insects that live in organized colonies. 2.	1. Bees in a hive work together, each doing a specific job. They depend on each other. 2.

Use the information in the chart to write a brief summary of the paragraphs in

three to four sentences. _____

_____

_____

_____

_____

Think about the details you used and the ones you left out. Explain why the details

in your summary should be included. _____

_____

_____

In my summary, I included the details that _____

_____

Continue reading the passage. Then answer the question.

A CLOSER LOOK
What is the role of older worker bees? Underline words and phrases that help you answer the question.

3 Worker bees are always female, and they are the most numerous type of bee in a colony. A healthy hive may have up to 100,000 worker bees in the summer. The work they do varies, but also depends on the age of the bee. Younger bees mostly stay home and do work around the hive. This means caring for the eggs and larvae in the nursery, or part of the hive for young bees. It also means caring for the queen bee and bringing her food. Younger workers also produce honey, and make the wax combs that honey is stored in. They repair the hive when necessary and keep it cool in the summer by fanning it with their wings. They also defend the hive against invaders. Older workers mostly leave the hive to gather nectar for making honey.

4 Drone bees are always male, and they have one job—to mate with the queen. After they mate with the queen, they die. Those that do not mate are banished from the hive before the beginning of winter.

5 Winter can be a tough time for a beehive. The colony must have enough honey for the bees to eat and enough bees to keep it warm in cold temperatures. The bees keep warm by staying together in a tight cluster. From time to time, the bees on the outside of the cluster change places with the bees on the inside. In this way, they maintain heat in the hive and keep the colony alive until warmer temperatures arrive in the spring.

Which answer choice is a minor detail?

Which statement is *not* a main idea that should be included in a summary of the article?

A Worker bees take care of the young bees and the queen, and they help make honey.

B The drones' only job is to mate with the queen.

C In winter, bees must have enough honey to eat and enough bees to keep warm.

D Eggs and larvae are cared for in the nursery part of the hive.

 DISCUSS IT
Think about the role or job of each bee in a hive. How does the fact that every bee has a specific job or task keep the hive running smoothly and efficiently? Turn to another student and summarize the points about how the hive is organized.

A CLOSER LOOK

What is each paragraph about? Circle words that show the main idea of each paragraph.

Read the passage. Then answer the questions.

Bee Swarms

1 Beehives are very busy colonies. When spring comes, the number of bees in the colony often soars. This creates a space problem. Bees do not like overcrowding. When there are too many bees in the hive, they do something about it—they swarm!

2 Bee swarms usually happen in the late spring, from April to June. Swarms happen after the queen lays thousands of eggs and new bees emerge. The queen communicates with the hive through chemicals. With so many new bees in the hive, the queen's messages are not passed to all the bees. The bees that do not get the messages do not know there is a queen. So they start preparing a new queen. They feed a larva special food to make it grow extra big. When this new queen emerges, the worker bees force the old queen out.

3 Bee swarms sound alarming, but actually they are organized, even planned, events. First, the old queen and up to 20,000 of the worker bees prepare to leave the hive. The worker bees fill up on honey so they will have enough energy to fly long distances, as much as several miles. Once the swarm leaves the old hive, it gathers on a tree or other site. Then a group of several hundred scout bees fly off to find a good location in a protected area. Each scout may find a separate location, and then begin the process of convincing the other scouts that their site is the best. They do this through dances that encourage other scouts to visit their site. The scouts seem to operate under a kind of democracy, as the site with the most visits wins. When the scouts return to the swarm, they communicate the location they have found and the swarm flies off to establish a new colony.

What happens in the spring when the queen bee lays thousands of eggs?

1 Which is the *best* summary of the first paragraph?

A Bees swarm because the hive has too many chemicals.

B Bees swarm because the hive has grown too crowded.

C Bees swarm because the bees are searching for a new queen.

D Bees swarm because the bees do not have enough to eat.

> One of the details in the chart is simply an explanation of a more important detail. Which one is not necessary to understand why bees swarm?

2 The chart below lists the main idea and some details from the second paragraph.

Main Idea	Details
• Bee swarms usually happen in the late spring after the queen lays thousands of eggs and new bees emerge.	• The hive is crowded, so some of the bees do not get the queen's chemical messages. • These bees don't know there is a queen. • They begin grooming a new queen. • They feed her special food to make her big. • The old queen is forced out of the hive.

Which detail from the chart is *not* important enough to include in a summary of the second paragraph?

A It happens in spring when the bees do not know there is a queen.

B The bees begin grooming a new queen.

C They feed her special food to make her really big.

D The old queen is displaced and forced out of the hive.

> How do the bees look for and decide on a new site for the hive?

3 Write a short summary of the third paragraph. Use at least two details from the text in your summary.

_____

_____

_____

_____

_____

_____

Read the passage. Then answer the questions.

Desert Swarm
by Abbas Samhadi

1   One of the most feared insects on Earth is the desert locust. It lives in the grasslands of northern Africa and southwest Asia. Most of the time, desert locusts don't bother anyone. They feed on the sparse grass of their homeland. When rain falls, however, the grass grows more abundantly. When that happens, the desert locust practically transforms itself into a different insect. The females lay more eggs in the sandy soil. When they hatch, the young locusts gather in large groups to feed. When their hind legs bump against each other, changes take place in their body chemistry. They change in color from green and brown to black, yellow, and pink. They give off a scent that causes them to swarm and fly off in search of food.

2   A locust swarm can be as small as a square mile or as large as several hundred square miles. A swarm that large darkens the sky. In each square mile, there may be anywhere from 60 million to 80 million locusts. One swarm is said to have had 250 *billion* locusts.

3   Locusts fly with the wind, so a swarm can travel as fast as the wind is moving. They can stay in the air for long periods of time. They can't fly much higher than 6,000 feet above sea level, so mountains can sometimes block their flight. But some swarms travel hundreds of miles. They can reach as far as Russia, Spain, and India. During the 1987–1989 outbreak, a swarm of locusts from Africa even crossed the Atlantic Ocean to the Caribbean region.

4   Locusts do not bite people or animals, but they eat just about any kind of plant. A single desert locust can eat its weight every day. Even a small swarm can eat three tons of food in a single day. They can breed up to five times a year. Each generation may have 10 to 16 times as many locusts as the last. One out of every ten people on Earth lives in danger of famine because of desert locusts. An outbreak in West Africa in 2004 led to severe food shortages in the region.

5   Locust species are found over most of the world. The Rocky Mountain locust was once as destructive as the desert locust. In the 1870s, it caused enormous crop damage in the central United States. However, by 1902 it had mysteriously gone extinct.

1 What is the passage *mostly* about?

   A   desert insects

   B   locust life cycle

   C   food shortages

   D   locust swarms

2 Complete the chart that lists details for a summary of the first paragraph.

Main Idea	Most Important Details
	• When the rain falls, the females lay more eggs. • The young locusts gather in groups to feed. • Changes take place in their body chemistry. • They give off a scent that causes them to swarm.

Which statement is a main idea that belongs in a summary?

   A   Locusts swarm when there are so many of them that they touch each other.

   B   The desert locust practically transforms itself into a different insect.

   C   Though the desert locust is normally harmless, it can change quickly.

   D   Desert locusts live in the grasslands of northern Africa and southwest Asia.

3 Part A

Which is the *best* summary of the last two paragraphs of the passage?

A   Locusts do not bite people or animals. Locusts can become extinct.

B   Locusts are destructive because they eat a lot of plants, causing food shortages. Most parts of the world are inhabited by locust species.

C   The problem with locusts is that they reproduce and travel quickly. They are even in the United States.

D   Even a small locust swarm can eat three tons of plants a day. The Rocky Mountain locust was once as destructive as the desert locust.

Part B

Which two quotations from the article *best* support the answer to Part A?

A   "However, by 1902 it had mysteriously gone extinct."

B   "They can breed up to five times a year."

C   "A single desert locust can eat its weight every day."

D   "Each generation may have 10 to 16 times as many locusts as the last."

E   "One out of every ten people on Earth lives in danger of famine because of desert locusts."

F   "Locust species are found over most of the world."

4 Write a brief summary of the passage, using at least two key details.

_____

_____

_____

_____

_____

_____

_____

_____

LESSON
10

Explaining Relationships in Text

1 **Introduction**

THEME: >>> The Power of Nature

Just as all literary texts are not the same so it is with informational texts. **Historical texts** explain events and people in the past. A **scientific text** tells about the natural world. A **technical text** tells how to make or do something. When you read informational text, it is important to identify how people, events, ideas, or concepts are connected. Sometimes authors state these relationships directly in the text, so the connections are explicit. Other times, the reader has to put together details to make connections. When you understand the interactions between people, events, ideas, or concepts, it helps you know what the author is trying to explain.

Read the following informational text.

The Eruption of Mt. St. Helens

Most people find volcanoes interesting, but few get to see one actually erupt. For two months, a volcano in Washington State named Mt. St. Helens had been spouting smoke and ash. Geologists watched it and were worried. They had noticed a bulge growing on its north side. Then, on the morning of May 18, 1980, Mt. St. Helens erupted.

With an incredibly loud explosion, hot gas and pieces of rock shot out of the north side of the volcano at 300 mph. In less than 5 minutes, all plants and animals within 18 miles of the mountain were killed.

The whole top of the volcano was blasted away. A landslide of rocks and debris rocketed down the mountain sides. When the blast was over, a huge crater had formed that was over a mile wide.

Think about what type of informational text you just read. Then answer the questions.

What type of text did you just read? _____

Underline the part of the text that tells what Mt. St. Helens had been doing for two months.

Now underline what happened on May 18, 1980.

You have now underlined two connected events. The author is explaining how the smoke and ash were clues that the volcano might erupt soon.

Draw a line from each event below to a connected event.

The top of the mountain was blasted away.   Geologists were worried.

A bulge was growing on the north side.   Plants and animals were killed.

Hot gasses and rocks shot out.   A huge crater formed.

As you read informational text, look for connections among the people, events, concepts, and ideas. Making these connections helps you understand the author's purpose for including them.

Read the first part of the passage. Then answer the questions.

Independence Rock: the "Register of the Desert"
by Edward Miller

1   Independence Rock stands above the high plains of Wyoming not far from the Sweetwater River. It's a rounded granite hill, rising about 120 feet high above the patchy dry grass. If not for the signs, travelers on State Highway 220 might not know that they were looking at history.

2   Independence Rock marked the halfway point of the famous Oregon Trail. Wagon trains of the years 1843–1869 made it their goal to reach this landmark by July 4. If they did, they would likely avoid autumn snow in the mountains farther west. Legend has it that that's how the rock got its name. In fact, it was called Independence Rock as early as the 1820s, when a group of fur trappers celebrated Independence Day there. Still, reaching the rock on the Fourth was a cause for celebration, as many pioneer diaries attest.

Think About It

What are the connections between Independence Rock and the people who were heading toward it? The question asks you to look for and make connections in the passage. To answer the question, look for details about people, things, events, ideas, or concepts. Think about how these details are related.

What is the relationship between Independence Rock and the Oregon Trail?

_____

What is the connection between the people in the wagon trains and reaching the

rock by July 4? _____

_____

What are two connections between the rock's name and the people who traveled

there? _____

_____

Explain how events in the 1800s connect to history.

In the 1800s, people named a hill in present-day Wyoming "Independence Rock"

because _____

_____

_____.

A CLOSER LOOK

In a text, the ways in which people relate to each other can reveal more about them and show how they get along. In paragraph 3, underline the ways in which the travelers interacted with each other.

Continue reading the passage. Then answer the question.

3 As Margaret Hecox wrote, "Being the Fourth of July, we concluded to lay by and celebrate the day. The children had no fireworks, but we all joined in singing patriotic songs and shared in a picnic lunch."

4 James Nesmith commented, "Had the pleasure of waiting on five or six young ladies to pay a visit to Independence Rock. I had the satisfaction of putting the names of Miss Mary Zachary and Miss Jane Mills on the southeast point of the rocks."

5 It's an easy climb to the top of Independence Rock. From there you can see the prairie, the mountains, and the westward course of the Sweetwater much as the pioneers saw them.

6 Like Mary Zachary and Jane Mills, many of the travelers left their names and other messages on the rock. About five thousand of them are still visible today, carved with chisels or written in axle grease.

Think about the relationships among these people.

What was the connection among James Nesmith, Miss Mary Zachary, and Miss Jane Mills?

A James helped the young ladies climb the rock.

B The young ladies wrote a message on the rock for James.

C James wrote the young ladies' names on the rock.

D James took the young ladies to see the fireworks.

 DISCUSS IT

Think about the 5,000 names and messages from the 1800s still visible today on Independence Rock. Turn to another student and talk about how early travelers on the Oregon Trail influenced those who came after them.

Read the passage. Then answer the questions.

The Ancient Redwoods

Oldest Tree on Earth

1   The redwoods are the oldest trees on Earth. Scientists believe they began growing about 240 million years ago. They live a long time, too. One redwood in California is thought to be more than 2,000 years old. Others may be even older.

A California Home

2   How do redwoods grow taller than any other tree? Scientists say redwoods have excellent growing conditions along the coast of California. In this climate, fog protects them from summer heat and drought. In the winter, there is plenty of rain, and the temperature is mild. Some redwoods have been measured at over 360 feet. A football field is 100 yards in length, equaling 300 feet. So a redwood could be taller than a football field is long. If the growing conditions are perfect, a redwood can grow two or three feet in one year. But many years don't have perfect conditions, and it takes hundreds of years for a redwood to reach 300 feet.

3   The roots of a redwood spread as far as 50 feet out from the trunk. The roots help to support the giant and keep it from falling in windstorms. Redwoods have a chemical called tannin in their wood. Tannin protects the tree from attacks by insects and disease. Redwoods also have very thick, rough bark that helps protect the tree from injury and fire. When a redwood dies, baby trees spring up around the base of the old tree. In this way, a new group of trees grows in a ring. These circles of redwoods are sometimes called fairy rings.

A CLOSER LOOK
What is a fairy ring? Underline the details that tell you.

Logging

4 Since settlers first found the redwoods, they have been cut down for lumber. In about 1850, logging began to be a big business. The gold rush of 1849 brought many settlers to California, and they needed lumber for homes. The trees were cut with axes and huge cross-cut saws. Horses and oxen hauled the logs to the ocean where they were put on sailing ships. The ships took the logs to mills where they were cut into timber and lumber. About 30 years later, trains pulled by steam engines began hauling the logs, and steam ships replaced the sailing ships. Today, most logging is done with huge pieces of heavy equipment. The logs are hauled away by huge log trucks.

5 Redwood lumber is valuable because of its resistance to insects and water. Logging has cleared many of the old redwood forests. Still many redwoods exist in state and national parks where they are protected. With care, these ancient trees will continue to live on the California coast for many more millions of years.

> How were the trees helpful to people coming to California for the gold rush?

1 What was the relationship between the redwoods and the gold rush?

_____

_____

_____

_____

> What are the conditions along the California coast?

2 One benefit of the relationship between the redwoods and the California coast is _____.

   A the trees have very long roots

   B the trees have resistance to fire and insects

   C it takes hundreds of years for the trees to grow

   D the fog protects the trees in summer

> Redwoods have characteristics that make them special.

3 How are redwoods different than other trees?

   A They are older.

   B They are not resistant to insects.

   C They grow in California.

   D They were used for lumber.

> Think about the connection between the redwoods and why many of them were cut down.

4 Explain the relationship between the redwoods and lumber.

_____

_____

_____

_____

_____

_____

Read the passage. Then answer the questions.

Should the Redwoods Be Preserved?

1 The California redwoods are the tallest and oldest trees on Earth. Redwoods can live as long as 2,000 years and have grown to 378 feet in height. They have existed for millions of years on the west coast of the United States. These trees are a national treasure and can't be replaced if harvested for lumber. The California redwoods should be preserved for future generations.

John Muir

2 John Muir was an environmental activist. He believed strongly in preserving the natural beauty of Earth. He was born in Scotland. When he was 11 years old, his family moved to Wisconsin. He worked hard on the family farm, but when he had free time, he roamed around the Wisconsin countryside enjoying the beauty of nature. When Muir grew up, he traveled many places, but when he saw California, he decided to make it his home. He soon realized that ranching and logging were destroying some of the area's most unique natural sites. He urged the government to turn these areas into national parks to preserve them. One of the parks he helped establish was Yosemite where California redwoods are found. Thousands of people visit Yosemite National Park each year to see the ancient trees.

3 As more people began to move to California in the 1800s, lumber was needed to build homes. Logging companies found the redwoods to be a wonderful source of lumber, and they began cutting them down. Redwood lumber is strong and resists water and insects. It is an excellent building material. When gasoline chain saws became available, the trees fell even faster. Trains were used to haul the huge logs to lumber mills. By the 1960s, 90 percent of all the redwoods in California were gone. Thanks to men like John Muir, some of the redwoods were saved inside parks where they could not be cut. Today, more land is being added to these parks. New redwoods are being planted. But it will be hundreds of years before the baby trees become giants.

4 The California redwoods have suffered more in the past 200 years than in the previous millions of years. Cut down and sawed into lumber, they became homes for people who moved west. Today, we realize that the supply of redwoods will not last forever. We need to remember the work of early environmentalists like John Muir and others who helped preserve some of the giant trees. And like Muir, we need to continue to preserve them also. People in the far future will want to enjoy seeing them, too.

1 **Part A**
   What was the relationship between John Muir and nature when he was a child?

   A He made California his home.

   B He worked on his family's farm in Wisconsin.

   C He decided to travel when he grew up.

   D He enjoyed nature from an early age.

   Part B
   Which statement from the article *best* supports the answer to Part A?

   A "When he was 11 years old, his family moved to Wisconsin."

   B "He worked hard on the family farm, but when he had free time, he roamed around the Wisconsin countryside enjoying the beauty of nature."

   C "When Muir grew up, he traveled many places, but when he saw California, he decided to make it his home."

   D "One of the parks he helped establish was Yosemite where California redwoods are found."

2 What does the passage say about John Muir's relationship to the redwoods of California?

   A He urged the government to protect them with parks.

   B He warned loggers not to cut them down.

   C He made a law that redwoods in parks could not be cut down.

   D He planted baby redwoods to take the place of those cut down.

3 Which relationship helped create national parks?

   A John Muir and the loggers

   B John Muir and the government

   C the ranchers and the government

   D the loggers and the government

4 Explain the connection between national parks and the redwoods.

   _____

   _____

Key Ideas and Details in Informational Text

Read the passage. Then answer the questions.

Bringing Back the Wolves to Yellowstone

1   In the 1800s, people moved westward to establish farms and communities. They cleared the land, claiming wilderness areas, and hunted game animals. But there were consequences. There were other residents in those western territories that became the states of Wyoming, Idaho, and Montana. Those residents were gray wolves. The wolves' territory quickly decreased, and the animals found themselves competing with ranchers for prey—elk, moose, bison, and deer. The wolves also began to attack and kill sheep and cattle, prompting the ranchers and farmers to fight back. They hunted and trapped the wolves and even poisoned them. Hundreds of wolves were killed in the early 1900s. By the mid-1900s, no wolf packs remained in Yellowstone National Park, a park that had been created in 1872 in parts of Wyoming, Montana, and Idaho. The gray wolf had virtually disappeared from the western United States. It did not make a return appearance for more than 70 years.

2   The gray wolf is the largest species of wild dog in the world. The wolves vary in size, with males generally larger than females. From the base of their paws to their shoulders, they are from 26 to 32 inches high. From their nose to their tail, they are from four to six feet long. They weigh between 50 and 100 pounds and are bigger than most domestic dogs. They look a bit like a German Shepherd, with a coat that is darker on the top and lighter on the bottom. The color can vary from black or brown to light gray. In the wild, most wolves live only about six to eight years, but some

can live up to 13 years. Wolves live in packs, and only the alpha, or dominant, male and female mate. Once a year, the female gives birth to a litter of four to seven pups, which are raised and cared for by the pack. When they are old enough, the pups join the other members of the pack in hunts, where they bring down large game like moose and elk. On their own, wolves hunt smaller animals like rabbits and mice. They may even scavenge for dead animals.

3   Decades after the gray wolf disappeared from Yellowstone, people noticed that other plant and animal populations in the park were declining. For example, certain types of trees were no longer so common, and beaver populations had decreased. When scientists looked into the cause, they found that with no wolves to kill the elk, these large animals were eating tree saplings, or young trees, that were food for beavers. The older trees were also used to build beaver lodges. Scientists believe that the decline of the trees also caused problems for some species of birds and insects.

4   In the 1960s and 1970s, laws were passed to correct these problems. One such law, the Endangered Species Act, required the government to restore native species that are endangered. In the 1990s, a plan was set in motion to bring the gray wolf back to the western United States. First, scientists trapped gray wolf families in Canada. Then, they brought them to Yellowstone and kept them in an enclosed area until they became used to their new surroundings. Finally, the officials set the animals free. Within a few years, the wolves' population began to increase. In fact, they are now doing so well that they have been taken off the Endangered Species List.

5   Scientists who have tracked the wolves have noticed changes in Yellowstone. The wolves hunt and kill large game. This enables smaller scavengers to feed on the leftovers after a wolf kill. As a result, the populations of small scavengers are increasing. The wolves have reduced elk and moose populations, which has allowed tree saplings to grow. Scientists predict that beaver populations will also increase as a result. It turned out that wolves were an important part of the Yellowstone ecosystem, and their return is helping to correct the mistakes of the past.

1   Which statement *best* explains the interaction between farmers and ranchers and gray wolves?

   A   Farmers and ranchers moved west, cleared the land, and claimed wilderness areas.

   B   Farmers and ranchers protected the wolves with new laws.

   C   Farmers and ranchers shot, trapped, and poisoned the wolves.

   D   Farmers and ranchers tracked the wolves and noticed changes in Yellowstone.

2   How does the author support the inference that when the gray wolf disappeared from Yellowstone, the entire ecosystem changed?

   A   by noting that the government passed the Endangered Species Act

   B   by explaining how a reduction in trees led to a lower beaver population

   C   by pointing out that small scavengers did not have enough to eat when the wolves were gone

   D   by emphasizing that people have become more aware of environmental issues

3 Write a paragraph that supports the main idea that the wolves' return to Yellowstone had a positive impact on the ecosystem of the park. Use at least three details to support the main idea.

_____

_____

_____

_____

Read the passage. Then answer the questions.

The Power of the Rain Forests

by James Evans

1 Tropical rain forests make up only about 6 percent of Earth's dry land. They also contain about 50 percent of all species of plants and animals on Earth! Amazingly, 80 percent of all insects are found in tropical rain forests. Also amazing is that 1.5 billion people depend, directly or indirectly, on the rain forests for their survival.

2 Earth's tropical rain forests stretch in a band across the equator. There, temperatures remain warm year round. The only continents with tropical rain forests are South America, Africa, and Asia. In these dense, humid areas, more than 75 inches of rain falls every year. This creates an environment that helps the rain forest plants grow and make leaves, which produce oxygen. Scientists estimate that rain forest plants produce as much as 20 percent of the oxygen in Earth's atmosphere.

3 While rainfall is essential in tropical rain forests, the rain forests themselves help to keep the environment wet through a process called *transpiration*. This process occurs when rain forest trees soak up rainwater through their roots and release as much as 200 gallons back into the air

each year. Their leaves, too, catch the rain as it falls. When the air temperatures rise in the afternoon, the water evaporates and hovers in a dense cloud over the trees. The cloud is the source of the next day's rainfall.

4 In the tropical rain forest, plants and animals are found in layers. At the bottom, along the ground of the forest, is the shrub layer. Here, taller trees have blocked out the sunlight and the dark conditions are not suitable to most plants. The next layer up is the under canopy. In this layer, sunlight is still scarce, and only a few young trees and vines grow. In the under canopy, the young trees wait for older trees to die and open up space for them. Here, the vines wind their way around taller trees to grow up into the top layers of the forest. The next layer is the canopy, formed by the upper parts of most of the trees. The canopy stretches out, blocking the sunlight below. But, it is home to diverse animal life. The top layer is the emergent layer. It consists of a few trees that extend far above the canopy.

5   Tropical rain forests are in trouble in many places. Farmers have cut rain forest trees to open up space for farm and grazing land. Loggers have cut trees to use for building supplies and fuel. Rain forests have been burned and cleared to make way for new roads and cities. The consequences of destroying the rain forest are dire. Deforestation will lead to the extinction of many of Earth's species that live in the rain forest. The burning of the rain forests also creates a buildup of greenhouse gases. This has led to climate change. And as the rain forests regulate water in an area, their destruction often leads to massive flooding.

6   More must be done to save Earth's tropical rain forests. Nearly all of Earth's people depend on the rain forests in one way or another. Rain forest plants have supplied the chemicals that have gone into making as many as 70 percent of cancer drugs. More chemicals in rain forest species have yet to be identified. Tropical rain forests produce foods and products that people depend on. These include coffee, cashews, pineapples, and many others. Rain forests are also home to many local people. These people have lived in the rain forests for generations. They depend on its plants and animals for their livelihoods and their culture.

4   Which detail from the passage *best* supports the inference that rain forests are important to the well being of all Earth's people?

A   "Farmers have cut rain forest trees to open up space for farm and grazing land."

B   "The consequences of destroying the rain forest are dire."

C   "Scientists estimate that rain forest plants produce as much as 20 percent of the oxygen in Earth's atmosphere."

D   "The only continents with tropical rain forests are South America, Africa, and Asia."

5 Which of the following provides the *best* summary of the passage?

   A Earth's tropical rain forests contain many different species of plants and animals. They also produce much of Earth's oxygen and many products people need. Therefore, more should be done to protect rain forests from destruction.

   B Tropical rain forests are only found in warm, rainy places around the world. We need to do more to save them because their destruction will make climate change worse.

   C Rain forests receive tremendous amounts of rain. The rain evaporates and hangs in clouds, falling again the next day as rain. Because of the amount of rain and the warm climate, rain forests are home to many different plant and animal species.

   D Earth's rain forests are found in a band around the equator. Temperatures here are warm and rain is plentiful. Though the plants in rain forests grow in four layers, most of the plant life can be found in the canopy.

6 How are the actions of people resulting in serious consequences for Earth's rain forests? Provide at least three details from the passage to support your answer.

_____

_____

_____

_____

_____

_____

Read the passage. Then answer the questions.

from What Is a Tropical Cyclone?

1   Tropical cyclones are among nature's most powerful and destructive events. If you live in an area prone to tropical cyclones, you need to be prepared. Even areas well away from the coastline can be threatened by destructive winds, tornadoes, and flooding from these storms.

What Is a Tropical Cyclone?

2   A tropical cyclone is a rotating, organized system of clouds and thunderstorms. These storms form over tropical or subtropical waters. Tropical cyclones rotate counterclockwise in the Northern Hemisphere.

- **Tropical Depression**—A tropical cyclone with maximum sustained winds of 38 mph (33 knots) or less.
- **Tropical Storm**—A tropical cyclone with maximum sustained winds of 39 to 73 mph (34 to 63 knots).
- **Hurricane**—A tropical cyclone with maximum sustained winds of 74 mph (64 knots) or higher. In the western North Pacific, hurricanes are called *typhoons;* similar storms in the Indian Ocean and South Pacific Ocean are called *cyclones.*
- **Major Hurricane**—A tropical cyclone with maximum sustained winds of 111 mph (96 knots) or higher. These are ranked as Category 3, 4, or 5 hurricanes.
- **Post-Tropical Cyclone**—A system that no longer has enough characteristics to be considered a tropical cyclone. Post-tropical cyclones can still bring heavy rain and high winds.

Where and When Tropical Cyclones Strike

3   Tropical cyclones forming between 5 and 30 degrees North latitude typically move toward the west. Sometimes the winds in the middle and upper levels of the atmosphere change. This steers the cyclone toward the north and northwest. When tropical cyclones reach latitudes near 30 degrees North, they often move northeast. Hurricane seasons and their peaks are as follows:

- Atlantic and Caribbean: June 1 to November 30 with peak mid-August to late October.
- Central Pacific (Hawaii): June 1 to November 30 with peak from July to September.
- East Pacific: May 15 to November 30
- Western North Pacific: Tropical cyclones can strike year round.

How Great Is the Danger from a Tropical Cyclone?

4   For 1970–2010, the average numbers of tropical cyclones per year were as follows:

- Atlantic Ocean, Caribbean, or Gulf of Mexico: 11 tropical storms, six of which became hurricanes.
- East Pacific Ocean: 15 tropical storms, eight of which became hurricanes.
- Central Pacific Ocean: 4 tropical storms, two of which became hurricanes.
- Over a typical two-year period, the US coastline is struck by an average of three hurricanes. Usually one of these is a major hurricane.

5   While hurricanes pose the greatest threat to life and property, tropical storms and depressions also can be devastating. Floods from heavy rains and severe weather, such as tornadoes, can cause extensive damage and loss of life.

7   What is the main idea of the first paragraph?

A   Wind causes a lot of destruction in a tropical cyclone.

B   Tropical cyclones are powerful and destructive events.

C   Inland areas are as vulnerable to hurricane damage as coastlines.

D   Tropical storms cause tornadoes and floods.

8   Which detail *best* supports the inference that tropical cyclones can only form over warm water?

A   Tropical cyclones rotate counterclockwise in the Northern Hemisphere.

B   Western North Pacific: Tropical cyclones can strike year round.

C   A tropical cyclone is a rotating, organized system of clouds and thunderstorms that originates over tropical or subtropical waters.

D   East Pacific Ocean: 15 tropical storms, 8 of which became hurricanes.

9 Explain why people who live inland may also be victims of a tropical cyclone.

_____

_____

_____

_____

10 Write a short summary of the passage.

_____

_____

_____

_____

_____

Have you ever borrowed a chapter book from the library? You've probably thought some books had chapters that were too long or too short! But the author did this for a reason. Authors make these choices about the different sections of a book or poem on purpose. They are also careful about the words they choose and the point of view from which a story is told. In this unit, you will determine the meanings of words and phrases, including figurative language. You will think about how writers split up the sections of their writing, and understand the difference between first- and third-person point of view.

LESSON 11 Word Meaning and Figurative Language is about determining the meaning of unfamiliar words and phrases as well as figurative language in stories and poems. You will use context clues to help you figure out what new words mean. You will also find and define metaphors, similes, idioms, and personification.

LESSON 12 Understanding Literary Structure examines the different structures of literary texts and how the pieces fit together. You will learn that poems are broken up by lines and stanzas, books are broken up by chapters, and plays are made up of acts and scenes with dialogue.

LESSON 13 Understanding Point of View looks at the point of view from which a story or poem is written and how this affects the events in the text. You will decide if the story or poem is told from the point of view of a first-person or third-person narrator.

Word Meaning and Figurative Language

 **Introduction**

THEME: >>> Travelers

There are many words in the English language, and new ones are added every day. You won't know every word you come across when you are reading. To understand unfamiliar words, it is useful to use **context clues.** Context clues are words and phrases around an unknown word that give you clues to its meaning.

Besides unfamiliar words, authors may also use colorful or descriptive language that helps you see, hear, taste, smell, or feel what they are writing about. This colorful language is called **figurative language.** There are many types of figurative language. One of the most common is the **simile.** A simile is a comparison of two unlike things using the word *like* or *as.* For example, in *the dancers swayed like tall grass in a breeze,* dancers are compared to tall grass moving in a breeze. The comparison helps you see how the dancers move.

A **metaphor** is another type of figurative language that compares two unlike things. A metaphor does not use *like* or *as.* Instead, in a metaphor, one thing is said to be another thing. An example of a metaphor is *Jessie's car was a dinosaur—it hardly ran at all.* The comparison of the car to a dinosaur tells you that Jessie's car is very old.

Another type of figurative language is **personification.** In personification, an author gives human or animal characteristics or qualities to objects or ideas. For example, in *hunger stalked the town as winter approached,* hunger is compared to a stalking animal. This helps the reader create a mental picture of desperation and fear.

Idioms are also a kind of figurative language. An idiom is a phrase that has a different meaning than its literal meaning. For example, have you ever told a friend that you were going to *hit the books?* If so, you were using an idiom. Another common idiom is *piece of cake.* These phrases are more colorful ways of saying that you're going to study or that something is easy.

Read the poem below.

The Sun Travels
by Robert Louis Stevenson

The sun is not a-bed, when I
At night upon my pillow lie;
Still round the earth his way he takes,
And morning after morning makes.

5   While here at home, in shining day,
We round the sunny garden play,
Each little Indian sleepy-head
Is being kissed and put to bed.

And when at eve I rise from tea,
10 Day dawns beyond the Atlantic Sea;
And all the children in the west
Are getting up and being dressed.

To understand figurative language, readers must think about the comparison the author is making.

Fill in the chart to help you understand how the poet uses personification to describe the sun and its movement around Earth.

Object Described	Words Used to Describe It	Picture the Figurative Language Creates
the sun		

Authors also use figurative language to help them express ideas, thoughts, and feelings. For example, in line 6 of "The Sun Travels," the line "We round the sunny garden play" helps create a happy image. It communicates to the reader how the poet feels about the sun's journey around Earth.

Read the first part of the poem. Then answer the questions.

The Railway Train
by Emily Dickinson

I like to see it lap the miles
And lick the valleys up,
And stop to feed itself at tanks;
And then—prodigious[1] step

5   Around a pile of mountains,
And, supercilious,[2] peer
In shanties by the side of roads;
And then a quarry pare

---

[1]**prodigious:** huge
[2]**supercilious:** proud and scornful

Think About It

Dickinson uses personification to help you visualize the train. To what is Dickinson comparing the train? Think about what the poet wants you to picture about the train.

List the author's descriptions of the train in this chart.

Object Described	Words Used to Describe It	Picture the Figurative Language Creates
a railway train	• • • • •	• • •

What is the poet *most likely* comparing the train to? How do you know?

_____

_____

A CLOSER LOOK
How does the poet use personification? Underline words and phrases that show that the train has lifelike qualities.

Continue reading the poem. Then answer the questions.

> To fit its sides and crawl between,
> 10 Complaining all the while
> In horrid, hooting stanza;
> Then chase itself down hill—
> And neigh like Boanerges;
> Then, prompter than a star
> 15 Stop—docile³ and omnipotent,⁴
> At its own stable door—

³**docile:** gentle
⁴**omnipotent:** all-powerful

Are the words and phrases the poet uses to describe the train positive or negative? What feeling do you get when you read the poem?

Part A

In comparing the train to a horse, you can infer that the poet _____.

A appreciates trains

B prefers animals to trains

C believes trains are horrid

D does not like to ride on trains

Part B

Which detail from the poem *best* supports your answer to Part A?

A "Complaining all the while"

B "To fit its sides and crawl between,"

C "Stop—docile and omnipotent"

D "Then chase itself down hill"

 DISCUSS IT

Think about the poet's description of the train. Remember that in Emily Dickinson's day, a train was a relatively new invention. Why do you think she compared the train to a horse? Turn to another student and talk about why the horse was or was not an appropriate personification.

Read the poem. Then answer the question.

Cavalry Crossing a Ford
by Walt Whitman

1 A line in long array where they wind betwixt[1] green islands;
2 They take a serpentine course—their arms flash in the sun—Hark to the musical clank;
3 Behold the silvery river—in it the splashing horses, loitering, stop to drink;
4 Behold the brown-faced men—each group, each person, a picture—the negligent rest on the saddles;
5 Some emerge on the opposite bank—others are just entering the ford—while,
6 Scarlet and blue and snowy white,
7 The guidon flags[2] flutter gaily in the wind.

_____

[1]**betwixt:** between
[2]**guidon flags:** small flags used to identify military units

---

A CLOSER LOOK

Notice the title of the poem. Underline words in the poem that help you picture the cavalry, or soldiers, on horseback.

How does the poet feel about the cavalry? Circle words that help show how the poet feels.

Remember the definition of a metaphor— something is described as if it is something else. Why does the poet call the men a picture?

---

1 Read this line from the poem.

   "Behold the brown-faced men—each group, each person, a picture—"

What does the poet *most likely* mean?

A He is looking at a picture of a group of men and describing it.

B He can see the men as if he had taken their picture.

C The men have stopped moving, so they are still like a picture.

D Words cannot describe the scene of the men crossing the river.

> The root of *serpentine* is "serpent." How might a course be like a serpent?

2 Part A

What does "a serpentine course" mean as it is used in the poem?

A direct

B frightening

C threatening

D curved

Part B

Which detail from the poem *best* supports your answer to Part A?

A "the negligent rest on the saddles"

B "their arms flash in the sun"

C "where they wind betwixt green islands"

D "Behold the silvery river"

> Think about what the poet is comparing the cavalry to in line 1 versus in lines 4 and 5. How is the mental picture of each scene different?

3 The poet is describing a cavalry crossing a river during the Civil War. Yet he gives different views of the cavalry, presenting different scenes. Explain how the first line of the poem provides a different view of the cavalry than the scene presented in lines 4 and 5. Use details from the poem to support your answer.

_____

_____

_____

_____

_____

_____

Read the story. Then answer the questions.

The Panhandle
by Sheila Rae

1 Zachariah looked out of the window and sighed deeply. "How much longer?" he intoned.

2 "Oh, we still have a ways to go," his mother replied. "We haven't even reached New Mexico yet."

3 Zachariah and his family were driving from Tulsa, Oklahoma, to Colorado Springs through Oklahoma, parts of New Mexico, and then into Colorado. The trip was supposed to take 11 hours, but it seemed to be taking longer, the road a shimmering black river that stretched on and on toward the distant horizon.

4 "Look!" his sister called out, pointing to something in the distance. "It's an old abandoned homestead."

5 Zachariah stared hard. "It's more like a hunchbacked giant, squatting in the dirt," he observed. Grass grew like hair from a dirt-covered roof and dark, vacant windows peered out at the grassland beyond. Tall buffalo grass whipped the skeleton of an old car nearby. The place had definitely seen better days. Zachariah shuddered. Parts of the panhandle were bleak and just a little bit scary, he thought.

6 "Why do they call it the 'panhandle' anyway?" he asked his sister.

7 "I guess because Oklahoma is shaped like a pan with a handle. And this part is the handle," his sister answered.

8 The car hummed and occasionally hiccupped as it hit small bumps in the highway. The soft, swaying motion made Zachariah sleepy. He leaned his head against the cool window and began to drift off to sleep.

9 "Look! Black Mesa!" his mother called out. Zachariah was jolted from his sleep. He rubbed his eyes, the scene in front of him slowly coming into view. Just ahead, a huge black table emerged from the prairie.

10 "What is it?" he asked.

11 "It's a mesa—a tall, wide, flat-topped mountain," his sister explained. "*Mesa* means 'table' in Spanish," she said knowingly.

12 "But how did it get like that?" he asked.

13 "Erosion," his mother said simply.

14 Zachariah frowned and studied the landform. "And?" he asked.

15 "The Cimarron River has sculpted this area. It has cut through the softest layers of rock and pinched the clay. In molding this mesa, the river has left behind a beautiful piece of art," she explained.

16 Zachariah watched as the mesa became a blur and slowly faded into the background. The sun, an enormous orange disk, burned through the windshield as the car rolled westward. Within a few miles, a "Welcome to New Mexico" sign on the side of the highway greeted them. Zachariah rolled down the window and inhaled deeply. The sweet smell of grass and the sharp, earthy smell of cattle wafted into the car. Cows grazed nearby, dotting the otherwise barren landscape and drinking deeply from a gray-green pond. Zachariah lay back against the seat and closed his eyes. Colorado Springs was still hours and hours away.

1   What two things does the simile "It's more like a hunchbacked giant, squatting in the dirt" reveal about the old homestead?

   A   It is modern.

   B   It is large.

   C   It is moldy.

   D   It is badly shaped.

   E   It is leaky.

   F   It is welcoming.

2   **Part A**
The phrase "The place had definitely seen better days" is an idiom that means _____.

   A   the place was a mess

   B   the place could see

   C   the place experienced a lot

   D   the place would soon look good

   Part B
Which detail from the text *best* supports your answer to Part A?

   A   "Zachariah shuddered."

   B   "Parts of the panhandle were bleak and just a little bit scary, he thought."

   C   "Grass grew like hair from the dirt-covered roof"

   D   "dark, vacant windows peered out at the grassland beyond"

3   Which phrase from the passage is a metaphor?

   A   "the road a shimmering black river"

   B   "The car hummed and occasionally hiccupped"

   C   "the sharp, earthy smell of cattle wafted into the car"

   D   "buffalo grass whipped the skeleton of an old car nearby"

4 How does the author's use of figurative language help you understand
what the mesa looks like and how it was formed? Use details from the text
to support your answer.

_____

_____

_____

_____

_____

_____

LESSON
12

Understanding Literary Structure

Introduction

THEME: >>> Travelers

The **structure** of a poem, story, or play refers to the way the author combines ideas to tell a story or create an image in the mind of the reader.

Poems are written in **lines** and sometimes in **stanzas.** Each line is not necessarily a sentence, and line breaks in a poem can help build suspense or create a rhythm. **Stanzas** are groups of lines set apart from other lines. Each stanza usually represents a separate key idea or image. The separation between stanzas also creates visual interest for the reader. Looking at how a poem is structured can help you understand the poet's ideas.

As you read each stanza of a poem, ask yourself what image or idea the poet is expressing. Then ask yourself how each stanza builds on the last one and why the poet put the stanzas in that particular order. Sometimes it helps to think of the stanzas as individual objects in a painting. Each object is important, but the placement of the objects in the painting helps create an image for the viewer. Note that some poems are written without stanza breaks. Instead, the poet develops images and ideas without separating them. In these cases, look at how the lines are organized to see how the ideas are connected.

Like a stanza in a poem, **chapters** in stories separate ideas and events. Some stories are actually collections of letters or journal entries, often arranged chronologically so that readers can follow the sequence of events. An individual chapter, letter, or journal entry usually presents one idea or event. The way the author arranges the chapters, letters, or journal entries helps to tell the story. Each section builds on the last, creating interest and suspense for the reader.

Most plays are made up of **acts** and **scenes.** Each act is a major section of the play. An act is made up of scenes that fit together and move the drama along as the act unfolds. Like chapters in a book, the acts build on previous acts. The **dialogue,** or characters' speech, and the characters' actions create suspense and tell a story.

Look at the illustrations below. Read the dialogue.

Remember, the way a story, poem, or play is structured helps convey the author's ideas.

Look at the illustrations again. What event is happening in the first picture?

_____

What event is happening in the second picture? _____

How do ideas in the two pictures fit together to tell a story? _____

_____

_____

_____

Now imagine that the second illustration appeared first. How would the story

change? _____

_____

_____

_____

_____

Read the first part of the song. Then answer the questions.

The Arkansas Traveler

an American popular song of the 1850s

Oh, once upon a time in Arkansas,
An old man sat in his little cabin door
And fiddled at a tune that he liked to hear,
A jolly old tune that he played by ear.
5 It was raining hard, but the fiddler didn't care,
He sawed away at the popular air[1]
Though his rooftree leaked like a waterfall,
That didn't seem to bother the man at all.

A traveler was riding by that day,
10 And stopped to hear him practicing away.
The cabin was afloat and his feet were wet,
But still the old man didn't seem to fret.[2]
So the stranger said, "Now, the way it seems to me,
You'd better mend your roof," said he.
15 But the old man said, as he played away,
"I couldn't mend it now, it's a rainy day."

———————————

[1]**air:** song
[2]**fret:** worry

Think About It

How does the second stanza build on the first? The question asks you how the two stanzas fit together to help tell a story. To answer the question, look for details that tell what is happening in each stanza.

Read the first two verses of the song again. Underline details in each verse that help tell the key idea or event in the stanza.

Now complete the chart using the details you underlined to tell the key idea or event in each verse.

First Stanza	Second Stanza
•	•
•	•
•	•
•	•

What is the setting of the song? _____

What is the problem in the first verse? _____

How does the traveler try to resolve the problem in the second verse?

_____

How do the two verses fit together to tell a story? _____

_____

_____

A CLOSER LOOK

Dialogue is one element that an author uses to connect ideas and tell more about characters. Underline what the traveler says, and circle what the old man says.

Continue reading the song. Then answer the question.

> The traveler replied, "That's all quite true,
> But this, I think, is the thing for you to do:
> Get busy on a day that is fair and bright,
> 20 Then pitch the old roof till it's good and tight."
> But the old man kept on playing at his reel,[3]
> And tapped the ground with his leathery heel.
> "Get along," said he, "for you give me a pain!
> My cabin never leaks when it doesn't rain!"

_____

[3]**reel:** dance

Think about the problem that was established in the first verse and the way the traveler tries to fix it in the second verse.

How does the third verse contribute to the overall structure of the song?

A   It shows that now there is a conflict to resolve between the old man and the traveler.

B   It adds a new setting, a sunny day, during which the old man decides to fix his roof.

C   It ends the story as the old man doesn't agree with the problem described in the first two verses.

D   It introduces a new character to the story of the traveler.

DISCUSS IT

Look at the dialogue in the third verse. What does it show about the traveler's point of view? What is the old man's attitude? Turn to another student and talk about what the dialogue shows about each character.

Read the story. Then answer the questions.

Emma's Journey

September 8, 1849

Dear Journal,

    Today, my family and I arrived at the port in Boston to board the ship the <u>Adam Alexander</u>. We packed up everything we had, as we're moving to New Orleans to be closer to Papa's family. Mama says the journey will be long. We will sail south around Florida and through the Gulf of Mexico until we reach New Orleans.

September 12, 1849

Dear Journal,

    Our cabin is below deck, and the air gets terribly stale. Papa tells us all to get fresh air up on deck, but we have to mind the railings. One of the crew members told us that a small child once slipped through the railings and off the deck right into the ocean. Can you imagine?

September 15, 1849

Dear Journal,

    Last night, a terrible storm rocked the boat. The captain said it was a hurricane churning up from the Gulf. The rain began shortly after dark, and then the winds soon picked up so that the boat was rocking violently. Mama got sick, and Abi and I cried, but Papa told us that this big, old ship wasn't going anywhere and not to worry. This morning, the weather seems calmer. The skies are brightening in the south. But still, some of the sails have been torn and the railing is broken in places. Water has swamped the deck, and so the sailors are cleaning it. The captain says it might take a long while before everything is back to the way it was.

September 18, 1849

Dear Journal,

The sails were all mended shortly after the storm. But the boat was badly battered, and the railings around the deck are splintered. Papa says we must stay away from the sides of the ship. So Abi and I hold on to the main mast and watch the seagulls and the waves rise and fall. This morning, as we were watching the white foam on the water, we saw dolphins! They were swimming in pairs, leaping up like dancers. They almost seemed to be smiling.

October 1, 1849

Dear Journal,

The <u>Adam Alexander</u> is limping along, and Papa says the bulk of the repairs will have to be done once we dock in New Orleans. Still, Papa says it won't be too much longer until we reach port. He says the weather there is warmer than in Boston, and that I'll hardly notice the winter months. I look forward to being with Papa's family, but I miss my friend Katherine.

October 6, 1849

Dear Journal,

Today we docked in New Orleans. What a lively city it is! Papa's sister, Aunty Lucy, met us at the dock, along with Uncle Henry and Cousin Martha. They took us to their house, a small wooden structure off the main shopping area. Aunt Lucy cooked up fish and rice, and served fresh fruit afterwards. We all ate until we could eat no more. It is so good to be standing without swaying, to drink fresh water, and to not be confined to that awful ship. I didn't think I'd say this when I left Boston, but New Orleans is a welcome sight!

> Look at the title of the story. What do you think this story is mostly about?

1 What is the *most* important thing you learn in the first journal entry?

   A Emma is sailing from Boston to New Orleans.

   B Emma is moving to be closer to her father's family.

   C The journey will be a long one.

   D The ship will sail around the coast of Florida.

> How does the journal entry of September 15 fit with the journal entries that follow it?

2 **Part A**

How does the journal entry of September 15 help contribute to the overall structure of the story?

   A It tells the reader more about the setting of the story.

   B It uses more figurative language than other entries.

   C It introduces an important problem in the story.

   D It tells the reader more about the other characters in the story.

Part B

Which detail from the story *best* supports your answer to Part A?

   A "This morning, the weather seems calmer."

   B "The skies are brightening in the south."

   C "Mama got sick, and Abi and I cried, but Papa told us that this big, old ship wasn't going anywhere and not to worry."

   D "Last night, a terrible storm rocked the boat."

> How does Emma describe her surroundings through each entry?

3 How does the journal show the progression of what happens during Emma's journey?

   A It shows how Emma gets more and more excited to get to New Orleans.

   B It shows how Emma's family gets along throughout the journey.

   C It shows how the ship changes through the journey.

   D It shows how the passengers react to the storm.

What does Emma do on October 6? How do you know?

4 Only five days pass between the journal entries of October 1 and October 6. How does the author show that much has changed for Emma in this time? How does the last journal entry contribute to the story? Use at least two details from the text to support your answer.

_____

_____

_____

_____

_____

_____

_____

Read the poem. Then answer the questions.

An Encounter
by Robert Frost

This poem describes a traveler's surprise when he sees a telephone pole where he doesn't expect to see one.

Once on the kind of day called "weather breeder,"
When the heat slowly hazes and the sun
By its own power seems to be undone,
I was half boring[1] through, half climbing through
5   A swamp of cedar[2]. Choked with oil of cedar
And scurf of plants, and weary and overheated,
And sorry I ever left the road I knew,
I paused and rested on a sort of hook
That had me by the coat as good as seated,
10   And since there was no other way to look,
Looked up toward heaven, and there against the blue,
Stood over me a resurrected tree,
A tree that had been down and raised again—
A barkless spectre.[3] He had halted too,
15   As if for fear of treading upon me.
I saw the strange position of his hands—
Up at his shoulders, dragging yellow strands
Of wire with something in it from men to men.
"You here?" I said. "Where aren't you nowadays
20   And what's the news you carry—if you know?
And tell me where you're off for—Montreal?
Me? I'm not off for anywhere at all.
Sometimes I wander out of beaten ways
Half looking for the orchid Calypso.[4]"

---

[1]**boring:** cutting through
[2]**cedar:** a kind of tree
[3]**spectre:** vision
[4]**Calypso orchid:** a rare flower

1   What structure has the poet used to write this poem?

   A   The poem is written in three acts.

   B   The poem is written as if each line were a chapter.

   C   The poem is written without stanza breaks.

   D   The poem is written as if it were a journal entry.

2   Reread the first seven lines of the poem. What two ideas does the poet present in these first lines?

   A   The poet is on a familiar road.

   B   It is a very hot day.

   C   It is late in the evening.

   D   The poet is walking through overgrown woods.

   E   The poet attempts to make a joke.

   F   The poet is worried about poisonous plants.

3   Reread lines 12 through 18. What event does the poet present in these lines?

   A   The poet has arrived in a new setting.

   B   The poet sees something in the woods that scares him.

   C   The poet has solved his problem of being weary and overheated.

   D   The poet is surprised to see a telephone pole in this wilderness area.

4   How does the dialogue in lines 19 through 24 contribute to the overall structure of the poem? Use details from the poem to support your answer.

_____

_____

_____

_____

_____

_____

LESSON 13

Understanding Point of View

Introduction

THEME: >>> Travelers

Every story has a **narrator,** that is, the voice that is telling the story. Every narrator has a **point of view,** or relationship, to events in the story. Sometimes a story is told in **first person.** That means the narrator is a main character in the story. The use of the pronouns *I, me, my, our, us,* and *we* are clues that the author is writing in the first person. You see the actions in the story through the eyes and feelings of the narrator.

Sometimes a story is told in **third person.** That means the voice telling what happens is not a character in the story. The use of the pronouns *he, she, his, her, them, they,* and *their* are clues that the author is telling the story in third person. The narrator describes characters and events by telling you what the characters are doing, seeing, and feeling.

Here is an example paragraph written in first person. Underline the pronouns.

> At the end of the day on Friday, I was so ready for the weekend. Jim and I were planning to get up early on Saturday morning and ride our bikes to Black Creek Park. Some of our friends were going to meet us there.

Here is an example paragraph written in third person. Underline the pronouns.

> At the end of the day on Friday, Carlos was so ready for the weekend. He and Jim were planning to get up early on Saturday morning and ride their bikes to Black Creek Park. Some of their friends were going to meet them there.

Use the chart below to list the pronouns you found in each paragraph.

First-Person Paragraph	Third-Person Paragraph

When you read a story, ask yourself, "Who is telling the story?" Is the narrator one of the main characters, or is the narrator someone outside of the story, describing the characters and events.

Read the first part of the story. Then answer the questions.

My Oregon Vacation

1 "Hi, Grandma and Grandpa!" I yelled from the airport entrance gate.

2 "Logan, you're finally here!" laughed Grandma as she hugged me. Grandpa grabbed my suitcase and gave me a high-five.

3 So excited after my long flight, I plastered my face to the car window as we drove through Eugene, Oregon. As we passed many huge trucks carrying logs, Grandma said, "This area is known for its tall fir trees. Those logs are going to a sawmill to be processed into lumber or telephone poles."

4 When we crossed a bridge, Grandpa said, "That's the Willamette River. We'll fish there for salmon, but first stop is a seafood restaurant for some lunch. We're only about 75 miles from the coast, so the seafood is fresh and delicious."

5 "Sounds wonderful to me, Grandpa. I'm starving because I got only one bag of peanuts on the plane."

6 After lunch, we stopped at my grandparents' house, and I carried my suitcase to the room my dad slept in as a boy. Then we piled back into the car to visit a rain forest park.

7 "This is Mount Pisgah Arboretum," said Grandpa as we pulled into the parking lot. "We'll walk one of the shorter trails today."

8 Hiking along the trail, I kept staring up at the towering trees. The trunks were fuzzy with moss and lichens. This part of Oregon gets huge amounts of rainfall, and plants grow on top of each other! Walking under some ferns taller than me, I nearly ran into an artist sketching a waterfall that was splashing into a sunlit pool.

Think About It

From what point of view is this story told? The question asks you to identify the point of view of the narrator.

Read the beginning of the story again. As you read, underline the pronouns you find. Then answer the questions below.

Who is telling this story? _____

Is this story being told in first person or third person? _____

How can you tell? _____

_____

What relationship does the narrator have to what is going on in the story?

_____

_____

Continue reading the story. Then answer the questions.

A CLOSER LOOK

The narrator is telling about his own thoughts and actions. Underline words and phrases that tell what he says and thinks.

9 The next morning, Grandpa and I went salmon fishing in the Willamette. The water was running fast and icy cold, and Grandpa said, "That's what salmon like. They've been out at sea the first part of their lives, and now they're swimming upriver to lay their eggs."

10 "Do they swim back out to sea then?" I asked.

11 "No, Logan," replied Grandpa, "after the eggs are deposited in a rocky streambed, the adults die. I know it seems sad, but that's the way salmon live their lives. Now let's see if we can catch one," he said as he cast his fly into the churning water. Well, we didn't catch a salmon, but a bald eagle swooped down and hooked one with its powerful talons! As we packed up our fishing gear, I noticed another artist farther down the river. *Sure are a lot of artists around here,* I thought.

12 On my last day in Oregon, we drove to the Pacific coast. We passed through the coast mountain range where acres of trees had been clear-cut from the mountainsides. Grandma said, "The lumber companies are required to plant new trees after they cut the old ones."

13 When we got to the coastal sand dunes, Grandpa bought tickets for a dune buggy ride. The buggy looked like a bus with gigantic tires and no roof. After all the passengers were seated, we zoomed off. The wind whistled around us, and the huge tires threw up clouds of gritty sand. The driver raced to the top of each dune and then dove down the other side. Grandma and some other ladies screamed. I loved every minute, but my hair and ears were crusted with sand when the ride was over.

14 Next stop was the sea lion caves. We rode an elevator from the top of the cliffs to the dark, damp, and smelly caves below. Through a viewing window, we watched gigantic sea lions swim in from the ocean and wallow on the stony cave floor.

15 At the end of the day, we walked along the rocky Pacific beach. Once again, I spotted an artist painting a picture, this time of the sunset.

16 I know I'm not an artist, but I like to write, so this is my word picture of my Oregon vacation.

Is the comment about the eagle part of dialogue in the story?

Who tells you that an eagle caught a salmon in the Wilammette?

A   Grandpa

B   Logan

C   an artist

D   another fisherman

What pronouns are used in the story?

How would the point of view be different if it was told by a narrator?

_____

_____

_____

_____

DISCUSS IT

Read this sentence from the story. *"I loved every minute, but my hair and ears were crusted with sand when the ride was over."* Turn to another student and talk about how this line of dialogue would be spoken if Grandpa were talking about the boy's experience.

A CLOSER LOOK
Underline pronouns in this story to help you determine the point of view. What point of view is used?

Read the story. Then answer the questions.

Oregon in Watercolor

1 Pete Lane is a well-known watercolor landscape artist. He travels around the country looking for beautiful places to capture in his paintings. Like many other watercolor artists, some of Pete's favorite places to paint are in Oregon. He has been to that state many times. On every visit, he has found new subjects for his paintings.

2 Watercolor painting is done on paper. The paints are usually mixed with water or brushed onto wet paper. The water gives the paintings a transparent look. This makes watercolors great for painting waterfalls, the ocean, and landscapes. Watercolors are more difficult to use than oil paints. An artist who uses oil paints can simply paint over mistakes. An artist who tries to paint over watercolors makes a muddy mess.

3 Last summer, Pete flew into Eugene, Oregon, to do some watercolor painting. His first stop was at the Salmon Fountain in the center of Eugene. He first took photos of the fountain from several angles. Then he did a quick sketch of the sculpture of bronze fish that appear to leap out of the fountain. He would complete the painting later with watercolors.

4 Pete's next stop was along the Willamette River. He likes the way the water moves over and around the rocks, and the way the sun sparkles on the ripples. Sometimes Pete includes people in his paintings. A recent painting shows fishermen casting for salmon. The Owen Rose Garden is Pete's favorite place to paint flowers. There are plenty of benches along the winding path where he has often set up his easel. People who pass by while he is painting stop to take a peek.

5 The Mount Pisgah Arboretum is another of Pete's favorite places to paint. Open fields as well as the temperate rain forest give a variety of landscapes to paint. He likes to capture the tall fir trees as the sunbeams fall through them late in the day. In several of his paintings, an eagle floats in the blue sky above.

6 On every Oregon trip, Pete drives to the Pacific coast. There are so many interesting views to paint that he never runs out of choices. He has painted the Heceta Head Lighthouse from many different angles and times of day. Each painting is unique.

7 Pete usually drives farther south along the shore. He sets up his easel along the rocky coast. One of his favorite times to paint is at sunset. Pinks, lavenders, and golds reflect in the water from the evening sky. The colors bounce off the rocky cliffs as well.

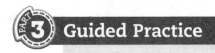

Sunset doesn't last long. Pete uses his camera to capture the quickly changing light. He completes his paintings later in his studio at home.

8 Pete often says that painting with watercolors is challenging. When he works outside, he has to watch the weather. Clouds move in, wind dries his paper, and the light changes quickly. Sometimes little bugs or sand get stuck to his paintings. Still, he continues to paint with watercolors. He loves the way his paintings capture the beauty of nature. And Oregon will always be one of his favorite places to paint.

> Pronouns can help you decide the point of view of the story.

1 The narrator of this story _____.

A participates directly in what is going on

B takes part in events of the story

C describes his own thoughts and feelings

D is an observer of events in the story

> Which sentence uses a third person pronoun to refer to Pete?

2 Which sentence is in the third person and could be included in this story?

A Besides painting along the river, I enjoy talking to the people fishing there.

B My favorite colors are the colors of the sunset.

C When people see Pete, they know they will get to see one of his paintings.

D I sometimes paint at the Mount Pisgah Arboretum.

> Change the pronouns and the verb ending.

3 Rewrite this sentence from the story in first person. *He completes his paintings later in his studio at home.*

_____

_____

Read the poem. Then answer the questions.

The Lake Isle Of Innisfree

by William Butler Yeats

I will arise and go now, and go to Innisfree,
And a small cabin build there, of clay and wattles made:
Nine bean-rows will I have there, a hive for the honeybee,
And live alone in the bee-loud glade.
5 And I shall have some peace there, for peace comes dropping slow,
Dropping from the veils of the morning to where the cricket sings;
There midnight's all a glimmer, and noon a purple glow,
And evening full of the linnet's wings.
I will arise and go now, for always night and day
10 I hear lake water lapping with low sounds by the shore;
While I stand on the roadway, or on the pavements grey,
I hear it in the deep heart's core.

1 What is the point of view in this poem?

A third person

B a narrator

C a poet

D first person

2 Why do you think the poet chose to write this poem from this point of view?

A to express his own thoughts and feelings

B to explain that he would build a cabin

C to describe how loud honeybees are

D to share the sounds of the water lapping at the shore

3 Which line from the poem tells the main reason why the poet wants to go to Innisfree?

    A "There midnight's all a glimmer,"

    B "I hear lake water lapping with low sounds by the shore;"

    C "And I shall have some peace there,"

    D "Nine bean-rows will I have there,"

4 How might the poem have been different if, instead of the poet Yeats writing it, someone else wrote it for him in the third person?

_____

_____

_____

_____

Craft and Structure in Literary Text

Read the story. Then answer the questions.

In the Footsteps of Lewis and Clark
from the Journal of Zack Peterson

July 15 Today we left St. Louis, Missouri, to trace the journey of Lewis and Clark. Zoe (my twin) and I had been studying about their journey in school. Since we live in Missouri, we convinced our parents it would be a fun vacation to follow the trail Lewis and Clark took. In 1803, President Jefferson asked them to explore the Louisiana Purchase and find a water route to the Pacific Ocean.

We started from St. Charles, Missouri. There the explorers left civilization behind. Beyond St. Charles, the land was like a puzzle. There would be only rivers to follow and directions from Native American tribes. Dad is driving our car, so we're moving as fast as a jet compared to the explorers. They traveled about 15–20 miles per day in canoes they paddled, pushed, and pulled.

Tonight, we are near Omaha, Nebraska. That's close to Fort Atkinson where the explorers met with western tribal chiefs. Speeches were made and a peace talk took place.

July 16 Today, we saw miles and miles of corn as tall as Dad! Tonight, we are in Stanton, North Dakota. Lewis and Clark spent the winter here. Tomorrow morning, we'll visit the Knife River Museum to learn more about the plains tribes.

July 17 After the museum, we stopped at Fort Mandan. Here Lewis and Clark first met Sacajawea and her French trader husband. They traveled on with the explorers and helped them speak with the American Indians. They helped Lewis and Clark find their way through unknown country.

We drove to Great Falls, Montana, this afternoon. We are close to the Rocky Mountains. Our car and interstate highways make our trip simple compared to that of the expedition. The Missouri River is a snake, and the explorers had to follow every twist and turn. Waterfalls presented a problem. The explorers had to portage. They carried the canoes around the falls, an 18-mile journey. Sacajawea was very sick, and there were grizzly bears all around. We didn't see any grizzly bears, but we did see beautiful rainbows painting the mist above the falls.

July 18 Topping the Rocky Mountain peaks, we reached the Continental Divide. From this point, all water flows east to the Atlantic Ocean or west to the Pacific Ocean. Lewis and Clark wanted to find a river to follow to the Pacific. However, only more mountains marched far into the distance.

July 19 We crossed more of the Rockies today. These mountains do seem to march on forever. The expedition traveled over them by foot, nearly starving to death. Then, they found the Clearwater River. The fast-moving waters sailed them through Idaho. We drove that part today and stopped at Lewiston, Idaho. We have left the Rockies behind. We are near where the Clearwater River joins the Snake River. The Snake took the explorers to the Columbia River.

July 20 We are driving through Oregon on Interstate 84. It follows the Columbia River through the Cascade Mountains. On the Columbia, the explorers portaged around dangerous rapids and crashing waterfalls. We stopped to see Multnomah Falls. It is the second-highest waterfall in the United States.

July 21 We are in Astoria, Oregon, tonight. Here the Columbia River enters the Pacific Ocean. Lewis and Clark camped near the river, traded with the coastal tribes, and explored the area. About ten days later, they built Fort Clatsop and set up a winter camp. It was November, and they couldn't begin their return journey until spring.

It has taken us seven days to follow the trail that took Lewis and Clark one year and six months to cover. What an exciting journey it has been, and one of the best vacations ever!

1 Read this sentence from the story.

"Dad is driving our car, so we're moving as fast as a jet compared to the explorers."

What type of figurative language is used in the sentence?

A idiom

B personification

C metaphor

D simile

2 **Part A**

Which sentence from the story uses personification?

A "Beyond St. Charles, the land was like a puzzle."

B "However, only more mountains marched far into the distance."

C "They carried the canoes around the falls, an 18-mile journey."

D "We crossed more of the Rockies today."

Part B

How can you identify personification? What is the meaning of the personification in Part A?

_____

_____

_____

_____

3 What is true about the structure of the journal?

A It presents events in stanzas.

B It helps the reader understand why good and bad things happen.

C It presents events in chronological order.

D It helps the reader understand more about Zack's family.

4 How does the narrator's point of view influence how the story is told? Use details from the story to support your answer.

_____

_____

_____

_____

_____

_____

Read the story. Then answer the questions.

Space Camp

1   Mariah took a deep breath as her mom pulled into the parking lot at the US Space Camp on Sunday afternoon. She could hardly believe she was finally here. It had been two months since her fifth-grade science teacher had told her she had won the scholarship. She still couldn't believe she had scored highest in science and math. But here she was, and her dream of becoming an astronaut might be coming closer to happening.

2   Mariah's first stop at Space Camp was the Habitat. This is the dorm where campers stay while at Space Camp. She got her bedding, T-shirts, and badge, and she was told to report to the fourth floor. There, she found her bunk bed with the other girl campers. She noticed the sign above the drinking fountain said H_2O REHYDRATION UNIT. There were space language signs everywhere! Later that afternoon, Mariah went on a tour of the whole complex. It was amazing to see all the spacecraft (including a space shuttle) and a training center with lots of space equipment for the campers to use.

3   The next morning, everyone was up at 7 a.m. Breakfast was at 8 a.m. Campers were assigned to teams they would work with throughout their stay. Then, Mariah had her first class in space history. She learned about how the space program began and how NASA chose the first astronauts. Mariah dreamed of her first day as an astronaut as the campers left the classroom.

4   After some fun swimming and a delicious lunch, it was time for the first astronaut activity. Mariah's team got to try out simulators that showed what life is like on the International Space Station (ISS). Then the campers saw a movie about the history of aviation.

5   Throughout the week, Mariah and her team had new adventures with space. One experience simulated landing on Mars for an exploration. Another day, they did experiments similar to those done on the ISS. A retired astronaut spoke to the campers about what life was like on the ISS. Mariah's brain was a huge sponge absorbing all the new things she was learning. She made friends with the other kids on her team as they studied and worked together.

6   Too quickly, it was Friday morning. After all the learning and experiences, the campers were ready for graduation. Proudly, Mariah stood under space shuttle *Pathfinder* with her team. She received a certificate and her flight wings! She knew she would be an astronaut someday. Her future was in space.

5   This story is told _____.

   A   in first person

   B   by the main character

   C   in third person

   D   by an astronaut

6   Which sentence from this story uses a metaphor?

   A   "Too quickly, it was Friday morning."

   B   "Proudly, Mariah stood under space shuttle *Pathfinder* with her team."

   C   "After all the learning and experiences, the campers were ready for graduation."

   D   "Mariah's brain was a huge sponge absorbing all the new things she was learning."

7   Explain how the author organizes Mariah's experiences so they fit together to tell a story.

_____

_____

_____

_____

Read the poem. Then answer the questions.

excerpt from In Praise of Johnny Appleseed
by Vachel Lindsay

      A boy
      Blew west
      And with prayers and incantations,
      And with "Yankee Doodle Dandy,"
5   Crossed the Appalachians,
      And was "young John Chapman,"
      Then
      "Johnny Appleseed, Johnny Appleseed,"
      Chief of the fastnesses, dappled and vast,
10   In a pack on his back,
      In a deer-hide sack,
      The beautiful orchards of the past,
      The ghosts of all the forests and the groves—
      In that pack on his back,
15   In that talisman¹ sack,
      Tomorrow's peaches, pears and cherries,
      Tomorrow's grapes and red raspberries,
      Seeds and tree souls, precious things,
      Feathered with microscopic wings,
20   All the outdoors the child heart knows,
      And the apple, green, red, and white,
      Sun of his day and his night—
      The apple allied² to the thorn,
      Child of the rose.
25   Porches untrod³ of forest houses
      All before him, all day long,
      "Yankee Doodle" his marching song;
      And the evening breeze
      Joined his psalms of praise
30   As he sang the ways
      Of the Ancient of Days.

_____

¹**talisman:** an object that brings good luck
²**allied:** working together with
³**untrod:** not traveled on

8 The structure of the poem _____.

    A follows Johnny Appleseed as he crossed the country with his seeds

    B tells about the pack Johnny Appleseed carried

    C praises Johnny Appleseed

    D tells the kinds of fruit seeds Johnny Appleseed planted

9 How can you can tell that the poem is written in third-person point of view?

    A It is written by Johnny Appleseed.

    B It uses the pronouns *he, him,* and *his.*

    C It describes fruit seeds that Johnny Appleseed planted.

    D It uses many adjectives.

10 What do you think "tree souls" means in line 18, "Seeds and tree souls, precious things."? Use context clues to help you answer the question.

_____

_____

_____

_____

Craft and Structure in Informational Text

Sometimes you will read two texts that are about the same topic, but written in completely different ways! In this unit, you will compare and contrast the structures of informational text. You will also use clues to find the meanings of academic words and words that are specific to certain topics. You will look at different sources and compare their treatment of the same event or topics.

LESSON 14 Understanding Word Meanings is about determining the meaning of words that are not familiar to you. By looking for context clues like synonyms, antonyms, and examples, in addition to prefixes and suffixes, you should be able to come up with definitions for new words.

LESSON 15 Comparing Informational Text Structure: Problem and Solution, Chronology focuses on comparing and contrasting texts written with a problem and solution structure to texts written with a chronological structure. You will think about the author's purpose in choosing a certain structure and learn about the signal words that help you know whether the text has a problem and solution or chronological structure.

LESSON 16 Comparing Informational Text Structure: Cause and Effect, Comparison analyzes texts written with a cause-and-effect structure and texts written with a comparison structure. You will consider how the text structure suits the author's purpose and what signal words help you recognize a text structure.

LESSON 17 Analyzing Relationships in Informational Text is about analyzing different sources on the same topic. As you are noting important similarities or differences, be on the lookout for positive or negative statements that show the author is biased.

LESSON 14

Understanding Word Meanings

Introduction

THEME: >>> **How Do Things Start?**

There are thousands of words in the English language, and new words are added every year. That means that you will come across many words you don't know, especially when reading informational text. Often, you will come across academic words, or words that are specific to a subject, that you may not recognize. But there are ways to determine the meaning of an unknown word.

First, look for **context clues.** Context clues are words or phrases in the sentence or surrounding sentences that help you infer, or make a logical guess about, the word's meaning. There are several different kinds of context clues. A **synonym** is a word that means the same or almost the same as another word. An **antonym** is a word that means the opposite of another word. **Definitions** tell information about what a word means. **Examples** are words that show what another word means. It is also important to look at the information in and around the sentence to help you understand the word's meaning.

Read the sentences. Then complete the chart on the next page.

1. Egyptian farmers kept excellent records about when the annual <u>inundation</u> of the Nile River started.

2. The ancients had a sort of <u>chronometer</u> that helped them tell time.

3. Scientists were <u>ecstatic</u>, delighted, at the latest discovery.

4. The Roman emperor was thought a <u>benevolent</u> ruler, not cruel like his father.

5. People have used the <u>celestial</u> bodies—the planets, moon, stars, and sun—to measure time.

Each sentence contains a context clue that will help you identify the meaning of the underlined word. Circle the context clue in the sentence, then write it in the chart. Tell what kind of clue it is. Then infer, or make a logical guess about, the word's meaning. The first one is done for you.

Word	Clues	Type of Clue	Word Meaning
inundation	*farmers, annual, Nile river*	more information	"flooding"
chronometer			
ecstatic			
benevolent			
celestial			

If you think you know a word's meaning, replace the word with the meaning in the sentence and see if it makes sense. If it does not, try another strategy: determine what part of speech the word is. Is it a noun, a verb, an adjective, or an adverb? Understanding the role the unknown word plays in the sentence can sometimes help you identify context clues you may have missed.

Read the first part of the passage. Then answer the questions.

Seasons

1   What's your favorite season? Do you like the warm days of summer the most? Or, do you prefer watching the snow fall in the winter? If you live in a place that has distinct seasons, you've probably noticed that each season has certain weather patterns that are different from the other seasons. Summer is the warmest season, and winter is the coldest. Spring and fall are somewhere in between the two. These weather patterns occur because Earth orbits the sun.

2   In one 24-hour period, Earth makes a complete rotation on its axis, the imaginary line that runs from the South Pole to the North Pole. Earth is tilted on its axis. As Earth travels around the sun, the hemisphere, or half of Earth, that points toward the sun experiences summer and receives more sunlight. The days are therefore longer, and the sun is higher in the sky, making the temperatures warmer. The hemisphere that points away from the sun experiences winter and receives less sunlight. This hemisphere has shorter days, and the sun is lower in the sky, helping to make the temperatures drop.

Think About It

***What is the meaning of the word* distinct?** The question asks you to determine the meaning of *distinct* in the context of the sentence. To answer the question, look for clues in paragraph 1 that help you understand the word's meaning.

Is the word *distinct* a noun, verb, adjective, or adverb as used in the sentence?

_____

Use this chart to list words, phrases, or details that help you understand the meaning of *distinct*. Note the type of clue. Then write the word meaning based on the context clues.

Word	Clues	Type of Clue	Word Meaning
distinct			

Reread the paragraph and substitute the definition you wrote in the chart for the word *distinct*. Does the definition make sense in the sentence? Does it help you understand the author's explanation of seasonal weather patterns?

Continue reading the passage. Then answer the question.

3　How does this affect you? If you live in the United States, you are in the Northern Hemisphere. Your summer begins on June 21, which is also the longest day of the year. Your winter begins on December 21, which is the shortest day of the year for you. If you lived in the Southern Hemisphere, say in South Africa, your winter would begin on June 21, and summer would start on December 21.

4　On September 22 and March 21, everyone in the world has about the same amount of sunlight and darkness—12 hours of each. This is the *equinox.* In the Northern Hemisphere, spring begins on March 21, and autumn begins on September 22. The reverse is true if you live in the Southern Hemisphere.

5　But what if you live at the equator? You wouldn't experience the change of seasons—no winter, no autumn, no spring. You would only have summer. That's because the sun at the equator is always high in the sky, so the weather is always warm.

A CLOSER LOOK

What happens on September 22 and March 21? Underline words that tell you what makes these days different from other days.

Look at the beginning of the word. What other words that you know begin the same way?

What is the meaning of the word *equinox?*

A　the first day of spring and fall, when everyone has equal amounts of sunlight and darkness

B　the band that runs around the center of the earth and that is always warm

C　the Northern Hemisphere, or northernmost part of the world, where the United States is located

D　the weather pattern that determines when summer begins in the Southern Hemisphere

 DISCUSS IT

Reread the article and underline unfamiliar words, such as *rotation, axis,* and *equator.* Turn to another student and talk about how to use what you know about figuring out word meanings to define these words.

Read the passage. Then answer the questions

Telling Time

1   When most people want to know what day it is, they check their computer or smartphone. Ancient peoples did not have these devices. They watched the positions of the sun and moon. They also kept track of the regular <u>recurrences</u> of certain events, such as the annual rains or the beginning of the dry season, to mark the passage of time.

2   Artifacts of Stone Age people suggest that they marked time by gouging holes in sticks and bones. Some people think they may have been counting days between phases of the moon.

3   The Egyptians based their earliest calendar on the moon's cycles. Later, they noticed that a major star rose next to the sun about once every 365 days. This happened to coincide with the annual inundation of the Nile River. Thus, in A.D. 3100, they developed a 365-day calendar. As far as historians know, it is the first calendar containing 365 days, which is approximately the same as a solar year.

4   The Roman calendar, which was put into practice by Julius Caesar in 46–45 B.C., was most like our own. The calendar divided each day into 24 hours, with 12 hours assigned to the day and 12 hours assigned to the night. The problem for the Romans was that there is more daylight in summer than winter. So summer hours were longer than winter hours.

5   Like the Egyptians and Romans, the Mayans also watched the sky, particularly the stars and sun. Their Haab calendar contained 365 days. However, the Haab calendar <u>comprised</u> 19 months. Of the months, 18 contained 20 days, and 1 month contained 5 days.

6   The ancient Chinese used both the sun and the moon to calculate the number of days in the year and to divide the year. They are said to have a *lunisolar* calendar, or a calendar based on both the sun and the moon. This calendar had 12 months; each month began on a new moon and lasted from 29 to 30 days. A new month was added to the calendar every two or three years to accommodate the extra days. Today, the People's Republic of China officially uses the same calendar that we use. However, people in the Chinese countryside still use the ancient calendar to mark festivals and to determine when to plant crops.

7   Today, we use the Gregorian calendar, which was originally created to mark the cycle of ceremonies of the Roman Catholic Church. The Gregorian calendar contains 365 days, with an

intercalary day every four years. A leap year, then, contains 366 days. Though the Gregorian calendar has been in use for a very long time, it is still used by most people around the world.

> What does the prefix *re-* tell you?

1 In paragraph 1, the author uses the term *recurrences* to mean _____.

   A   times of rainy and dry weather

   B   events that happen again and again at certain times

   C   devices that mark the passage of time

   D   natural disasters

> Which definition makes the most sense when you use it in place of *comprised?*

2 **Part A**

Read paragraph 5. What does the word *comprised* mean as it is used in this paragraph?

   A   pointed out

   B   was the same as

   C   was very long

   D   was made up of

Part B

Which detail from the article provides the *best* clue for the meaning of *comprised?*

   A   19 months

   B   contains

   C   the same

   D   the stars and sun

> What other words start with *inter-?* What word does the second part of the word, *-calary,* look like?

3 Explain the meaning of the word *intercalary* in the last paragraph and list details from the text that helped you determine the meaning of the word.

_____

_____

_____

Read the passage. Then answer the questions.

adapted from Navigation and Related Instruments in 16th-Century England

Instruments for Measuring Time

1 Explorers in the 16th century used different navigational instruments than today's sailors. To navigate a ship, most navigators used the dead-reckoning method of navigation. The word *dead* in the phrase is short for "deduced." The navigator began at a known or assumed position and then measured as best he could the position of the ship. He measured the heading and speed of the ship. He measured the speeds of the ocean currents and the leeward (downwind) drift of the ship. He measured the time spent on each heading. From this information, he could compute the course he had made and the distance he had covered.

2 Accurate time is essential to dead reckoning. So the sandglass or hourglass was the timepiece most often used in navigation. The most common glasses were the four-hour and half-hour sizes. Days at sea were divided into 6 four-hour shifts, or watches. A ship's boy carefully tended the half-hour glass, turning it as soon as the sand had run through. He called out or struck a bell for all aboard to hear. At the end of four hours, he turned the four-hour glass. (Hence, the system of bells and watches still used aboard many vessels.)

3 The glass was used in combination with the *log*. The log was a piece of wood attached to a line knotted at uniform intervals. A sailor heaved the log from the stern of the ship and let the line pay out freely as the ship pulled away. When the sailor felt the first knot pass through his fingers, he shouted a signal to another sailor. The other sailor turned a one-minute glass. The first sailor counted aloud the number of knots that passed until the sand ran out. A timer of one minute (1/60 of an hour), knots spaced 1/60 of a nautical mile apart, and simple arithmetic easily gave the speed of the ship in nautical miles per hour (or knots).

Other Tools

4 The traverse board was used to approximate the course run by a ship during a watch. It consisted of a circular piece of wood on which the compass points had been painted. Eight small holes were evenly spaced along the edge to each point. Eight small pegs were attached with string to the center of the board. Every half-hour, one of the pegs was stuck into the hole for the compass point closest to the heading the ship. At the end of that watch, a general course was determined from the position of the pegs. The traverse board served as a crude dead-reckoning computer reminiscent of those used to this day aboard aircraft.

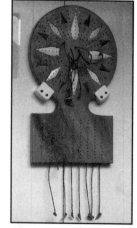

Replica Traverse Board

5 The lead and line was an ancient, but highly useful, navigational aid. It was used to find depth and seabed characteristics. It consisted of a sounding lead attached to a line. It had evenly-spaced knots or bits of colored cloth worked into it. The lead was tossed overboard and allowed to sink to the sea floor. Each mark was distinctive. The distance between successive marks was constant. Water depth could easily be measured ("by the mark") or estimated ("by the *deep*").

6 Although not a navigational instrument, the *boatswain's pipe* was a tool of great value. This peculiarly shaped whistle was used by the boatswain to pipe orders throughout the ship. (The contraction *bos'n,* which stands for "boatswain," was not used in the 16th century.) Its high-pitched sound was usually <u>audible</u>, even above the howling of the wind, to crewmen working high in the rigging.

7 The ship's log contained a record of courses, speeds, soundings, and other relevant information. A good log was accurate and comprehensive enough to allow the navigator to check his dead reckoning.

1 Which choice is the *best* definition of the word *vessels* as it is used in paragraph 2?

   A containers

   B veins

   C ships

   D systems

2 The word *interval* means "a space between things." Which detail from paragraph 3 provides the *best* clue to the meaning of the word *interval?*

   A "The first sailor counted aloud the number of knots that passed until the sand ran out."

   B "The glass was used in combination with the *log.*"

   C "Simple arithmetic easily gave the speed of the ship."

   D "A sailor heaved the log from the stern of the ship and let the line pay out freely as the ship pulled away."

3 Part A

Read paragraph 6. What does the word *audible* mean as it is used in this paragraph?

A   irritating

B   unusual

C   able to be heard

D   able to be understood

Part B

Which details from the passage provide the *best* clue for the meaning of *audible?*

A   "peculiarly shaped whistle…to pipe orders throughout the ship"

B   "high-pitched sound…even above the howling of the wind"

C   "navigational instrument…crewmen working high in the rigging"

D   "boatswain's pipe…a tool of great value"

4 The word *reminisce* means "to remember past events." Explain the meaning of the word *reminiscent* as it is used in paragraph 4. Tell how you used context clues and the meaning of the word *reminisce* to determine the definition.

_____

_____ . _____

_____

_____

CCLS RI.5.5: Compare and contrast the overall structure (e.g., chronology, comparison, cause/effect, problem/solution) of events, ideas, concepts, or information in two or more texts.

LESSON 15

Comparing Informational Text Structure: Problem and Solution, Chronology

Introduction

THEME: ⟫⟫ How Do Things Start?

If you were going to write about how to grow tomatoes, you probably wouldn't start by describing tomato plants. You would likely explain what the reader should do first, then second, and so on. You would think carefully about the **text structure,** or the way you organized your article, so that it made the most sense to the reader, because your purpose for writing would be to explain a process.

Recognizing text structure is important in reading nonfiction. It will help you understand the **author's purpose,** or what the author wants to accomplish in the article. That will help you understand what you are reading about and anticipate, or expect, what you will read next. It also helps you locate ideas in a nonfiction text.

The text structure that you would likely use to explain how to grow tomatoes is called **chronological,** or **sequential.** This text structure explains ideas in time order or as a series of events or ideas in order. For example, a diary records events in the order in which they happen. Most how-to guides use a sequence of steps to explain how to do, make, or fix something. You can often recognize chronological or sequential text structures because they contain signal words such as *first, second, next, then, last,* or *finally.* A series of dates, or a time line, can also signal a chronological order.

Sometimes, other text structures are more useful in presenting information. For example, if your purpose was to explain everything that can go wrong when you are growing tomatoes and what you should do to correct the problems, you might arrange the information in a **problem and solution** text structure. In this organization, the author tells about the problem and then explains the solution. As a reader, you would be able to locate information that you need quickly by glancing at the problems. Problem and solution text structures also use signal words, including *problem, solution, question, answer, because, cause, since,* or *as a result.*

Read the paragraphs. Then answer the questions.

If you want to start a business, you must first determine if there is a need for your product or service. Next, make a business plan that will help you set goals. Then determine how you will finance, or pay to start and run, your business. Finally, think of a name for your new business.

Can't get your new business off the ground? The problem could be the economy. But there might also be too much competition in the area. One solution is to move your business to an area with a greater need for your product. You might also look at the name of your business. Catchy names are an important part of making a business successful.

How is the information in the first paragraph organized? _____

_____

What signal words help you identify the type of text structure? _____

_____

How is the information in the second paragraph organized? _____

_____

What signal words help you identify the type of text structure? _____

_____

What information does the first paragraph contain? _____

_____

What information does the second paragraph contain? _____

_____

If you wanted to start a new business, the information in the first paragraph would be more useful and easier to follow. If you were having trouble with your new business, you'd want to read the second paragraph. Its text structure provides information arranged in a way that would be more helpful to you.

Read the first parts of two passages. Then answer the questions.

adapted from The Story of the West Point Mint

Yesterday

1   The name "West Point" reminds many people of the United States Military Academy at West Point, New York. But did you know that the town of West Point is also home to the United States Mint? In fact, the United States Mint and the Academy are neighbors.

2   The United States Mint at West Point wasn't always a mint where coins were made. It was built in 1938 to store silver, and that was its only job for many years as the "West Point Bullion Depository." A depository is like a storehouse, where coins are not made—like the depository at Fort Knox, Kentucky, that stores bullion, or brick-shaped bars of gold and silver. In fact, the West Point facility has been called "the Fort Knox of silver." But things do change, and change came to West Point as well.

3   This facility became the first new mint in more than 100 years!

More Duties

4   At first, silver was always stored in the West Point Bullion Depository in the form of bullion. But changes began in 1970.

- Some 3 million Carson City silver dollars were found in New York City and moved to West Point.
- From 1973 to 1986, West Point minted some of our one-cent coins (pennies).
- In 1980, West Point began striking gold medallions, then storing gold in its vaults.
- In 1983, West Point began minting gold coins.

Battling Counterfeit Currency

1   The money in circulation in the United States is backed by the Federal Reserve Bank. That means that when counterfeit, or fake, money goes into circulation, it creates problems for the economy. Finding and preventing counterfeit money is an important job of the government and an important issue for Americans. It has the potential to affect everyone.

2   Paper money was once incredibly easy to counterfeit. To solve the problem, the Secret Service was established to root out counterfeit money and pursue the counterfeiters. The Federal Reserve Bank also has a role in rooting out counterfeit money. *The Fed,* as it is called, removes counterfeit money from circulation when it is detected. How is it detected? High-speed machines that contain sensors detect certain qualities in counterfeit bills. The Fed puts bills through these machines to count them. Then they shred the bills they find to be counterfeit.

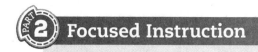

3 The Secret Service and Federal Reserve are the government's answer to detecting counterfeit money. But not all counterfeit money goes through the Federal Reserve or comes under the scrutiny of the Secret Service. This is where new printing techniques come in.

Think About It

How are the two articles organized? The question asks you to determine the text structure of the two passages. To answer the question, look for signal words in the texts.

Read the first part of each article again. Use this chart to list any signal words that help you identify the text structure of each article.

The Story of the West Point Mint	Battling Counterfeit Currency
•	•
•	•
•	•
•	•
•	•

What information is presented in the first passage? _____

_____

What information is presented in the second passage? _____

_____

What text structure do the authors use for each passage?

Passage 1 _____

Passage 2 _____

Continue reading the two passages. Then answer the question.

The Story of the West Point Mint *continued*

5 With all that minting going on at the West Point Bullion Depository, it was time for a name change. A law was passed in 1988 that changed this bullion depository into the nation's first new mint facility in more than 100 years! It became known as The United States Mint at West Point.

6 And then there was another first in 1997. The West Point facility struck collectible coins from platinum, making it the first mint facility in the United States to make coins out of platinum.

7 In 2000, the West Point facility enjoyed another first: It struck the nation's first coin made from two metals. In such a *bimetallic* coin, the metals are not mixed together as an alloy, but one metal is used in the center of the coin, and the other surrounds it. That ten-dollar coin, made of gold and platinum, honored the Library of Congress.

Today

8 The United States Mint at West Point is still a depository, but it also makes bullion coins and commemorative coins, or coins that are struck to honor something. To keep all that gold, silver, and platinum safe, no tours are held. Only people who work in the building are allowed to enter it.

Battling Counterfeit Currency *continued*

3 As sophisticated computers and printers become more widespread, counterfeiting has become easier, and the quality of counterfeit bills has improved. But the Bureau of Engraving and Printing (BEP) found a solution. They have added a number of new features to the bills that are now in circulation in the United States. These include a watermark, which contains a change in paper density that is hard for counterfeiters to duplicate. Another solution is color-shifting inks. These inks change colors when viewed from different angles and are not readily available for counterfeiters. Fine-line printing patterns are also used on currency, as they are difficult for most scanners and printers to replicate. Newer bills also contain a larger, off-centered portrait that includes more details, details that are also more difficult to reproduce. And you've probably noticed the security thread, or thin colored ribbon that runs through your dollar bills. This detail is also difficult for counterfeiters to reproduce.

4   What if counterfeiting becomes more sophisticated? Then perhaps more solutions will be incorporated into our currency. Perhaps, each currency will include a computer chip or some other means of identifying it as government issued. But that solution has yet to be presented.

> Look at the title of each passage. How might the title help you determine the author's purpose for writing each passage?

Which statement *best* explains why the authors organized their information the way they did?

A   The author's purpose in the first passage is to compare the ways the West Point Mint has functioned, and the purpose in the second passage is to explain how the government's approach to counterfeiting has changed.

B   The author's purpose in the first passage is to ask questions and then provide answers, while the purpose in the second passage is to explain the steps in the process of finding and preventing counterfeiting.

C   The author's purpose in the first passage is to tell how the West Point Mint became a mint, while the purpose in the second passage is to examine how the government has tried to solve the problem of counterfeit money.

D   The author's purpose in the first passage is to solve the issue of what the West Point Mint should be used for, and the author's purpose in the second passage is to compare the ways that the government battles counterfeit money.

DISCUSS IT

Think about how the authors organized the information in the two texts. Turn and talk with a partner about why these two text structures work for these passages. Discuss whether the text structure of the second passage would work with the first passage, and vice versa.

Read two passages. Then answer the questions.

Bell's Telephone

by Alex Davies

1   Alexander Graham Bell is widely credited with inventing the telephone. Born in Scotland in 1847, Bell moved with his family to Canada and soon afterwards to Boston. Bell's father was a respected teacher of the hearing impaired. He encouraged Bell to explore various interests, including photography, music, and anything having to do with electricity.

2   In Boston, Alexander took a job as a teacher at a school for the deaf. Though he was a committed teacher, he became interested in creating a device that would transmit a human voice over wires. Recognizing that he lacked the necessary technical abilities to produce such a device, Bell hired an assistant named Thomas A. Watson. Then in February 1876, Bell filed a patent. A patent is the right of an inventor to be the sole maker and seller of an invention. But even with his patent, Bell still didn't have a workable telephone. He just had an idea and a general notion of how the idea would work. But Bell was tireless and confident. He experimented with different devices. And on March 10, 1876, with Watson's help, Bell was able to send the first message over the wires. The inventor spoke these words: "Watson, come here. I want you."

3   Bell and Watson tinkered with their new device, ironing out the problems and perfecting it. They even took the new invention on a kind of tour, demonstrating its use around the country. Later in 1876, Bell was part of the first long-distance phone call. It was transmitted over a telegraph wire from Brantford, Ontario, to Paris, Ontario.

4   Anticipating great commercial success with Bell's device, a businessman started the Bell Telephone Company to make telephones available to the general public. The company hired Bell to be the technical advisor. Bell continued in this role until the early 1880s, at which point he became bored with the telephone. Bell continued his scientific pursuits, including experimenting with other versions of the phonograph, a device to play back sound recordings. However, Bell was no longer so involved in the telephone industry. He continued to work tirelessly in his efforts to help the deaf and hearing impaired. Alexander Graham Bell died in 1922 at the age of 75.

A CLOSER LOOK

Remember that signal words can help you identify text structure. Circle words in the text that signal a chronological structure or problem/solution text structure.

Underline words and phrases that help you identify the author's purpose for writing.

Who Got There First?
by Steve Smith

1   While most people think of the inventor of the telephone as Alexander Graham Bell, many people believe that the real credit should go to another inventor, Elisha Gray. Gray, who was born in Ohio in 1835, was interested in electricity and began experimenting with reproducing writing at a distance. Bell, who was born in 1847, began experimenting with transmitting telegraph messages. Both men eventually began working on a device that would transmit sound. This device would lead to the telephone. Both filed patents on the same day: February 14, 1876. The problem is, nobody is quite sure which one should *actually* be credited with inventing the telephone.

2   How do you solve this vexing historical problem? Some historians have looked at the time line. For example, according to some reports, Alexander Graham Bell had been working for quite a while on his telephone, but he could not get the device to transmit sound. Then on March 8, 1876, he tried something new, and suddenly, he found success. It turns out that Bell had visited the US Patent Office just days before and may have looked at Gray's patent caveat, or the paper Gray filed announcing the device he was working on. The caveat contained the plans for a device that explained in detail how sound would be transmitted using the same procedure that Bell used. And Bell's drawings of the device look remarkably similar to Gray's drawings. Bell, it should be noted, was awarded the patent for the telephone, even though Gray had submitted his patent caveat first.

3   But other people argue that to solve the problem, you have to look at court records—hundreds of them. That's because Bell's patent was legally challenged in hundreds of cases. Over the course of several years, Gray suggested that Bell bribed the patent officer to win the patent for the telephone. But every time the case came up, Bell won. Time after time, the courts ruled in Bell's favor.

4   So what's the answer? Perhaps in the years to come, historians will uncover more information that helps definitively decide who actually invented the telephone. But until then, the mystery remains unsolved.

How are the dates important in the first passage?

1 In the first passage, the author tells about the invention of the telephone by _____.

A   comparing Bell's work on the phone to Watson's

B   pointing out all the problems Bell encountered

C   explaining events in the order that they occurred

D   describing the process of inventing something

How does the topic sentence in the second passage help you understand the author's purpose?

2 In the second passage, the last paragraph *mainly* _____.

A   explains that the inventor of the telephone will never be known

B   points out who got credit for the invention of the telephone

C   suggests how the problem might be solved in the future

D   provides a step-by-step guide for determining the inventor

What is each author's purpose in writing the passage?

3 Compare how the two passages discuss the same event: the invention of the telephone.

_____

_____

_____

_____

_____

_____

Read the passages. Then answer the questions.

Sir Isaac Newton and the Apple

1 Sir Isaac Newton was a great thinker. No other man of his time knew so much about the laws of nature. No other man understood the reasons of things so well as he. He learned by looking closely at things and by studying hard. He was always thinking, thinking.

2 Although Newton was a wise man, he felt that he knew but very little. The more he learned, the better he saw how much there was still to be learned.

3 When he was a very old man he said, "I seem to have been only like a boy playing on the seashore. I have amused myself by now and then finding a smooth pebble or a pretty shell, but the great ocean of truth still lies before me unknown and unexplored."

4 It is only the very ignorant who think themselves very wise.

5 One day in autumn, Sir Isaac was lying on the grass under an apple tree and thinking, thinking, thinking. Suddenly, an apple that had grown ripe on its branch fell to the ground by his side.

6 "What made that apple fall?" he asked himself.

7 "It fell because its stem would no longer hold it to its branch," was his first thought.

8 But Sir Isaac was not satisfied with this answer. "Why did it fall toward the ground? Why should it not fall some other way just as well?" he asked.

9 "All heavy things fall to the ground—but why do they? Because they are heavy. That is not a good reason. For then we may ask why is anything heavy? Why is one thing heavier than another?"

10 When he had once begun to think about this, he did not stop until he had reasoned it all out.

11 Millions and millions of people had seen apples fall, but it was left for Sir Isaac Newton to ask why they fall. He explained it in this way:

12 "Every object draws every other object toward it."

13 "The more matter an object contains, the harder it draws."

14 "The nearer an object is to another, the harder it draws."

15 "The harder an object draws other objects, the heavier it is said to be."

16 "The earth is many millions of times heavier than an apple; so it draws the apple toward it millions and millions of times harder than the apple can draw the other way."

17 "The earth is millions of times heavier than any object near to or upon its surface; so it draws every such object toward it."

18 "This is why things fall, as we say, toward the earth."

19 "While we know that every object draws every other object, we cannot know why it does so. We can only give a name to the force that causes this."

20 "We call that force gravitation."

21 "It is gravitation that causes the apple to fall."

22 "It is gravitation that makes things have weight."

23 "It is gravitation that keeps all things in their proper places."

24 Suppose there was no such force as gravitation, would an apple fall to the ground? Suppose that gravitation did not draw objects toward the earth, what would happen?

25 To you who, like Sir Isaac Newton, are always asking "Why?" and "How?", these questions will give something to think about.

The Scientific Method

by Benjamin Evans

1 Scientists ask a lot of questions about the world, and they seek to find answers through observation and experimentation. But each scientist can't have his or her own rules and methods for finding out answers and solving problems. That's why the scientific method is so important. It's also why scientists around the world use it to explore their world.

2 The scientific method is a process by which scientists try to figure out how the world and the universe work. There are several steps in the scientific method.

3 The first step is to make an observation. For example, you might observe that a heavy ball rolls down a hill faster than a light ball.

4 The next step is to form a hypothesis, which is an educated guess based on what you have observed. Your hypothesis might be that the heavy ball rolls down a hill faster than the light ball because gravity pulls the heavy ball down faster.

5 The third step in the scientific method is to design an experiment. An experiment is a test of your hypothesis using a step-by-step procedure that changes only one variable or element of the experiment at a time. An experiment for your ball hypothesis might be to drop balls of different weights down a smooth slope. The variable might be changing the material from which the balls are made.

6 The fourth step is to collect your data, or record the results of your experiment. Your data for the ball experiment would likely include the weight of the balls, the materials from which the balls were made, the distance the balls had to travel, and the time it took each ball to reach the bottom of the slope.

7 The last step is to make a conclusion. This step involves reading over the data and comparing your findings with your original hypothesis. What did you find when you did your experiment? Did your data support your hypothesis? Present your findings in written form, explaining your experiment and noting whether or not it supported your hypothesis.

8 The scientific method helps scientists ask and answer questions about the world. But it also helps students of science create real science experiments that can produce real results.

1 Which of these *best* describes what the first passage is mostly about?

    A   the life and career of Sir Isaac Newton

    B   how to be a scientist like Sir Isaac Newton

    C   how Sir Isaac Newton was not like other scientists

    D   how Sir Isaac Newton approached scientific questions

2 How does the author *mainly* organize information in the second passage?

  A by stating a problem and how it can be solved

  B by stating a point of view and then comparing ideas

  C by explaining a series of causes and effects

  D by explaining the sequence of a procedure

3 **Part A**

Which statement *best* describes the overall structure in the first passage?

  A It describes the series of steps that scientists follow.

  B It explains how one scientist sought answers to scientific questions.

  C It describes the rules of all scientific study.

  D It compares the scientific questions that Sir Isaac Newton asked.

Part B

In the first passage, in what way do paragraphs 8–10 contribute to the overall structure in Part A?

  A They provide an example of Newton's determination to solve scientific problems.

  B They provide the first step in one of Newton's most famous experiments.

  C They provide contrasting questions to the ones that Newton had previously asked.

  D They provide the most important question that Newton asked during his career.

4 How does the organization of the second passage help you to understand the ideas in the first passage?

_____

_____

_____

_____

LESSON 16

Comparing Informational Text Structure: Cause and Effect, Comparison

Part 1 Introduction

THEME: ≫ How Do Things Start?

Authors of informational text use text structures to organize the information they are presenting. This helps you understand the events, ideas, and concepts discussed in the text. Identifying the text structure the author is using helps you better understand what you are reading.

Compare-and-contrast text structure is used to tell how two or more similar events, ideas, or concepts are alike and different. For example, an author might use this type of structure to show how evergreen and deciduous trees are similar and different.

An author uses a different text structure to tell how an event influences a particular outcome. This **cause-and-effect** text structure discusses a cause and then gives a description of events, or effects, that result from that cause. For example, an author may use this type of structure to tell about a hurricane and the effects that resulted from the hurricane's powerful rains and winds.

One way to help identify the text structure is to look for signal words. Here are some examples.

Text Structure	Signal Words
compare/contrast	similarly, on the other hand, alike, also, in contrast, in comparison, both
cause/effect	therefore, because, since, so that, as a result, if-then, due to, thus

Read the paragraphs. Then answer the questions.

Some scientists believe that 65 million years ago, a huge asteroid struck Earth. Because giant clouds of dust were thrown into the air, sunlight was blocked. As a result, Earth's climate changed quickly. It became dark and cold so that most plants and many animals died.

Tornadoes and hurricanes both form in hot, humid weather. A tornado forms over land unlike a hurricane that forms over the sea. Both have high-speed, destructive winds. Hurricanes usually move slowly and can last for days. In contrast, a tornado moves quickly and lasts for minutes.

How is the information in the first paragraph organized? _____

What signal words help you identify the type of text structure? _____

_____

What was the cause? _____

What were the effects? _____

_____

What text structure does the author use in the second paragraph?

_____

What signal words help you identify the text structure?

_____

Authors use a particular text structure to organize information and present it clearly. It can be useful to compare and contrast the text structures of two or more texts to see how events, ideas, concepts, or information relate to each other.

Read the first parts of two paired passages. Then answer the questions.

Electricity

1   To understand electricity, you need to know about atoms. Atoms are so small, they can only be seen with the most powerful microscopes. Everything is made of atoms, and atoms are made of electricity. There are even smaller particles inside atoms called neutrons, protons, and electrons. The neutrons and protons are gathered tightly together in the center of the atom called the nucleus. The electrons orbit around the nucleus in a way that is similar to how the planets orbit around the sun.

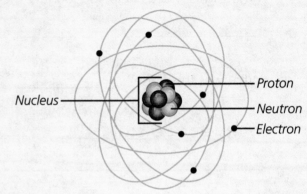

2   Sometimes an electron flies out of its orbit around the nucleus of the atom. If an electron escapes, it releases a tiny bit of electricity. Then the electron is attracted to the orbit of another atom and joins it. So we can define electricity as energy that is produced when electrons move. There is electricity everywhere because electrons are constantly escaping from their orbits around atoms.

3   Benjamin Franklin believed that lightning was a powerful form of natural electricity. In the 1750s, he performed experiments that proved his idea was correct. Lightning is a result of electrons flying from one cloud to another or from a cloud to the ground. People began to wonder how to capture the power of lightning, so that they could make it work for them. But it is only in the last 200 years that people have learned how to make and use electricity.

Ovens Old and New
by Zadie Jones

Early Ovens

1   At first, early people ate whatever food they could find. Plants, meat, and fish were eaten raw. Later, when people discovered how to make and control fire, they learned to cook food. They probably cooked the food by holding them on a stick over a fire, much like you roast a marshmallow. Then people realized they could place food in the hot coals of a fire to bake. Some people still use this method today. But food cooked in hot coals is often burned on the outside and raw on the inside. Eventually, early people began to build ovens to bake food. In contrast to open-fire cooking, ovens kept the temperature steady so that the food cooked all the way through.

2 Native Americans constructed ovens of stones and clay. A fire was built inside the oven and allowed to burn for an hour or more. Then the fire was put out by throwing sand or dirt on it. Next, bread dough was placed on the hot stones inside the oven, similarly to the way you would put bread in a hot oven today. Then a rock was placed over the opening so that the heat would remain inside. In the last step, the rock covering the opening was pulled away, and the well-baked bread was removed from the oven.

Think About It

How are the two passages organized? The question asks you to compare the two passages. To answer the question, look for signal words in each passage to help you identify the text structure.

What signal words are used in the passage about electricity? _____

_____

What text structure is the author using? _____

How does the text structure help support the information in the passage?

_____

What signal words does the author use in the passage about ovens?

_____

The title of the article on ovens gives a clue about what text structure the author is using. Look at the signal words you underlined. What text structure is this article

using? _____

How does the text structure help support the information in the article?

_____

_____

Continue reading both passages. Then answer the question.

Electricity *continued*

4 Once people learned about electricity, they invented ways to use it. The idea of inventing a way to use electricity to create light was especially exciting. Until the late 1800s, people used candles and oil or gas lamps for lighting. Thomas Edison, as well as other inventors, conducted experiments to try to make an electric light bulb. Edison's improvements on the light bulb and his system of generating and distributing electricity helped make the use of electric light practical. As a result, streets, stores, factories, and houses that were once dimly lit with gas lamps were able to have bright, electric lights.

5 Today, electricity powers many of the machines we use. Everything from small battery-operated toys to huge factory machines use electricity for power. Thus our lives are much different than those of people who lived just 200 years ago. And electricity has had a major influence on those changes.

Ovens Old and New *continued*

Modern Ovens

3 Today's modern kitchens have a stove for cooking foods. Most stoves include an oven for baking foods. The modern oven and the Native American oven are alike in that they both cook foods in a chamber that has been preheated. In contrast to the early oven, most modern ovens are heated by natural gas or electricity. Now you don't need to build a fire before you bake bread. You simply flip a switch on the stovetop to turn on the oven. In contrast to the heat in the wood-burning oven, the heat in a modern oven is easily controlled by adjusting the temperature control dial. Turning the dial up increases the flow of electricity or gas and raises the temperature. Turning the dial down decreases the flow of electricity or gas and lowers the temperature. Most modern ovens can be set to temperatures from 170 to 500 degrees so that foods are cooked just right.

> How do the authors organize information in the articles?

Which of the following statements tells why the authors of these passages chose to use the text structures they used?

A You need to understand how electricity works before you can invent things to use it. A modern oven is similar in some ways to a Native American oven.

B Electricity should be compared to lightning. The effects of using a wood-burning oven need to be understood.

C Life without electricity should be compared to life with electricity. Cooking in hot coals causes foods to be burned.

D Readers should compare the work of Benjamin Franklin and Thomas Edison. The reason modern ovens were invented was to prevent burned foods.

DISCUSS IT

Think about how the authors organized these two passages. Turn to a partner and talk about why the text structures used for these passages were good choices. Discuss whether the text structure of the second passage would work with the first passage, and vice versa.

Read two passages. Then answer the questions.

adapted from Notes on the Origins of American Animation, 1900–1921

A CLOSER LOOK
Look through both passages and underline any signal words you find. Now think about the purpose of each passage.

1   George Méliès, a Frenchman, was a stage magician who enjoyed amazing people with his magic tricks. After some time as a performer, he bought his own theater in Paris. Huge crowds came to see the magic and other shows he put on there.

2   When George saw the first moving pictures, he knew he had to have a movie camera. When he couldn't buy one, he studied the cameras of other people and made an even better one! With his camera, George began making films of all types. He still loved amazing people with magic. As a result, many of his films were similar to magic shows. These films used "trick" photography to produce films that seemed to show something impossible.

3   In 1896, George was the first to show that objects could appear to be set in motion through single-frame exposures. He would take a photo of an object, move it slightly, take another photo, move the object slightly, take another photo, and so on. When the frames were run together as a film, the object appeared to move. Therefore, this was the beginning of animation—that is, the creation of artificial moving images.

4   Filmmakers began to experiment with other ways to use animation. They made drawings of people or animals with each film frame showing a slightly different pose. Winsor McCay made between 4,000 and 10,000 line drawings for each of his three one-reel films between 1911 and 1914. As technical problems were solved, making animated cartoons became a big money-maker.

5   Below are some early animated films from 1900–1915. You can watch some of them on the Internet.

6   *The Enchanted Drawing* by Thomas Edison and J. Stuart Blacktop. The film was photographed in Thomas Edison's New Jersey studio. Blacktop performed a routine known as the "lightning sketch." Camera tricks brought drawn objects to life.

7 *Fun in the Bakery Shop* by Thomas Edison and Edwin S. Porter. This film uses "lightning sketch" with claymation. One picture was taken of the scene, a change was made to the scene, and then another picture was taken.

8 *Humorous Phases of Funny Faces* by J. Stuart Blackton. This is the earliest surviving American animated film. It uses chalkboard sketches and cut-outs.

9 *Keeping Up with the Joneses* by Harry S. Palmer. This was a series of films about styles for women and men. It was based on a comic strip in the newspapers, *Keeping Up with the Joneses.*

The Development of Animation

1 You may think that cartoons and other forms of animation have been around for a long time. But it's only been a little more than 100 years since the first animations were made.

Early Days of Animation

2 The first animations were painstakingly slow to create. An artist would draw a series of pictures. Each picture would show a slight change of movement. Then each picture would be photographed. The photographs were then linked together in a strip of film. When the photographs were viewed in rapid succession, the human eye perceived it as smooth movement. It took 24 drawings to make one second of film! The artists were kept busy drawing endless numbers of the same picture with only slight changes. It took hundreds of drawings to produce one minute of film. In 1910, Winsor McCay made a cartoon film titled *Gertie, the Trained Dinosaur.* It took 10,000 drawings to make the film. No wonder animated films were short in those days!

3 Around 1913, a new material called celluloid became available for filmmakers. Celluloid was one of the first kinds of plastic. It was thin and transparent, and artists could paint on it. It speeded up the making of animated films tremendously. The artist would paint a background and a foreground on two sheets of celluloid. Then figures could be placed between the two sheets and a photograph taken. In this way, the artist didn't need to spend time carefully redrawing the same scene around a character. The foreground painting on the celluloid gave an impression of depth so that scenes did not look so flat. If you watch an old cartoon film today, you may see that the characters move, but the foreground and background remain the same.

Computer Animation

4   You've seen cartoons or movies where the impossible happens. A spaceship shoots through the galaxy with alien saucers following. How can animation do that? In contrast to hand-drawn and celluloid animation, these films seem unbelievable. It is with the magic of computer technology that animated films can make the unbelievable believable.

5   There are two ways computers are used to create animation. One is computer-assisted animation. The artist draws the characters by hand or using a computer similarly to the way animation used to be created. But in contrast to older methods, the characters are placed in key frames. These are the frames where the most important movements take place. The computer then is programmed to fill in the frames in between the important frames. This is called tweening, and it can be done much faster with the computer than an artist could ever draw them by hand.

6   The other type of computer-assisted animation is called computer generated. The animator programs the computer to do things like break the law of gravity so people can fly. Or the animator might use a picture of one bird and create a huge flock of birds flying through the sky. The possibilities are limited only by what the animator can dream of.

7   Today, movies often mix real actors with scenes that are animated. It is all done with computer-assisted technology. Some examples are the *Star Wars* films, *Jurassic Park,* and *The Lord of the Rings* trilogy.

What did George Méliès want so he could start making animated films?

1 You can tell the first passage uses a cause-and-effect text structure because _____.

A artists had to make many drawings

B a movie camera led to making animated films

C a magician showed his magic tricks on film

D an animated film caused a movie camera to be created

What big change has happened recently in animated films?

2 You can tell the second passage uses a comparison text structure because _____.

A movie making is being compared to cartoon making

B painting on celluloid made animation easier

C a description of early animation is followed by one of computer-assisted animation

D in one type of computer animation, artists still draw pictures

These passages were written with different text structures because they had different purposes. Think about the author's purpose.

3 Compare and contrast the events in the first passage with the events in the second passage. Tell why the authors chose the text structure for each passage.

_____

_____

_____

_____

_____

_____

Read both passages. Then answer the questions.

adapted from Myth #38
Levi's 501 Jeans: A Riveting Story in Early Reno

You wouldn't be alone in thinking that Levi Strauss invented blue jeans with copper rivets. Even as late as 1999, a newspaper reporter for the Associated Press wrote that it was Strauss. Other legends also point to Strauss. Not so. Jacob Davis deserves the credit. Trial testimony in a patent-infringement case brought by him in 1874 tells the true story. Davis was living in Reno, Nevada, when he created the iconic American pants.

1 By 1869, Jacob Davis had opened a tailor shop on the town's main thoroughfare, Virginia Street. He began fabricating wagon covers and tents from a rugged off-white duck cloth sold by San Francisco's Levi Strauss & Co.

2 Events in January 1871 changed Jacob Davis' life forever and made him a wealthy man. His trial testimony told of a woman who needed a sturdy pair of pants for a husband too big to wear ready-made clothes. "She, his wife, said she wanted to send him to chop some wood," Davis testified, "but he had no pants to put on."

3 Davis went on to testify that he was paid three dollars in advance for the pants which he made of white duck purchased from Levi Strauss & Co. The woman wanted the trousers made as strong as possible.

4 There were copper rivets in the tailor's shop used to attach straps to horse blankets made for teamsters. "So when the pants were done—the rivets were lying on the table—and the thought struck me to fasten the pockets with rivets," Davis recounted. "I had never thought of it before."

5 As word of the new pants began to spread, orders first trickled in, but soon Davis was deluged[1] with requests. In the following

18 months, he made and sold 200 pairs to persons in need of heavy work clothing. Some of the pants were made of denim. Concerned that his idea might be pirated[2], Davis asked Levi Strauss to help him with a patent application. A preliminary application was approved in July 1872, and the full patent granted on May 20, 1873.

6 Davis sold his tailor shop property to Levi Strauss on May 27. The frame building was destroyed on October 29, 1873, in Reno's first great fire.

7 The truth in this story lay undiscovered for 100 years until Ann Morgan Campbell, chief of the San Bruno branch of the National Archives, brought it to light in an article in the *Nevada Historical Society Quarterly* in 1974.

8 Davis is also mentioned in a brief biography of Levi Strauss in the *World Book Encyclopedia*. Actually all the AP reporter in San Francisco needed to do was call the corporate headquarters of Levi Strauss & Co. Historian, Lynn Downey, would have set the record straight.

9 Anyway, we now know the facts thanks to a federal court case. The next time you look at your Levi 501 blue jeans, think of Jacob Davis and Reno, Nevada.

---
[1]**deluged:** flooded
[2]**pirated:** copied without permission

How the Forty-Niners Affected Life in California

1 In 1848, James Wilson Marshall was working as a carpenter in Coloma, California. He had been hired by John Sutter to supervise the building of a water-powered sawmill on the American River. Lumber was needed in the new territory. Settlers were arriving daily who needed houses, barns, and other buildings. The water in the American River would be used to power the mill. On January 24, Marshall was working on a ditch that was used to carry the river water into the mill. He happened to look down and see something shiny in the water. Amazed, he scooped up what he was sure were a few flakes of gold. And he was right!

2 Marshall told Sutter about what he had found. The two men tried to keep others from learning about the gold discovery, but somehow word leaked out. Rumors about the discovery spread quickly. Soon area newspapers began reporting that huge amounts of gold had been found near Sutter's Mill. Some reports say that 90% of the men living in San Francisco immediately rushed to the area around the mill, looking for gold.

3 Less than eight months after Marshall had scooped up those first flakes of gold, 4,000 miners had poured into the area around Sutter's Mill. They were digging everywhere, living in tents and quickly-built shacks. By the end of the year, "gold fever" had spread to the East Coast. Newspapers there reported that a man could gain unbelievable riches in California.

4 Many families used their life savings to send a father or brother to the gold fields to get rich. These adventurers called themselves '49ers for the year the gold discovery was made. Women and children were usually left behind to take care of farms and businesses.

5 As more and more miners poured into the area of the gold fields, stores and other businesses sprang up to take care of the miners' needs. Many shopkeepers became far richer than the miners who worked so hard to find gold. But it wasn't easy for stores to get the supplies they needed. Everything had to be hauled from the East over the Rocky Mountains by wagon train. Some supplies were shipped around the tip of South America on sailing ships. Stores could charge outrageous prices for their goods because miners did not want to leave the mines to go shopping elsewhere.

Item	Gold Rush Prices	In Today's Prices
Eggs	$3.00 each	$84.00 each
Butter	$20.00 per pound	$560.00 per pound
Flour	$13.00 per bag	$365.00 per pound
Rice	$8.00 per pound	$225.00 per pound
Boots	$6.00 per pair	$170.00 per pair
Shovel	$36.00 each	$1,010.00 each

6 There were fights over gold claims, and many of the shantytowns that grew up around the gold fields were lawless. Law officers were in short supply, and those who did patrol did not always enforce the law equally. Sometimes groups of people, called vigilantes, got together to enforce the law as they saw fit. Few doctors were available, and diseases like cholera spread quickly through the towns. Many miners were hurt or killed in mining accidents. The gold fields were not a safe place for anyone, and for the most part, only men lived there.

7 In 1849, California applied for statehood. It became the 31st state to be admitted to the union in 1850. By 1852, the gold rush was pretty well over, but that didn't stop people from heading to California. It is estimated that by 1855, 300,000 settlers from all over the world had arrived. Many of them came to farm the rich land, and others came to build railroads. As a result, California has developed into the diverse, multicultural state it is today.

1 Part A
Which sentence *best* tells how the two passages illustrate cause and effect?

   A   They are about a historical time.

   B   They tell about an event with lasting consequences.

   C   They both take place in California during a particular time.

   D   They both tell about an invention.

Part B
What text evidence *best* supports your answer to Part A?

_____

_____

_____

_____

_____

2 Which sentence describes both passages and explains the text structure choice?

  A The articles explain why we need to remember things from the past.

  B The articles teach a lesson about how to avoid problems.

  C The articles give important information about California history.

  D The articles seek to show how a historical event affected the future.

3 Explain why the cause-and-effect text structure works well for historical articles such as these.

_____

_____

_____

_____

4 Using both passages, identify a cause and explain what effects resulted from it.

_____

_____

_____

_____

_____

_____

LESSON
17

Analyzing Relationships
in Informational Text

① Introduction

Everyone has a point of view. **Point of view** is shaped by what someone thinks, believes, or feels. Sometimes people may share a similar point of view, and sometimes they may disagree. When you read, you should determine the different points of view being expressed. Look for **opinion** words that signal what the author believes or feels about a subject. Notice the type of statements the author makes. Are they positive or negative? Authors often write to **persuade,** or convince, you to do or believe something so it is important to understand the author's point of view and then develop your own point of view about the event or topic.

Look at the illustration. Then answer the questions.

Describe the two points of view shown in the illustration.

What is the point of view of the team in white? _____

_____

What is the point of view of the team in black? _____

_____

An author's point of view takes into account how the author feels about a subject. Whey you compare and contrast different authors' points of view on a similar topic or event, you can see how the authors' perspectives are alike or different. You can also learn more about the subject since each author has something unique to offer.

Read the first parts of two paired passages. Then answer the questions.

How to Grow Tomatoes

1   Every year, Americans plant more tomatoes than any other kind of vegetable. Taste is the number one reason people love to grow tomatoes. Compared to a grocery-store tomato, a home-grown tomato has a far superior flavor. And then there is the attraction of all the varieties that can be grown—more than 7,500! There are all sizes and shapes, and each one has its own special tomato flavor. Another reason tomatoes are prized is for all the vitamins they have in them that help keep you healthy.

2   Tomatoes are easy to grow, but like any plant, they need certain growing conditions. In most of the United States, tomatoes are a summer crop. Plants are set in the soil after the last frost in spring. The tomatoes are ripe and ready to pick in mid to late summer. The plants will die at the first frost in fall. In some southern states, where the temperature doesn't drop below freezing, tomatoes are grown as a fall and winter crop.

3   Tomatoes need sunshine, so you can't plant them in shady places. They need good soil to which compost and fertilizer have been added. Rain is also essential to tomato growth. But if it doesn't rain, you can always water plants with a hose.

Growing Your Own Vegetables

1   Over one-third of the people in the United States plant a vegetable garden every year. Why would they want to when grocery stores are filled with beautiful fresh vegetables? Gardeners give a variety of answers, but one thing is almost always true. Once people start growing their own food, they almost always continue. Let's look at some of top reasons for growing what you eat.

1. One of the best reasons for growing your own vegetables is that you know everything about those vegetables. You know all about the soil where they were planted. You know what fertilizer was used. You also know which (if any) pesticides were applied to them. You know whether they are safe to eat. Grocery store vegetables look beautiful, but if you are purchasing them, you are trusting that someone else raised them safely and carefully.

2. Growing your own vegetables will save you money. Seeds cost only pennies a piece, and vegetable plants are usually inexpensive. Because you do the work of raising them into edible size vegetables, the cost is very low. If you preserve some of your vegetables by canning, freezing, or drying them, you can

make the savings last throughout the year. Sometimes there is bad weather in a part of the country that produces vegetables. Prices rise quickly. If you don't have your own vegetables, you have to pay whatever the stores charge.

Think About It

How are the two authors' points of view similar or different? Look for opinion words that help you understand what the author believes or feels.

How does the author of "How to Grow Tomatoes" feel about growing tomatoes?

_____

_____

What text evidence reveals the author's point of view? _____

_____

_____

_____

How does the author of "Growing Your Own Vegetables" feel about growing your

own vegetables? _____

_____

What text evidence reveals the author's point of view? _____

_____

_____

Continue reading both passages. Then answer the question.

> **A CLOSER LOOK**
> Underline sentences in each article that illustrate the author's point of view.

How to Grow Tomatoes *continued*

4   There are two types of tomato plants—determinate and indeterminate. Determinate plants grow to a certain height and then stop growing. Determinate plants are great for growing in pots and small spaces because they don't take up as much room. Indeterminate plants never stop growing until frost kills them. These tall-growing plants will produce many more tomatoes than the smaller determinate plants. Indeterminate plants take a little more work because they must be grown in cages or tied to stakes to keep them from flopping over as they get taller.

5   Once the plants are set into the soil, weeds will begin to sprout around them. You need to remove the weeds so that the plants get all the sunlight, water, and food from the soil they need. Although tomatoes don't suffer from many pests, you will need to watch closely for the tomato hornworm. This large caterpillar with a horn on its head will eat the leaves off your tomato plants in a hurry.

6   Some diseases will also attack tomato plants. These diseases often live in the soil. One of the best ways to avoid diseases is to plant tomatoes in a different location each year.

7   By mid-summer, small yellow flowers appear on the tomato plants. These will develop into small green tomatoes. As soon as the tomatoes begin to ripen, watch the plants daily. Pick tomatoes when they are brightly colored but firm. Remember that not all tomatoes are red when ripe. Some varieties may be yellow, orange, or even light green. Tomatoes are best eaten immediately. However, they will keep in the refrigerator for several weeks. The longer they are kept, the more flavor they lose. Tomatoes may also be cooked and frozen for later use.

Growing Your Own Vegetables *continued*

3. Working in your vegetable garden is good for your health. Your body gets the benefit of exercise from planting, cultivating, weeding, and harvesting a garden. Working outside in the sunlight lifts your spirits. People are less likely to get depressed while they are gardening. Stress from school, work, or other sources is relieved as you concentrate on raising your plants.

4. There is something exciting and satisfying about eating what you have grown. Your vegetables are picked when

they are perfectly ripe and have the best flavor. You are more likely to eat your own vegetables. That means you get more nutritious foods into your diet. Fresh vegetables contain more vitamins than those that have been picked the week before and shipped across the country.

5. You can grow vegetables that are almost impossible to find in grocery stores. Some of the most delicious have fragile skins and taste best when ripened on the plants. Growers with far-away farms don't grow those kinds of vegetables because they don't ship well.

6. Home-grown vegetables can be shared. Most gardeners will have extras that they can share with family, friends, and neighbors. Fresh vegetables are a thoughtful and healthy gift. Most food pantries and homeless shelters welcome fresh vegetables.

7. You can take pride in your vegetable garden. You have produced at least some of your own food without relying on others. And you can show younger children or even adults how you did it. Gardening is a great way to show your appreciation for our planet.

2 Now you know some of the many benefits of raising your own vegetables. If you don't have space for a garden, many communities have garden plots you can use. Or, you can share a garden space with a friend or neighbor by helping with the work. Any way you do it, raising your own vegetables will bring you many rewards.

> Look for words in the passages that express the authors' opinions.

How are the authors' points of view similar or different?

A   The first author gives facts; the second author discusses benefits.

B   The first author discourages people from planting; the second author encourages people to plant.

C   Both authors believe that the tomato hornworm is bad for plants.

D   Both authors believe that planting vegetables is good for you and the plants.

DISCUSS IT

Turn to a partner and talk about how the authors' points of view compare. Cite text evidence to support your answer. Talk about whether you agree or disagree with the authors' points of view.

Read two paired passages. Then answer the questions.

Tomatoes

A CLOSER LOOK

These passages have something in common—they are making both positive and negative statements about a subject. Underline words in each passage that tell something positive and something negative.

1 If you thought tomatoes first came from Italy, you would be wrong. Tomatoes were first found growing wild in the South American countries of Peru, Bolivia, Chile, and Ecuador. These wild tomatoes were yellow and as small as cherries. The English word *tomato* comes from *tomatl,* the name given to this plant by the Aztec people who lived in the area.

2 In the 1500s, Spanish explorers sailed their ships to the Americas. They took new plants home with them, and that is how tomatoes first came to Europe. Some people called them Peruvian apples. They planted them in their gardens because they thought the vines and fruits were pretty. At first, most people thought the plants and fruits were poisonous! They were actually close to correct. Tomatoes belong to a family of plants called Solanaceae. Many fruits of plants in that family are poisonous. The fruits of the tomato plant are not poisonous, although the stems and leaves do contain enough poison to give a stomachache. Potatoes, eggplants, and chili peppers are also in the Solanaceae family.

3 The Spanish were the first people to eat tomatoes. They fried them with squash and onions to serve with meat. It took a while, but eventually people in other European countries began to realize tomatoes were delicious. In the 1700s, recipes began to be written using tomatoes. By the 1800s, Italian cooks were inventing all kinds of ways to use tomatoes. They began to make the pasta sauces and pizza still popular today. By the late 1800s, farmers were raising tomatoes to sell in markets.

4 Settlers brought tomato seeds to North America in the 1700s. At that time, they were still being grown mostly in flowerbeds. Our third president, Thomas Jefferson, ate some tomatoes in Paris. He liked them so well that he sent seeds home to his farm and grew them in his large vegetable garden. By the mid-1800s, people were growing them in their gardens in the United States— and eating them.

5 Tomatoes became larger and tastier through the work of A. W. Livingston. He crossed different plants and produced 17 different varieties of tomatoes during his lifetime. Livingston, along with other plant breeders, is responsible for the thousands of tomato varieties available today.

A Few Words About Ketchup
by Bryan Hollowell

1   What foods do you eat with ketchup? It is certainly America's most popular condiment. According to one survey, 96 percent of American households keep ketchup on hand. Certainly no Fourth of July barbecue would be complete without it. Yet ketchup (or "cat-si-up," as it was originally called) isn't American at all. It comes to us from Southeast Asia. It was brought to Europe by traders in the 1600s and from there to colonial America. This ketchup was not made with tomatoes. Tomatoes were native to Mexico and unknown to the rest of the world until the 1500s. Instead, "cat-si-up" was made from pickled fish. Mushrooms, nuts, and spices were added to give it flavor.

2   The first tomato ketchup may have been made in Canada in the 1700s. In 1801, a recipe for it appeared in an American cookbook for the first time. But few Americans were eating tomatoes then. Common belief had it that they were poisonous! There's a story that in 1820 one grower, Colonel Robert Johnson, proved that people's fears of tomatoes were nonsense by eating a whole basket of them on the steps of a New Jersey courthouse.

3   As tomatoes became a popular food, tomato ketchup also became popular. Farmers made it from tomatoes that had become too ripe to sell. They sold it in jars at local markets. Making ketchup is hard work, so when Jonas Yerks began bottling and advertising it in 1837, it sold and sold across the country. The ketchup you know was born.

4   "Shake and shake the ketchup bottle; nothing comes and then a lot'll." Richard Armour wrote this rhyme in 1949. It describes a problem every ketchup eater once knew. Ketchup is a kind of liquid that scientists call *thixotropic*. That means it doesn't flow unless acted upon by an outside force (like your hand, or a knife), and then it can be hard to stop.

5   Another problem with ketchup is that people often eat it with foods that are not very good for them. Around 1990, people were eating fewer burgers and fries due to concern for their health. Ketchup sales fell. Then in 1991, an inventor named Paul Brown came up with a kind of valve. It fit into the cap of a plastic bottle. Squeezing the bottle made the ketchup flow easily. When you stopped squeezing, air sucked the ketchup back in, and the valve closed. Brown's valves are used in shampoo bottles (another thixotropic liquid) and in babies' sippy cups. It was the ketchup makers, however, who made him rich. Soon they were selling ketchup in enormous bottles. They were displayed upside down on store shelves. Ketchup sales soared.

Think about how the topics of these passages are the same and different.

1 One way the authors' points of view in these passages are the same is that they _____.

   A tell about the invention of something

   B tell about using tomatoes

   C tell about something poisonous

   D tell about Spanish explorers

Skim both passages and underline how tomatoes and ketchup developed.

2 How do the authors feel about the popularity of tomatoes and ketchup?

   A They both became more and more popular.

   B Italians popularized tomatoes and ketchup.

   C Ketchup led to the popularity of tomatoes.

   D Paul Brown and A. W. Livingston made them popular.

Underline opinion words in the passages that show feelings about the subjects.

3 What are the authors' points of view about their subjects?

_____

_____

_____

_____

Read the passages. Then answer the questions.

adapted from One-Cent Coin (Penny)

The Story

1 Every penny you've ever spent probably had Abraham Lincoln on it. That's because his picture has been there for more than a 100 years! But when the US Mint was created in 1792, one of the first coins it made was the one-cent coin, and it looked very different from a modern cent.

2 The image on the first cent was of a lady with flowing hair, who stood for liberty. The coin was larger and made of pure copper, while today's penny is made of copper and zinc.

3 In 1857, Congress told the US Mint to make the cent smaller and to mix the copper with nickel (12 percent). People found the smaller cent easier to use. The new cents showed a flying eagle on the front and a wreath on the back.

4 At the same time, Congress stopped people from using money from other countries, though we had used foreign coins for many years. But the US Mint could melt them down and make them into US coins.

5 One foreign currency we were using was British money. The British pound was not divided into 100 cents like our dollar, but its smallest part was called a penny, and that's why we call our cent a "penny" today. But for more than one, the British called them "pence" while ours are called "pennies."

6 The man on our pennies today is Abraham Lincoln, our 16th president. During the time the Lincoln design has appeared on the obverse (front), several different designs have been used on the reverse (back): first a wheat design, then the Lincoln Memorial. Four designs were used in 2009, and the union shield design first appeared in 2010.

7 As a 2005 law directs, the shield design symbolizes President Abraham Lincoln's preservation of the United States as a single country. The familiar portrait of Lincoln remains on the front of the coin. The union shield used in the design dates back to the 1780s.

8 In the current coin design, a banner inscribed "one cent" is draped across the shield. The 13 vertical stripes on the shield represent the states joined in one union to support the federal government, represented by the horizontal bar above. The bar is inscribed with the national motto "E Pluribus Unum" ("out of many, one").

The 2009 Pennies

9 Abraham Lincoln's image has been on the front of the penny since 1909. That image remained in place for all four coins in the 2009 program. On the back, four different images highlight four parts of Lincoln's life. These coins were issued about 3 months apart in the order they happened.

- His birth in Kentucky (1809 to 1816)
- His youth in Indiana (1816 to 1830)
- His professional life in Illinois (1830 to 1861)
- His presidency in Washington, DC (1861 to 1865)

Should the Penny Be Saved?

1 How many times have you seen a penny on the sidewalk? Did you pick it up? A lot of people don't. The truth is that in today's economy, a penny is worth practically nothing. Can you think of anything you can buy for one penny? Your grandparents may be able to tell you about buying a penny piece of gum or candy, but today that piece of gum or candy would cost at least ten cents. Many people say the penny has outlived its usefulness.

2 Pennies are made of nickel covered with copper. Copper is a pretty reddish-gold metal, and it is valuable. In fact, in 2013 it cost 1.8 cents for the US Mint to make each penny. That means each one cent coin cost almost two cents to make, and the US Mint makes over 20 million pennies each day. In a year, the cost of making pennies was over $50 million more than they were worth.

3 There are other costs associated with having penny coins in circulation. Consider the time that bank employees spend handling pennies and the time store employees spend making change with them. These are just bits of time, but banks and stores are paying wages for those bits of time. Even charities that have put out boxes and cans to collect pennies are changing their efforts. The time spent collecting the pennies and counting them is hardly worth it. Charities are shifting their efforts to appeals for electronic contributions.

4 Several suggestions have been made about what to do with the penny. Some people favor doing away with it altogether. In fact, Canada did discontinue pennies in 2006 after costs of manufacturing them exceeded their worth. Another suggestion is that pennies be made of cheaper metals. During WWII, some pennies were made of zinc-coated steel so that the copper supplies could be used for the war effort.

5 Let's say that the US government did decide to discontinue the use of pennies. How would that affect our everyday lives? All those items priced at $1.99 would be rounded up to $2.00. One study showed that when all purchases in one year are taken into account, rounding could cost US customers $600 million more.

6 Should the penny be saved or dropped from circulation? There seem to be many reasons for dropping it, however, Americans are sentimental about their coins. Pennies have been around since the US Mint first started making coins in 1792. When you've had something for more than 200 years, it's hard to let it go.

1 Which statement *best* expresses the overall point of view of the author of the second passage?

   A The penny is a valuable coin.

   B Canada should not have given up its penny coin.

   C Americans are sentimental about pennies.

   D There are many arguments for dropping the US penny.

2 Part A

Which sentence *best* describes the overall point of view of the first passage?

A The author wants the reader to understand the design of the penny.

B The author wants the reader to know how the penny has changed over time.

C The penny shows the head of our 16th president, Abraham Lincoln.

D The back of the penny has changed more than the front.

Part B

What text evidence *best* supports your answer to Part A?

_____

_____

_____

_____

_____

3 The title of the second passage is a question. Does the author's viewpoint defend or counter whether the penny should be saved? Explain using text evidence in your answer.

_____

_____

_____

_____

4 Compare and contrast the points of view of the authors of these passages. Use details to explain how they are alike and different.

_____

_____

_____

_____

Craft and Structure in Informational Text

Read both passages. Then answer the questions.

adapted from Advantages of Wind Power

1   Wind energy offers many advantages over other sources of power. In fact, it's the fastest-growing energy source in the world. Scientists are constantly researching ways to produce and use more wind power.

Wind Turbines

Here are some important facts about wind power.

- It's a clean fuel source. Wind energy doesn't pollute the air like power plants that rely on fossil fuels, such as coal or natural gas. Wind turbines don't pollute the air. They don't cause acid rain or greenhouse gases.

- Wind energy comes from the air around us. The United States doesn't need to buy wind energy from other countries. The United States is now producing more wind energy than other countries.

- Wind energy will never be used up. Earth has only so much coal, gas, and oil. When they are used up, there is no more. But there is no end to wind energy. Wind is formed when the sun heats the atmosphere, Earth rotates, and air moves over landforms and oceans. For as long as the sun shines and the wind blows, wind energy can be produced and turned into electricity.

- Wind power is cost effective. Making electricity with wind power is cheaper than using many other sources of power.

- The best places for wind turbines are flat lands where winds blow constantly. That means turbines can be built on farm or ranch land. The companies that put up wind turbines pay the land owners rent for having turbines on their land. Farmers and ranchers can continue to work the land because the wind turbines take up only a small amount of space.

Here are some ways the United States benefits by increasing the use of wind energy.

- Burning fuels like coal and gas produces carbon dioxide. Too much of this gas is bad for Earth's atmosphere. Using wind energy keeps millions of tons of carbon dioxide out of the atmosphere.

- By using wind power, not as much water is needed to make electricity. Trillions of gallons can be saved for other uses.
- When people use wind energy, they don't need as much natural gas to heat their homes and run appliances. The price of natural gas will go down.
- As many as 30,000 people will find jobs making wind turbines and their parts.
- Wind power companies will pay land owners millions of dollars to rent land to set up turbines. The land owners will pay taxes on the income. The tax money will help governments meet the needs of citizens.

2 Wind power is already being used in many areas of the country, and more turbines are added every day. This clean, form of free energy is the energy of today and of the future.

Challenges of Wind Power

1 Many people think wind power is the answer to many problems from a shortage of fossil fuels to the problem of global warming. But before we get too enthused about wind power, let's look at some interesting facts.
- It is true that wind is free. However, every place on Earth does not have an equal amount of wind. And it takes wind to drive the turbines. Wind turbines are expensive, and the cost to erect them is high. If a location does not have much wind, it is not cost effective to put wind turbines there. So some places on Earth may never be good locations for turbines.
- Many locations with high year-round winds are far from cities where electricity is needed most. That means lines to carry the electricity must be set up over long distances to carry the power to where it is needed. Those lines are expensive to install and need to be maintained.
- Flat land is usually the best location for turbines because wind builds up speed as it sweeps across flat surfaces. A lot of flat land is already being used for farming, ranching, housing developments, and other uses. Power companies must rent or purchase the land to erect wind turbines. If the land is more valuable for another use, it won't be used for turbines.
- Many people who live near the turbines have objected to them. They don't like the noise the rotary blades make as they turn.
- Some people don't like the way the turbines look as they rise above the landscape. In fact, some people think they are ugly and pollute the beauty of nature.
- There have been occasions when birds and bats have been killed by flying into the rotary blades.

- There have been a few cases when wind turbines have caught fire. This has happened when fluids used to oil the machine have leaked.
- To erect the wind turbines, roads must to be built across farm and ranch land to get to the location.
- Wind turbines need maintenance to keep them running well. That requires trained workers to climb the 200-foot towers to get to the machines that turn the blades.

2   Now that you know some of the challenges to using wind power, you need to compare them to the advantages. Everything new is usually looked at with suspicion until it proves itself. Will wind power prove to be the answer to the world's energy needs? Only the future can bring us that answer.

1   Which sentence tells the opposing points of view about the cost of using wind to make electricity?

A   Flat land rather than hilly land is better for turbines.

B   Wind turbines and the land to put them on are expensive.

C   Wind is free but building lines to the cities is expensive.

D   Burning fuels produces carbon dioxide, but some turbines have caught fire.

2   What does the word *turbines* mean in these passages?

A   jet engines

B   engines with rotary blades

C   large fans

D   electric machines

3   Compare and contrast the text structures of the two passages. Explain why each is effective in expressing a particular point of view.

_____

_____

_____

_____

Read the two passages. Then answer the questions.

adapted from How NASA Studies Water

1   The National Aeronautics and Space Administration (NASA) missions collect information about Earth's water cycle. This includes data on rain, floods, and tides. Scientists then develop ideas about how air, water, temperature changes, and gravity interact. To test their ideas, they send up satellites. The satellites collect information to help us understand more about the changes in Earth's water resources. We also learn how human behavior affects Earth.

Terra: the EOS Flagship

2   An international program called Earth Observing System (EOS) has set up a program to monitor changes to Earth's climate and environment. Over the next 15 years, it will be collecting and analyzing data. The leading (flagship) satellite is called Terra. Terra will send back data on how Earth's land, oceans, air, ice, and life function together.

Seawifs

3   The Sea-viewing Wide Field-of-view Sensor (SeaWiFS) Project puts a sensor in space. Like an eye in the sky, it gives scientists a view of the oceans. The color of the oceans in different areas can show how many phytoplankton (microscopic plants) are living in certain areas. The number of these plants helps explain how pollution, carbon dioxide, and other greenhouse gases are affecting the oceans.

Tropical Rainfall Measuring Mission

4   Rainfall in the tropical zones affects the weather in the rest of the world. The Tropical Rainfall Measuring Mission (TRMM) satellite measures tropical rainfall. TRMM is the first NASA mission dedicated to measuring tropical and subtropical rainfall. This data helps scientists better predict weather patterns.

5   Measurements are used to find out where it's raining and how hard it's raining. Not all clouds cause rain. Rain falls from different heights in the atmosphere. Sometimes it doesn't reach the ground at all.

6   We have never known before just how much rain actually falls across Earth. However, it is something we need to know. The data will help us predict wind patterns, ocean currents, floods, and droughts.

7   TRMM won't be used to measure daily rainfall in your city. Instead, scientists and weather forecasters will use it to understand how rainfall happens and why. This can improve forecasts in the future.

NASA Project Terra

1   The National Aeronautics and Space Administration (NASA) launched a satellite on Dec. 18, 1999. Its name is Terra. *Terra* means "earth" in Latin. Terra is about the size of a small school bus. Terra's job is to keep an eye on Earth from 438 miles above. It takes 99 minutes for Terra to make each orbit. That means it circles Earth 16 times each day. Scientists expect it to keep orbiting well into the 2020s.

2   Terra's mission is to find out how Earth is changing and what those changes mean for life on Earth. In the last 60 years, scientists have found that the carbon dioxide in Earth's atmosphere has increased. They have also seen increases in other gases containing chlorine, bromine, and fluorine.

3   Scientists know that these changes do not happen separately from each

other. They are connected. So to find out what is going on, scientists need to study Earth's land, water, and atmosphere. Terra is equipped with instruments that take measurements of all of them. With the measurements, scientists will be able to understand how the water, land, and atmosphere work together as a system.

4   One instrument on Terra is called CERES. It makes a colored picture of Earth that shows what temperatures are in various places. Blue represents the coolest temperatures, and red and yellow represent the hottest. By comparing maps over time, scientists can tell whether areas are becoming warmer or cooler.

5   Another instrument on Terra is called MISR. Among other things, it measures the interactions between sunlight and cloud cover. MISR tracks these measurements over months, seasons, and years.

6   A third instrument is called MODIS. With cameras pointed in nine different directions, MODIS takes pictures of every part of Earth. From high in space, scientists can see powerful hurricane clouds. They can spot smoke and ash from forest fires and volcanoes. They can also see huge dust storms over desert areas.

7   All the data that Terra's instruments collect is sent back to Earth. It is analyzed by computers and studied by scientists around the world. One day soon, science may be able to tell us how we can keep our Earth a safe and healthy place to live.

4   **Part A**

What does the word *mission* mean in these passages?

A   a place where people work far from home

B   an orbit in space

C   a set of instruments on a satellite

D   work that needs to be accomplished

Part B

Which context clues from both passages *best* support your answer to Part A?

_____

_____

_____

_____

5 Which state the authors' points of view in the passages?

   A Both claim that studying water is NASA's most important mission.

   B Both highlight Terra as NASA's most important satellite.

   C Both focus on NASA's tropical rainfall measurement satellite.

   D Both inform about NASA studies about water.

6 Which text structure is used in these two passages?

   A Passage one uses chronology, and passage two uses cause and effect.

   B Passage one uses comparison, and passage two uses problem and solution.

   C Both passages use problem and solution.

   D Both passages use comparison.

7 What point do the authors both agree on? Use details from both passages to support your answer.

   _____

   _____

   _____

   _____

   _____

   _____

UNIT 5
Integration of Knowledge and Ideas in Literary Text

It's easy to compare different shapes and sizes, but what about comparing characters in a story? Or settings and tones? These are a little bit harder to think about. But when you do, you can come up with new information and ideas that help you understand the text better. This unit is about looking closely at visuals for clues that will tell you more about a story, and about comparing and contrasting stories in the same genre.

LESSON 18 Understanding Visual Elements in Literary Texts looks closely at how visual elements can add to your understanding of a text. You will think about how pictures can set a tone, and how the images in graphic novels and comic books help to tell the story.

LESSON 19 Comparing and Contrasting Stories is about the different types of genres in literature and about learning how to identify them. You will compare the similarities and differences between characters, settings, morals, and tones in similar stories written in the same genre.

LESSON 18

Understanding Visual Elements in Literary Texts

 Introduction

THEME: ≫ **Wondrous Creatures**

You've probably read books with pictures. In these tales, beautifully illustrated pictures help tell the story that the author has set down in words. Think about some of the books you've read. How did the illustrations help you understand the ideas and characters in a way that the text did not?

Some stories are told mostly in pictures. Graphic novels, for instance, are stories told in panels, much like a comic book. Speech and thought bubbles and captions help tell the story, but the illustrations carry most of the author's ideas.

Of course, not all stories are accompanied by illustrations on every page. Some stories contain just a few illustrations or pictures. But these illustrations can still add to a reader's understanding and appreciation of a text. They can provide details about characters, setting, events, and even **tone**—the author's attitude—that the words cannot.

Read the paragraph and then look at the illustration.

Jasmine stopped and turned toward the soft shaking noise that came from beneath the stairs. She hesitated, as she was already late for school. But the noise was insistent and growing louder. She peered around the stairwell, her eyes adjusting to the dark. And there, in the corner, was what Jasmine first thought was a snake until she looked closer. The creature had the body of a snake, but it had the head of something resembling a bird. It didn't seem angry or mean, just interested in her. Jasmine took a step toward it.

Read the paragraph again. What does the text tell you about the setting? _____

_____

What does the illustration show you about the setting that the words do not say?

_____

What does the text tell you about the creature Jasmine finds? _____

_____

What does the illustration show you about the creature that the text does not say?

_____

Stories are enriched by more than just pictures. You may have listened to a recording of a book. The person reading the story may add drama and emphasis. Maybe the storyteller made a character sound sad and lonely by speaking the character's dialogue in a soft, hushed tone. Or perhaps the storyteller made a storm seem particularly threatening by reading the description of it in a loud, fast, dramatic voice. These kinds of **multimedia** elements help readers understand and appreciate a story.

When you read, pay attention to how the illustrations add to the text. When you listen to a multimedia presentation, notice how the storyteller's voice expresses feelings and mood. What illustrations show and the tone of a speaker's voice can help you better understand a story.

Read the first part of the story. Then answer the questions.

adapted from The Book of Dragons
by E. Nesbit

Long, long ago in England, a young girl named Effie came across something unusual—

1   At teatime another thing happened. Effie's brother Harry fished something out of his tea, which he thought at first was an earwig.[1] He was just getting ready to drop it on the floor, and end its life in the usual way, when it shook itself in the spoon—spread two wet wings, and flopped onto the tablecloth. There it sat, stroking itself with its feet and stretching its wings, and Harry said: "Why, it's a tiny newt!"[2]

2   The professor leaned forward before the doctor could say a word. "I'll give you half a crown for it, Harry, my lad," he said, speaking very fast; and then he picked it up carefully on his handkerchief.

3   "It is a new specimen," he said, "and finer than yours, Doctor."

4   It was a tiny lizard, about half an inch long—with scales and wings.

5   So now the doctor and the professor each had a specimen, and they were both very pleased. But before long these specimens began to seem less valuable. For the next morning, when the knife-boy was cleaning the doctor's boots, he suddenly dropped the brushes and the boot and the blacking, and screamed out that he was burnt.

6   And from inside the boot came crawling a lizard as big as a kitten, with large, shiny wings.

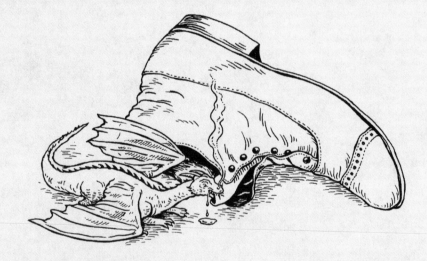

---

[1]**earwig:** an insect that has long, thin feelers and two curved, pointed parts at the end of the body
[2]**newt:** a small animal that lives mostly in water and that has four short legs; a long, low body and tail; and soft, wet skin

7 "Why," said Effie, "I know what it is. It is a dragon like the one St. George killed."

Think About It

What does the illustration help you understand about the dragon when it comes out of the boot? To answer the question, reread the text and look at the illustration.

Complete the chart with details from the text and illustration.

Details in the Text	Details in the Illustration
a lizard as big as a _____ with _____ wings	

What details are in the illustration that are not in the story?

1. _____

2. _____

3. _____

A CLOSER LOOK

Descriptions of the dragons and their actions will help you understand how the author feels about them. Underline words and phrases that describe the dragons. Think about the author's attitude toward them.

Continue reading the story. Then answer the question.

8   And Effie was right. That afternoon Effie's dog, Towser, was bitten in the garden by a dragon about the size of a rabbit, which he had tried to chase, and the next morning all the papers were full of the wonderful "winged lizards" that were appearing all over the country. The papers would not call them dragons, because, of course, no one believes in dragons nowadays—and at any rate the papers were not going to be so silly as to believe in fairy stories. At first there were only a few, but in a week or two the country was simply running alive with dragons of all sizes, and in the air you could sometimes see them as thick as a swarm of bees. They all looked alike except as to size. They were green with scales, and they had four legs and a long tail and great wings like bats' wings, only the wings were a pale, half-transparent yellow, like the gear-boxes on bicycles.

9   They breathed fire and smoke, as all proper dragons must, but still the newspapers went on pretending they were lizards, until the editor of the *Standard* was picked up and carried away by a very large one, and then the other newspaper people had not anyone left to tell them what they ought not to believe. So when the largest elephant in the Zoo was carried off by a dragon, the papers gave up pretending—and put ALARMING PLAGUE OF DRAGONS at the top of the paper.

How does the illustration add to or change this tone?

How does the dragon in the illustration compare with the description of dragons in paragraphs 8–9?

A   The dragon in the illustration is eating a boot, which sets a scary tone.

B   The dragon in the illustration is cartoonish, which sets a funny tone.

C   The dragon in the illustration has bat-like wings, which sets a realistic tone.

D   The dragon is a creature of fantasy, which sets a fantastic tone.

 DISCUSS IT

Think about details the artist could have included in another illustration for this story. Turn to another student and talk about the details and how the illustration might change the way you understand the story.

Read the movie review. Then answer the questions.

The Book of Dragons Comes Alive

A CLOSER LOOK
Look at the illustration. Circle words and phrases in the text that help describe the scene in the illustration.

1   How can a movie improve on one of the great classics of children's literature? E. Nesbit's *The Book of Dragons* contains all of the features of a magical tale of mystical creatures, but the newly released film improves on the classic book. Filmgoers might be surprised at the producer's departure from some elements the book, which was first published in 1900. But that surprise will turn to wonder at the film's beautiful animation.

2   In the movie's opening scene, Effie's younger brother Harry is fishing a winged lizard baby out of his drink. The lizard is small and cute. Harry is immediately offered money for the rare creature by the professor, who has coveted a similar specimen picked up by the doctor. The movie's opening scene is funny, serene.

3   The next scene cuts to dark humor as the doctor's boots are cleaned by a maid. She drops the boots and screams loudly, as a larger and more menacing specimen crawls out of the boot. The audience instantly recognizes what Effie loudly announces—the lizard is a dragon. And soon, these creatures transform from harmless winged lizards to enormous winged dragons with jagged scales, tails that can flatten a grove of trees, and breath that can torch a city.

4   Cut to the next scene—a swarm of dragons has popped up almost overnight in rural and urban gardens and houses, in the alleyways of cities and in dark, quiet forests. At first, one has the impression of watching an invading air force. The animator has done a magnificent job of capturing the dragons' menacing force. These dragons fly in formation, dipping and diving over houses and coming too close to children. They wreak havoc on the villages and cities of England, carrying away grown men and large animals, even elephants. They spew smoke and fire, leaving the countryside blackened and charred.

5   It is at this point in the action that the audience comes to know the real star of the movie, the heroine, Effie. She has both the nerve and courage that children expect from their movie heroes. Effie is in charge, and the voice actress portrays the character as inquisitive and authoritative, smart and sassy. Of course, one of the most impressive features of this film is the original score. The music is at times jarring and soaring, carrying viewers along through the dark skies of London. Will England be safe from this onslaught of dragons? Moviegoers can find out Friday, when the film opens nationwide.

What details support what the movie reviewer has said about the dragons and their portrayal in the film?

1 How does the illustration help you better understand the tone of the movie?

A   It depicts a cold, wintry scene that sets a threatening tone.

B   It depicts fierce, savage dragons that set an unkind tone.

C   It depicts a frightened young girl, which sets a timid tone.

D   It depicts a strong city, which sets a determined tone.

What idea do you get about the 1900s setting from the first passage "The Book of Dragons"?

2 The author writes that "Filmgoers might be surprised at the producer's departure from some elements of the book." Which detail in the illustration *best* supports the idea that this film is quite different from the book?

A   an elephant being carried away by a dragon

B   the modern London setting

C   the snow on the ground

D   dragons that can fly

What does the author say about the character of Effie? What details in the illustration show these character traits?

3 Explain how the illustration helps you better understand the character of Effie. Use at least two details from the text and two details from the illustration to support your answer.

_____

_____

_____

_____

Read the poem. Then answer the questions.

excerpt from The Fairies of the Caldon-Low[1]

by Mary Howitt

"And where have you been, my Mary,
And where have you been from me?"
"I've been to the top of the Caldon-Low,
The midsummer night to see!"

5 "And what did you see, my Mary,
All up on the Caldon-Low?"
"I saw the glad sunshine come down,
And I saw the merry winds blow."

"And what did you hear, my Mary,
10 All up on the Caldon-Hill?"
"I heard the drops of the water made,
And the ears of the green corn fill."

"Oh, tell me all, my Mary—
All—all that ever you know;
15 For you must have seen the fairies
Last night on the Caldon-Low!"

"Then take me on your knee, mother,
And listen, mother of mine:
A 100 fairies danced last night,
20 And the harpers they were nine.

"And their harp-strings rang so merrily
To their dancing feet so small;
But, oh! the words of their talking
Were merrier far than all!"

---

[1]**Caldon-Low:** a town in central England

1 Which line does the picture *best* illustrate?

   A "For you must have seen the fairies/Last night on the Caldon-Low!"

   B "A 100 fairies danced last night,/And the harpers they were nine."

   C "And their harp-strings rang so merrily/To their dancing feet so small;"

   D "But, oh! the words of their talking/Were merrier far than all!"

2 The table below lists a detail from the text about the setting of the story.

Detail from the Text	Detail from the Illustration
The story takes place in Caldon-Low.	

Which of the following is a detail that appears in the illustration but not in the text?

   A The setting is at night.

   B The setting is on a hill.

   C The setting is in the summer.

   D The setting is near a forest.

3 Which idea does the illustration *most* help you understand?

   A Caldon-Low is a town in England.

   B Fairies are small, human-like creatures with wings.

   C Midsummer night is the shortest night of the year.

   D Corn grows in the area around Caldon-Low.

4 How does the illustration help support the tone that the author creates in the poem? Use details from the text and the illustration to support your answer.

_____

_____

_____

_____

Comparing and Contrasting Stories

 **Introduction**   THEME: >>> **Wondrous Creatures**

Genre refers to the type of literature. Literature can be categorized into different genres based on the subject matter. For example, mysteries have certain characteristics that distinguish them from other genres. A mystery typically involves a crime or a puzzle that must be solved. Stories in a particular genre may have similar themes and topics.

Look at the chart below and pay attention to the characteristics of the different genres that are described.

Realistic Fiction	• has characters who could be real • has settings and problems that could happen in real life
Historical Fiction	• features realistic characters and problems but the setting is an earlier time period.
Science Fiction	• has settings and problems that probably could not happen in real life, but usually involve a real life science concept or problem • characters may be nonhuman or people living in the future
Fantasy	• features imaginary settings • characters with extraordinary powers • fantastic creatures like unicorns
Traditional Literature	• includes stories that have been passed down orally from generation to generation • **fables** are short folktales but have talking animals that teach a lesson or moral • **folktales** are stories of ordinary people that contain a lesson about human behavior • **myths** explain something about nature or a people's beliefs or customs, characters are often heroes or gods • **fairy tales** involved magical creatures and places

Sometimes, comparing and contrasting texts in the same genre can help readers understand important features of each text. For example, authors might develop similar themes, tones, settings, and even types of characters.

Look at the two illustrations from two stories. Then answer the questions.

What genre are the two stories? _____

How are the settings different? _____

_____

What is similar about the characters in the two stories? _____

_____

_____

How are the problems in each story similar or different? _____

_____

_____

_____

Read the first part of the story.

How the Monkey Became a Trickster

by Elsie Spicer Eells

1   Once upon a time there was a beautiful garden in which grew all sorts of fruits. Many beasts lived in the garden, and they were permitted to eat of the fruits whenever they wished. But they were asked to observe one rule. They must make a low, polite bow to the fruit tree, call it by its name, and say, "Please give me a taste of your fruit." They had to be very careful to remember the tree's correct name and not to forget to say "please." It was also very important that they should remember not to be greedy. They must always leave plenty of fruit for the other beasts who might pass that way, and plenty to adorn the tree itself and to furnish seed so that other trees might grow. If they wished to eat figs, they had to say, "O, fig tree, O, fig tree, please give me a taste of your fruit;" or, if they wished to eat oranges, they had to say, "O, orange tree, O, orange tree, please give me a taste of your fruit."

2   In one corner of the garden grew the most splendid tree of all. It was tall and beautiful and the rosy-cheeked fruit upon its wide spreading branches looked wonderfully tempting. No beast had ever tasted of that fruit, for no beast could ever remember its name.

3   In a tiny house near the edge of the garden dwelt a little old woman who knew the names of all the fruit trees which grew in the garden. The beasts often went to her and asked the name of the wonderful fruit tree, but the tree was so far distant from the tiny house of the little old woman that no beast could ever remember the long, hard name by the time he reached the fruit tree.

4   At last, the monkey thought of a trick. Perhaps you do not know it, but the monkey can play the guitar. He always played when the beasts gathered together in the garden to dance. The monkey went to the tiny house of the little old woman, carrying his guitar under his arm. When she told him the long, hard name of the wonderful fruit tree he made up a little tune to it, all his own, and sang it over and over again all the way from the tiny house of the little old woman to the corner of the garden where the wonderful fruit tree grew. When any of the other beasts met him and asked him what new song he was singing to his guitar, he said never a word. He marched straight on, playing his little tune over and over again on his guitar and singing softly the long, hard name.

Now read the first part of the poem. Then answer the questions.

The Monkey
by Marmaduke Park

The animals, on the death of the lion,
    During his life, prince of the country,
Resolved to elect a king to try on
    The regal crown, and chose a monkey.
5   Because after the animals had all
Tried on the regal crown, or let it fall,
Because their heads were all too big,
Or too small, too horned, or too thick,
The monkey slipped through it;
10   And with it cut up many a trick,
Which they all thought refined[1],
And chose him with one mind.
Only the fox regretted the election,
And swore to reign in his defection.

――――――――――――――

[1]refined: fine

Think About It

How is the character of the monkey similar and different in the poem and the story? To answer the question, look for details in the text about each monkey.

How is the character of the monkey in "How the Monkey Became a Trickster"

similar to and different from monkey in "The Monkey"? _____

_____

_____

What details from the two texts support your comparison? _____

_____

_____

_____

Continue reading the story and then the poem. Then answer the questions.

A CLOSER LOOK

Reread the last two paragraphs of the story and the last nine lines of the poem. Circle words and phrases that tell what happened to the main character and what the main character may have learned.

How the Monkey Became a Trickster *continued*

5   At last, he reached the corner of the garden where the wonderful fruit tree grew. He had never seen it look so beautiful. The rosy-cheeked fruit glowed in the bright sunlight. The monkey could hardly wait to make his bow, say the long hard name over twice, and ask for the fruit with a "please." What a beautiful color and what a delicious odor that fruit had! The monkey had never in all his life been so near to anything which smelled so good. He took a big bite. What a face he made! That beautiful sweet-smelling fruit was bitter and sour, and it had a nasty taste. He threw it away from him as far as he could.

6   The monkey never forgot the tree's long, hard name and the little tune he had sung. Nor did he forget how the fruit tasted. He never took a bite of it again; but, after that, his favorite trick was to treat the other beasts to the wonderful fruit just to see them make faces when they tasted it.

The Monkey *continued*

15   He came and made his compliment;
"Sire," said he, "I know a treasure meant
For your high majesty. I will show
The spot where it lies hid."
The monkey went at Reynard's bid—
20   And was caught in a trap.
The fox exclaimed,
"How do you think to govern us,
When, after all, with all your fuss,
You cannot well, do what you may,
25   Keep e'en yourself out of harm's way."
The animals agreed,
That royal power suits very few indeed.

Think about the lesson that the monkey learns about the fruit and the point the fox makes about being a leader. How are they similar?

How are the lessons of the two stories similar?

A Both teach that monkeys are not reliable leaders.

B Both teach that animals can never really trust a fox.

C Both teach that tricking others never leads to good outcomes.

D Both teach that some things are not as good as they first seem.

Think about the descriptions in the genre chart on page 219.

What characteristics of the two stories help you determine the genre?

_____

_____

_____

_____

DISCUSS IT

In the poem and story, the monkeys do not end up getting what they want. Turn to another student and talk about how things ended for the monkey in the first story and the monkey in the poem.

Read the two stories. Then answer the questions.

A CLOSER LOOK

Underline details in each story that tell about the setting.

Circle words and phrases in each story that tell what the characters learn.

What The Yen Tzi Taught The Hunter

1   ONE day a hunter was looking for a fox in the wilderness, when suddenly he saw thousands of birds coming toward the river, and he lay quite still and waited for them all to come.

2   The Yen Tzi[1], or Kind Birds, were talking together, and the hunter listened. One asked, "Is all our company here?"

3   And the Leader Bird said, "No, little One-Month-Old and Two-Month and Mrs. This-Year are not here yet."

4   And the Leader Bird said to the Lookout Birds, "You must go after them and help them to the river before five days. Our boats are dried and ready to sail. It is growing cold, and we must all go south together."

5   So the Lookout Birds flew all around the country to hunt the lost birds. They found one with a broken wing, and a little one with not enough wing feathers to fly far, and one with a wound in his leg made by a hunter, and others that were tired or very hungry. They found every missing bird, and this great family of friends were soon all together again.

6   But while the Lookout Birds were seeking the lost ones from their own family, they heard another bird cry, "Save me! Save me, too!" They stopped and said, "Who is calling? Someone must be in trouble." They flew to a lemon tree and saw a Tailor Bird with her leg all covered with blood. The Kind Birds said, "Friend, how came you in such trouble? What is your name, and where do you live?"

7   The Tailor Bird said, "I live in the South Province, 800 miles away. I came here to see my friends and relatives. Three of my children are with me, and we were on our way home to the south. We had gone 60 miles, when I asked my children to stop and rest in this lemon tree, and now I do not even know where they are. I fear the hunter got them. I am hurt, too, and I do not think I shall ever see my home again. I shall lose my life here, I fear."

8   The Yen Tzi heard all the Tailor Bird said. They talked together and were sorry for her who had no one to care for her, for they knew her children had been killed by the hunter. "If we do not save her life, she will surely die," they said.

---

[1] **Yen Tzi, or Kind Bird:** a species of the fly-catcher family found in China. They are very gentle, never fight among themselves or with others, share their nests with each other or even with other birds. Hence the name "Kind Birds."

9 So they asked, "Would you like to go with us? We know you eat different food. We live on rice and fruit and a few bugs. We do not know that you can live as we do. And we must ride on our boats, many, many hours."

10 The Tailor Bird answered, "Yes, I will go gladly, and will eat what you have and cause you no trouble."

11 The Kind Birds helped the Tailor Bird to their company and put her in one of their boats, and two or three birds fed her and cared for her until she was well.

12 The hunter who told this story said, "I have learned many things by watching and studying the habits of the Kind Birds. I will never kill birds again."

13 EE-SZE (Meaning): In time of trouble, man should help not only his own, but others.

The Squirrels of Central Park

1 Ben was the absolute ruler of Central Park. No one questioned his authority, for no other squirrel knew the park like he did. When Ben told the others to back away from a bag of popcorn dropped by a screaming child, they listened and they obeyed. When they were told to stay out of the big oak tree near Columbus Circle, they did.

2 One day, a new squirrel happened into the park. She was reddish brown, like the others, but she had a white splotch on the tip of her tail. The other squirrels were intrigued. They gathered around the newcomer. Her name was Sheila, and she told them she had come from Battery Park. She described her harrowing journey along the streets of New York, dodging cars and avoiding barking dogs. She showed the other squirrels how she had climbed over snow banks along the side of the road, and how she had stood near subway vents to keep warm. The other squirrels listened intently, for they had never met such a brave squirrel.

3 But Ben was not so impressed. "You cannot stay here, for it's winter and we do not have enough food for even one extra mouth," he said firmly.

4 Slowly, reluctantly, the others began to turn and run away. But Sheila moved closer to Ben. She flicked her whiskers and said in a strong steady voice, "I would like to stay right here. I have traveled a long way, and I need a new home. I can help you find a new source of food."

5 The other squirrels turned around quickly to glance at Ben. They wondered what he would say and do. But Ben, too, was confused. A new source of food? It can't be, he thought. I know every oak tree in this park, every trash can along its paths.

6 But Sheila turned and walked toward a shrub, one the others hadn't noticed before. It was prickly and green, but Sheila was undeterred. She scampered under the shrub and called to the others. "This plant here has soft green stems near the base. They are tender and delicious, even in winter." The others crept close to Sheila and tasted the stems themselves. She was right, they were soft and nutty tasting.

7 The other squirrels turned to Ben, who hesitated, but just for a moment. "Oh, I suppose you can stay," he grumbled. "You might even be a good addition to our community."

8 Moral: Do not turn your back on newcomers, for they likely have something to contribute.

> Who are the main characters of both stories, and what does this tell you about the genre?

1 Part A

How is Ben's reaction to Sheila joining their group different from the Kind Birds' reaction to the Tailor Bird joining their group?

_____

_____

_____

_____

Part B

Why might the author of "The Squirrels of Central Park" have taken this approach?

_____

_____

_____

_____

> What ideas do you get from the hunter and from the mention of the subway?

2 Part A

How are the settings of the two stories different?

A   One is set in the spring, and one is set in the autumn.

B   One is set in the morning, and one is set in the evening.

C   One is set long ago, and one is set in modern times.

D   One is set in the wilderness, and the other is set in a city park.

Part B

Which details from the stories *best* support your answer to Part A?

A   "It is growing cold, and we must all go south together;" "it's winter, and we do not have enough food"

B   "Our boats are dried and ready to sail;" "dodging cars and avoiding barking dogs."

C   "a hunter was looking for a fox in the wilderness;" "Ben was the absolute ruler of Central Park"

D   "we must ride on our boats, many, many hours;" "One day, a new squirrel happened into the park."

> Think about what the hunter learns and what the squirrels learn. How will the characters benefit from what they have learned?

3 Explain how the morals or lessons of the two stories are alike and how they are different.

_____

_____

_____

_____

_____

_____

Read two passages. Then answer the questions.

THE MACHINE STOPS
by E. M. Forster

I

THE AIR-SHIP

Written in 1909, E. M. Forster's short story forecasts a futuristic world where people no longer live on Earth's surface, but instead in underground cells. In this scene, a mother and son talk to each other through a platelike invention that projects their images.

1 An electric bell rang.

2 "I suppose I must see who it is", she thought, and set her chair in motion. The chair, like the music, was worked by machinery, and it rolled her to the other side of the room where the bell still rang.

3 "Who is it?" she called. Her voice was irritable, for she had been interrupted often since the music began. She knew several thousand people, in certain directions human intercourse had advanced enormously.

4 But when she listened into the receiver, her white face wrinkled into smiles, and she said:

5 "Very well. Let us talk, I will isolate myself. I do not expect anything important will happen for the next five minutes—for I can give you fully five minutes, Kuno. Then I must deliver my lecture on 'Music during the Australian Period.'"

6 She touched the isolation knob, so that no one else could speak to her. Then she touched the lighting apparatus, and the little room was plunged into darkness.

7 "Be quick!" She called, her irritation returning. "Be quick, Kuno; here I am in the dark wasting my time."

8 But it was fully 15 seconds before the round plate that she held in her hands began to glow. A faint blue light shot across it, darkening to purple, and presently she could see the image of her son, who lived on the other side of the earth, and he could see her.

9 "Kuno, how slow you are."

10 "I have called you before, mother, but you were always busy or isolated. I have something particular to say."

11 "What is it, dearest boy? Be quick."

12 "I want you to come and see me."

13 Vashti watched his face in the blue plate.

14 "But I can see you!" she exclaimed. "What more do you want?"

15 "I want to see you not through the Machine," said Kuno. "I want to speak to you not through the wearisome Machine."

16 She replied that she could scarcely spare the time for a visit.

17 "The air-ship barely takes two days to fly between me and you."

18 "I dislike air-ships."

19 "Why?"

20 "I dislike seeing the horrible brown earth, and the sea, and the stars when it is dark. "

21 "I want to see the stars. They are curious stars. I want to see them not from the air-ship, but from the surface of the earth, as our ancestors did, thousands of years ago. I want to visit the surface of the earth."

22 She was shocked again.

23 "Mother, you must come, if only to explain to me what is the harm of visiting the surface of the earth."

24 "No harm," she replied, controlling herself. "But no advantage. The surface of the earth is only dust and mud, no advantage. The surface of the earth is only dust and mud, no life remains on it, and you would need a respirator, or the cold of the outer air would kill you. One dies immediately in the outer air."

25 "I know. Of course, I shall take all precautions."

26 "And besides—"

27 "Well?"

28 She considered, and chose her words with care. Her son had a strange temper, and she wished to dissuade him from the expedition.

29 "It is contrary to the spirit of the age," she asserted.

30 "Do you mean by that, contrary to the Machine?"

31 "In a sense, but—"

32 His image in the blue plate faded.

33 "Kuno!"

34 He had isolated himself.

35 For a moment, Vashti felt lonely.

The Colony

1 Aisha inspected the almond tree. Yes, it definitely has some kind of disease, she thought, something that we never saw back on Earth.

2 The little colony on Venus had prospered beyond anyone's wildest dreams. And they had Aisha to thank for it. She had been the one to determine that their need for oxygen could be supplied by growing vegetable plants and fruit trees. It was Aisha who suggested the excess food could be sent back to Earth to help feed the hungry.

3 But now the crops were dying in the Venus colony. The dome that protected them from the sun's powerful rays and helped keep the colony cool was also fostering an environment perfect for funguses and bacteria. If the almond trees were dying, what next? Maybe the orange groves, maybe the apple trees. Aisha sat back on the rocky soil. The thought sent a shiver through her body. She knew the colony depended on the food. Without it, they would go hungry right here on Venus, for it was nearly impossible to think of returning to the overcrowding and fighting that had characterized Earth in the last century.

4 "Aisha," a voice called. Aisha stood up and went to say hello to the scientist she had asked to examine the almond leaves. "I'm afraid we have some bad news," he reported. Aisha waited, and the scientist went on. "It seems that this is a fungus inherent in the soil here, something with which we have no experience. I guess the sun's rays kept the fungus dormant, but now that we have the dome, this fungus has sprung to life. There's really nothing we can do to combat it. I figure we have two, maybe three years at best."

5 Aisha thanked the scientist and walked toward the marketplace, forcing a smile at the friendly faces she passed. It was bustling, a community that was so different from and better than the one they had left back on Earth. She couldn't bear to think what it was destined to become—desperate gangs of people fighting over every last resource, poisoned by the environment around them.

1 In what way is Aisha's situation different from Kuno's?

    A Aisha wants to leave Venus, while Kuno does not want to live below the earth's surface.

    B Aisha doesn't want to leave Venus, while Kuno wants to stay below the earth's surface.

    C Aisha is unhappy living on Venus, while Kuno is happy living below the earth's surface.

    D Aisha is content with living on Venus, but may have to leave, while Kuno is not content with living below the earth's surface, and wants to leave.

2 Complete the chart about the settings of the stories.

The Air-ship	The Colony	Both Stories
An earth that is cold and devoid of life.	A colony on the planet Venus that is protected by a dome.	

Which of the following would go in the blank space in the chart?

    A occur sometime in the recent past

    B are set in a place other than the surface of the earth

    C are set in a place that is cold, rocky, and very dusty

    D occur at a time when Earth's people are at war

3 Part A

Which of the following *best* describes how the tone of the two stories is similar?

A Both stories have a dark, depressing tone.

B Both stories have a sharp, sarcastic tone.

C Both stories have a wistful, hopeful tone.

D Both stories have an angry, aggressive tone.

Part B

Which details from the stories *best* support your answer to Part A?

A Passage 1: "'Kuno, how slow you are.'"
  Passage 2: "'I'm afraid we have some bad news,' he reported."

B Passage 1: "'I want to see the stars.'"
  Passage 2: "If the almond trees were dying, what next?"

C Passage 1: "For a moment, Vashti felt lonely."
  Passage 2: "desperate gangs of people fighting over every last
      resource"

D Passage 1: "Her voice was irritable."
  Passage 2: "But now the crops were dying in the Venus colony."

4 What is similar and what is different about the way the authors write about the futuristic society? Provide two details to support your answer.

_____

_____

_____

_____

_____

_____

Integration of Knowledge and Ideas in Literary Text

Read the poem. Then answer the questions.

The Satyrs and the Moon
by Herbert S. Gorman

Within the wood behind the hill
The moon got tangled in the trees.
Her splendor made the branches thrill
And thrilled the breeze.

5 The satyrs in the grotto bent
Their heads to see the wondrous sight.
"It is a god in banishment
That stirs the night."

The little satyr looked and guessed:
10 "It is an apple that one sees,
Brought from that garden of the West—
Hesperides[1]."

"It is a cyclops' glaring eye."
"A temple dome from Babylon."
15 "A Titan's cup of ivory."
"A little sun."

The tiny satyr jumped for joy,
And kicked hoofs in utmost glee.
"It is a wondrous silver toy—
20 Bring it to me!"

A great wind whistled through the blue
And caught the moon and tossed it high;
A bubble of pale fire it flew
Across the sky.

25 The satyrs gasped and looked and smiled,
And wagged their heads from side to side,
Except their shaggy little child,
Who cried and cried.

---

[1]**Hesperides:** a garden in Greek mythology

1   What is the *best* reason for including the illustration with this poem?

   A   It helps the reader read the poem.

   B   It helps the reader understand the poem.

   C   It makes the poem fun to read.

   D   It adds something funny to the poem.

2   The illustration helps the reader understand that the tone of the poem is _____.

   A   sad and depressing

   B   calm and peaceful

   C   magical and enchanting

   D   evil and scary

3   What did you learn about satyrs from the illustration that you do not learn from the text?

   _____

   _____

   _____

   _____

Read the story. Then answer the questions.

The Snake

a tale from West Africa

1   One cold winter day, a woman was walking home along a lonely country road. Suddenly, she heard a soft hissing sound. She looked and saw a cobra trapped between two rocks.

2   "Lady, please help me," the snake hissed. "I'm cold, I'm hungry, and I'm trapped here. If you don't help me, I'll die."

3   The woman felt sorry for the poor serpent. She carefully moved the rocks and freed it.

4   "Thank you," said the snake. "Now, won't you please take me home with you? All I need is some food and a warm place to spend the night, and I'll be on my way in the morning."

5   The kindhearted woman carried the snake home, warming it with her hands. She lit a fire in her stove and gave the snake some food. Soon it was fit and healthy and slithering about the floor of her house.

6   The woman sat down in her chair and held the snake on her lap. The snake sprang up and bit her savagely. "Oh!" cried the woman. "How could you do such a thing? I saved your life! I took you in and fed you, and now I may die from your poisonous bite!"

7   "Lady," the serpent hissed, "I'm a snake. Didn't you know that before you took me in?"

4   The illustration helps you understand that the woman in the folktale _____.

   A   is in Africa

   B   has a warm home

   C   is surprised by the snake's behavior

   D   is not suspicious of the snake

5   How does the illustration show that the snake is not what it seems to be?

   A   The snake has a mean look on its face.

   B   The snake lets the woman carry it.

   C   The snake coils around the woman.

   D   The snake is lighter than it looks.

6   How does the illustration help you understand the snake's actions at the end of the story?

   _____

   _____

   _____

   _____

Read the story. Then answer the questions.

The Reptile Education Center

1   I had always been afraid of snakes. Even though I was told the little garter snakes I saw in the garden weren't dangerous, I didn't like the way they slithered quickly through the grass. I wasn't too happy when, on our class field trip to the zoo, we headed into the Reptile Education Center. I decided I would look straight ahead until we came out the door on the other side.

2   Inside the building, it was dark and cool. We passed by display areas covered with glass windows. I was relieved to see there was no way the snakes and other reptiles could escape. The docent (that's what they call the zoo guide) told us that the reptiles came from all over the world. I enjoyed seeing the frogs, toads, lizards, and other reptiles. When we got to the snakes, I tried not to look.

3   The docent was obviously a snake fanatic. She talked enthusiastically about how snakes are helpful. Their ways of capturing prey are natural and essential to their lives. She described how some, such as rattlesnakes, inject poison when they bite. The poison is meant to stun the prey. Then they swallow their prey—whole! Other snakes, such as the boas and pythons, squeeze and suffocate their prey. They also swallow their prey whole. The docent pointed out a snake that recently had been fed a rat. We could see the bulge in the snake's body where the rat was being digested.

4   I was still having trouble seeing how snakes were helpful animals. Just the sight of them gave me a shivery feeling on my skin.

5   Then the docent explained that if it weren't for snakes and other predators, rats, mice, and other vermin would take over the world! A female mouse will have five to ten litters of five to six young in one year. Each of the female babies will begin having her own babies when only four weeks old. So even though a mouse only lives about one year, there are plenty more to take its place.

6   Our last stop was beside the display of the zoo's largest snake. Her name is Goldie. She is a reticulated python. These pythons are the longest snakes in the world, and Goldie is about 10 feet long. Pythons eat lots of rats and mice, but they are so big they can eat a deer or wild pig. The docent lifted a lid and took Goldie out of her display. Goldie wrapped around the docent's body. We were allowed to pet Goldie. When it was my turn, I ran a finger along Goldie's back. She was very smooth. I was amazed at how friendly and calm she was.

7   I still don't like snakes very much. But after our trip to the zoo, I understand how they play an important part in our world.

7 Part A

Both the "The Snake" folktale and the "Reptile Education Center"
story teach a lesson about _____.

A picking up snakes

B feeding snakes

C trusting animals

D judging animals

Part B

What evidence from both stories *best* supports your answer to
Part A?

_____

_____

_____

_____

_____

_____

8 Explain the lesson the author teaches in "The Snake" folktale.

_____

_____

9 What lesson does the author teach in the "Reptile Education
Center" realistic fiction story?

_____

_____

Integration of Knowledge and Ideas in Informational Text

Have you ever had to do research for a project? There can be so many sources to choose from! Don't feel discouraged. There are strategies to help you decide between articles and to identify the important information in a text. In this unit, you will practice skimming and scanning for important information, choosing articles that are the most helpful, and watching out for authors who state their opinions instead of facts.

LESSON 20 Drawing Information from Multiple Sources is about using different sources to find information. You will learn abut skimming and scanning articles to find important information. You will also compare articles, decide which gives you the most information, and think about what details helped you decide.

LESSON 21 Identifying Supporting Information helps you evaluate claims to decide if they are fact or opinion. You will also reread information and look for evidence to support the author's claim.

LESSON 22 Integrating Information from Multiple Sources focuses on comparing research articles and skimming to find specific information in them.

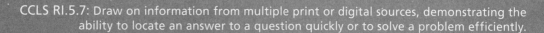

LESSON
20

Drawing Information from Multiple Sources

Introduction

THEME: >>> From Distant Shores

Sometimes you read informational texts to find answers to specific questions or to solve problems. But when you're looking for answers, it's not always possible to read an entire text. For example, say you want to know where the capital of the Cherokee Nation is located. An article on Cherokee history might provide the answer. But a passage on Cherokee cultural festivals might also provide the answer. To find the answer, you would have to skim or scan the articles. **Skimming** involves quickly looking over the text to figure out what it's about. You'd read the title and the first sentence of each paragraph to get the main ideas. This technique might lead you to the answer you're looking for. But you could also scan the article. **Scanning** involves glancing over the text to find specific words. In this case, you would look for the word *capital.*

Identifying and reading **text features** is also useful in locating information in nonfiction texts. Titles and headings are like signposts that help you figure out if you're looking in the right place. Information in graphs, charts, illustrations, maps, and captions can be accessed quickly and easily.

At other times, you need to really understand a topic. If you needed to understand the role of Chinese immigrants in building the railroad, you might want to read an article about Chinese immigrants in the 1800s as well as an article about the construction of the railroads. Together, both texts would give you facts and ideas about the topic that reading only one of the articles would not. But even when you read several sources to understand a topic, you must look for main ideas and key details and constantly check to make sure you understand the author's main points.

Read the passage and the sidebar below.

The Big Idea Behind the Erie Canal

Going West Before the Canal

In the late 18th century, traveling west was difficult and took a lot of time. The roads were bad and there were few places to stop for supplies. As a result, most people stayed near the coast, where there were roads and cities. But plenty of people had looked for a water route to the west—one that would help settlers and traders move quickly and easily from east to west.

The Planning Phase

But then in 1807, a flour merchant wrote an essay that described his vision of moving his flour to markets in a faster, cheaper way. He imagined a water route that went from Buffalo on the eastern shores of Lake Erie to Albany, nearly 400 miles away. And the idea for the Erie Canal was born.

> **The Erie Canal: Quick Facts**
> - Begun in 1817
> - Completed in 1825
> - 363 miles long
> - Cost $7 million to build
> - Built using men and horses
> - Originally 40 feet wide and 4 feet deep
> - Later enlarged for bigger boats

Imagine that you have to write a report about the Erie Canal. You need to find out why the canal was built. Would the passage or the sidebar provide the answer?

_____

How would you know where to look in this passage? _____

_____

Would you use the passage or the sidebar to determine the length of the canal?

_____

Would the passage or the sidebar likely be easier to scan? _____

_____

Both the passage and the sidebar are about the Erie Canal, but both cover very different kinds of information. The only information they have in common is the approximate length of the canal. If you wanted to write a report about the Erie Canal, or even if you just wanted to learn about it, you would need to read both.

It is often useful to draw on multiple sources to find complete information about a topic. By skimming and scanning the text and text features, you can find answers to your questions quickly.

Read the first parts of two passages. Then answer the questions.

Hard Traveling

by Harry Thelen

1   In 1842, two men crossed America in opposite directions. They never met, but together they helped add the Pacific Northwest region to the United States.

2   John Charles Frémont was a 29-year-old lieutenant in the United States Army. He was on a scouting mission to the West. With a well supplied party of soldiers and guides, Frémont started out in May along the Oregon Trail. This was an old fur-trader's path that since 1836 had become a route west for settlers in covered wagons. Frémont explored passes in the Rocky Mountains. He climbed a mountain in Wyoming that he named for himself. When he returned on October 29, he was convinced that the far West had to become part of the United States. With the help of his talented young wife, Jessie, he wrote a book about his adventures and his idea that the country should expand westward. It became a best seller.

3   Dr. Marcus Whitman, 40, was a missionary at a tiny settlement he and his young wife, Narcissa, had started near today's Walla Walla, Washington. Six years earlier, the Whitmans had been part of the very first wagon train to travel west on the Oregon Trail. They ran a school for American Indian children and also sought to convert the American Indians to Christianity. In 1842, Whitman and the few other American settlers in the region heard some disturbing news. A British trading company was about to claim the whole of the Oregon Territory, which included today's states of Washington and Oregon, part of Idaho, western Montana and Wyoming, and much of western Canada.

from Journal of a Trip to Oregon in 1852

by Abigail Jane Scott

June 29, 1852

1   We came 20 miles. We struck the Sweet water about two o'clock and about three came to Independence Rock; The Sweet water is about 100 feet in width; The water is clear and palatable but is warmer during the day than the water of the Platte.

2   Independence Rock is an immense mass covering an area of, I think about ten acres, and is about 300 feet high; My sisters and I went to the base of the rock with the intention of climbing it but we had only ascended about 30 feet when a heavy hail and wind storm arose obliging us to desist. We then started on after the wagons and before we reached them they had all crossed the river except the last to overtake. They had intended to let us wade it (it was waist deep) to learn us not to get so far behind the team; I would have liked the fun of wading well enough but did not like to get joked about being left. Immediately after leaving Independence Rock we came in sight of the well known Devil's Gate five miles ahead of us and when we came near enough we turned off the road about one mile and halted for the night opposite to it in a bend of the river.

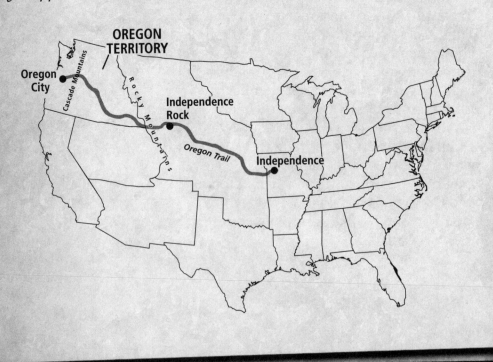

Think About It

How would you use both passages to understand the history of Oregon?
The question asks you to determine which parts of the passages would provide you
with information about Oregon's history.

What does the first map "Oregon Country/Columbia District 1818–1846" tell you?

_____

_____

What does the second map of the United States tell you? _____

_____

When you reread the first passage and skim for main ideas, what do you find it is

mostly about? _____

_____

When you reread the second passage and skim for main ideas, what do you find it

is *mostly* about? _____

_____

**Now determine how you would use each passage to understand the
history of Oregon.**

I would use the first passage to _____

_____.

I would use the second passage to _____

_____.

Continue reading both passages. Then answer the questions.

Hard Traveling *continued*

A CLOSER LOOK

Why did Whitman run into heavy snow on his journey? Underline the answer.

4   Whitman had planned to go east in the spring to persuade his church not to close his mission. Now he took it upon himself to persuade the government to "keep Oregon American." He started on October 3—very late in the year for a Rocky Mountain crossing. He headed south to Santa Fe, which was then part of Mexico. He ran into heavy snow in the mountains and swam his horse through broken ice in Colorado's Grand River. From Santa Fe he headed east. He reached Washington, DC, in March 1843 after a 3,500-mile journey. He met with President John Tyler and Secretary of State Daniel Webster. Then Whitman went to New York and told his story to a newspaper. In the spring, Whitman headed back to his mission. He found himself part of the biggest wagon train that had ever followed the Oregon Trail.

5   Many Americans were ready to go to war over Oregon. It was an issue in the 1844 campaign for president. But two years later, a treaty divided the territory peacefully between Britain and the United States.

Journal of a Trip to Oregon in 1852
continued

A CLOSER LOOK

When did most of the travelers visit Independence Rock? Underline the answer.

3   *We in company with many others paid this gate a visit; It is indeed a sight worth seeing. The Sweet water passes through it, and it really seems left by providence for the river to pass through as we can see no other place where it can find its way through the rocks. The cliffs of rock on either side are at least 400 feet in height and on the South side almost perfectly perpendicular; The rocks are in many places covered with names of visitors to this place a few of which were of as early date as '38 a great many were dated '50 and '51 but the majority were '52. We passed seven graves.*

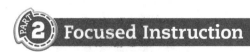

Look at the map in the second passage. What information does it provide that is explained more in the first passage?

How does the first passage better help you understand the journey of the people in the second passage?

A It provides a map of the journey.

B It tells where the people were going.

C It explains what the Oregon Trail was.

D It points out what the weather was like.

What do you learn from the second passage about the Oregon route?

How does the second passage help you understand more about Whitman's return journey to Oregon?

_____

_____

_____

_____

DISCUSS IT

Think about the information in the second passage. What questions does a journal entry answer that a history of a region does not? Turn to another student and talk about how this journal helps you understand people, places, and events.

Read two passages. Then answer the questions.

The Native People of Alaska

A CLOSER LOOK

What did the Interior Indians trade with other peoples? Circle the information in the text that answers the question.

1   Today, the Native people of Alaska make up about 16% of Alaska's population. But this number does not represent one group. In fact, Alaska's first people can be divided into five major groups. They are the Aleuts, the Interior Indians, the Northern Eskimos, the Southern Eskimos, and the Southeast Coastal Indians. All the people within each group have similar languages and cultural traditions. At one time, they all lived in the same general area.

The Aleuts

2   The Aleuts lived mostly in the Aleutian Islands and the Alaska Peninsula. They are the smallest group of natives in Alaska, but they are one of the better known. That's because they have been hugely successful at making a living from the sea. In fact, just about everything they wore, ate, and even lived in came from the sea. Sometimes they paddled for miles to hunt seal and other sea creatures.

The Interior Indians

3   The Interior Indians lived in the interior of Alaska and what is now Canada. Weather conditions could be harsh here, and the Interior Indians did not have sea animals to depend on for food. Instead, they followed herds of caribou and fished in the rivers for salmon. They also gathered roots and berries. Their fringed and beaded skin clothing was admired by other native groups. The Interior Indians often traded these items.

The Northern Eskimos

4   The Northern Eskimos lived mostly in the northernmost part of Alaska in the Arctic Circle. The weather here is bitter cold and unforgiving. These Northern Eskimos were at the mercy of the land and its climate. They depended on sea birds and mammals for food, and on the caribou that roam the area. They also foraged for roots and berries during the very brief summer.

The Southern Eskimos

5   Originally the largest group of natives, the Southern Eskimos lived in an area from the north Pacific Coast to St. Lawrence Island in the central Bering Sea. Like the other groups, the Southern Eskimos also depended on the sea for their tools, food, clothing, and even materials for their homes. As a result of their dependence on the sea, they were skilled hunters and fishers.

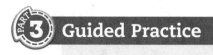

The Southeast Coastal Indians

6 The Southeast Coastal Indians inhabited a region blanketed by lush forests and a mild climate. Game animals were plentiful, and the rivers teemed with fish. But the natives of this area didn't solely depend on the forests for their food. They hunted and fished along the coast, paddling out for miles to kill seals and whales. Perhaps best known for their elaborately carved totem poles, the Southeast Coastal Indians also produced ceremonial costumes and intricate blankets.

The Aleutian People

1 More than 4,000 years ago, the first group of native peoples paddled from what is now mainland Alaska to the Aleutian Islands. Once on the islands, they built small partially underground homes near the coast. They depended on boats for hunting and transportation. They also lived near the coast so they could see any surprise attacks that might be launched from the sea. As the years progressed, the people of the Aleutian Islands continued to live along the coast and continued to rely on the sea.

2 The Aleutian Islands are a volcanic chain of islands, with steep rocky coastlines. About 70 volcanoes exist on the islands. Both volcanic activity and earthquakes played a role in the history of the Aleut people. The climate is milder than in other parts of Alaska. Summertime temperatures average 50 degrees Fahrenheit and winter temperatures average 30 degrees Fahrenheit.

3 Villages were made up of related families, with large family groups living together in each snug home. The people traced their relatives through their mother's line. The chief was usually a good hunter and fisher, and he often ruled over a village or sometimes an entire island.

4 Because the sea rarely froze in the winter, it was a source of food and transportation year round for the Aleut people. The men hunted seals, sea lions, sea otters, whales, and sometimes walruses. They used one- and two-man boats made of skin. The men also hunted bears and caribou. The women collected fish, shellfish, berries, roots, and wild plants. They were also adept at weaving baskets from grass. The women of the villages turned the bones and ivory they collected from walruses and other sea animals into needles, containers, and other useful objects.

5 The Aleut people spent most of their time gathering food. But the work required cooperation. For this reason, the Aleuts were known for their ability to work together and to share. For example, hauling a large fish into a small boat required two men. Similarly, pulling in a fishing net and collecting the fish required two or more women. Even older and younger members of the group helped in gathering foods.

How has the author chosen to divide the information in the first passage?

1 What feature of the first passage is *not* found in the second passage?

_____

_____

_____

What is the most important feature of the Aleutian culture?

2 Which information can be found in both passages?

   A The Aleutian people lived in semi-underground houses.

   B The Aleutian people depended a great deal on the sea.

   C The Aleutian people were the smallest group of Natives in Alaska.

   D The Aleutian people were known to work cooperatively.

Where did each group live, what did they eat, and what kinds of art did they produce?

3 Skim and scan the articles to compare the Southeast Coastal Indians with the Aleutian people. Use at least three details from each passage in your response.

_____

_____

_____

_____

_____

_____

Read both passages. Then answer the questions.

Huge Machine Harnesses the Tides

1   Energy is everywhere. It's in the sunlight. It's in the wind. It's in the ocean.

2   The ocean has heat energy from soaking up the light energy of the sun. Like the wind, the ocean has energy of motion in the form of waves and currents.

3   Another form of energy in the ocean is tidal energy. The energy for Earth's tides comes mostly from the moon's gravity and a little from the sun's gravity. The part of the ocean facing the moon bulges out. The part of the ocean on exactly the opposite side of Earth bulges out, too. As Earth turns, the ocean surface seems to rise and fall. Usually, there are two high tides and two low tides each day.

4   With all that water moving up and down, we ought to be able to capture some of that tidal energy. And we can! We can use tidal energy to supply electricity to our homes and businesses. We can use tidal energy in some places instead of burning coal and oil that contribute to global warming.

5   Tidal generators (or turbines) work like wind turbines, except it is ocean currents, not wind, that turns them. The spinning turbine is connected to another device that produces electricity. The electricity then travels through wires to a city where people need it.

6   Now the world's biggest tidal energy generator is being placed off the coast of Invergordon, Scotland. The new tidal generator in Scotland is huge. The turbine blades are 59 feet across. It weighs 143 tons and stands (almost 74 feet high. It is capable of generating enough electricity to power more than 1,000 homes.

7   It is important to put tidal generators near where people actually live. That's another reason Scotland and other locations around the United Kingdom are ideal for capturing clean, renewable tidal energy.

8   In the US, most of the tidal energy resources are along the coast of Alaska where populations are small. Still, tidal energy could power their small cities.

9   Unlike the wind, the tides are very predictable. So it's easy to decide where to put tidal turbines and figure out how much energy they will generate.

10 Another plus, the turbines are usually completely under water, so no one can complain about them spoiling the view!

adapted from Hydro Power

1   When it rains in hills and mountains, the water becomes streams and rivers that run down to the ocean. The moving or falling water can be used to do work. Energy is the ability to do work, so moving water, which has kinetic energy, can be used to make electricity.

2   For hundreds of years, moving water was used to turn wooden wheels that were attached to grinding wheels to grind, or mill, flour or corn. These were called gristmills or water mills.

3   In the year 1086, the *Domesday Book* was written. The multivolume books are very large. Handwritten on the pages of the books are lists of all properties, homes, stores and other things in England. The *Domesday Book* listed 5,624 waterwheel-driven mills in England south of the Trent River. That was about one mill for each 400 people.

4 Water can either go over the top of the wheel or the wheel can be placed in the moving river. The flow of the river then turns the wheel at the bottom.

5 Today, moving water can also be used to make electricity.

6 *Hydro* means "water." *Hydroelectric* means "making electricity from water power."

7 Hydroelectric power uses the kinetic energy of moving water to make electricity. Dams can be built to stop the flow of a river. Water behind a dam often forms a reservoir. Dams are also built across larger rivers but no reservoir is made. The river is simply sent through a hydroelectric power plant or powerhouse.

8 Hydro is one of the largest producers of electricity in the United States. Water power supplies about 10 percent of the entire electricity that we use. In states with high mountains and lots of rivers, even more electricity is made by hydro power. In California, for example, about 15 percent of all the electricity comes from hydroelectric.

9 The state of Washington leads the nation in hydroelectricity. The Grand Coulee, Chief Joseph, and John Day dams are three of six major dams on the Columbia River. About 87 percent of the electricity made in Washington state is produced by hydroelectric facilities. Some of that electricity is exported from the state and used in other states.

1 Which is the definition of *hydroelectric?* Scan the passages to find the definition.

   A energy that comes mostly from the moon's gravity

   B water behind a dam that forms a reservoir

   C making electricity from water power

   D using tides, which are very predictable

2 How are tidal generators different from hydroelectric plants?

   A Tidal generators rely on the predictable flow of water.

   B Hydroelectric plants use energy from moving water.

   C Tidal generators can be used to power homes and cities.

   D Hydroelectric plants capture energy from rivers.

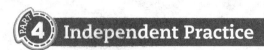

3 Which statement incorporates statements from both passages?

    A Hydro power was first used in England many years ago.

    B Hydro power comes from moving water.

    C Hydro power can be captured by putting dams on rivers.

    D Hydro power is generated most in places with many rivers.

4 Explain how moving water can be used to generate electricity. Use at least two details from each passage in your response.

_____

_____

_____

_____

_____

_____

LESSON 21

Identifying Supporting Information

1 **Introduction**

THEME: >>> **From Distant Shores**

If you saw a television commercial for a skateboard that claimed to "defy gravity and literally make you sail through the air," would you believe it? Why not?

You see and hear claims all the time, from advertisers, speakers, and authors. But you know that what you see and hear isn't always true. Your job is to tell fact from opinion. A **fact** is a statement that can be proven. But an **opinion** is what someone believes or feels. Opinions aren't necessarily bad, but writers who state opinions must back them up with reasons and evidence. How do you know that an author has done this? You have to **evaluate** the information. That means you have to ask hard questions about a text as you read it. Some questions include:

- Who is the author, and what do I know about him or her? Does he or she have a background in the area he or she is writing about?
- What is the author's point of view or opinion about the subject?
- Does the author provide facts, evidence, and examples to support her claims?
- Where did the author get the information she uses to support her ideas?
- Can the author's sources be trusted, or are they are partial to one side or the other?

Read the passage. Then answer the questions to help you evaluate the passage.

Build More Rail Lines
by Sandra Cooper, president of the Train Consortium

More needs to be done to improve train travel in the United States. At present, far fewer people travel by train than by plane. That's mostly because the current system makes train travel expensive and time consuming. Why? Government records show most train tracks are owned by freight companies, so freight trains have the right of way. That means passenger trains often have to stop and let freight trains go by. This takes time and makes train travel unappealing. A recent comparison of train tickets versus plane tickets shows that train travel is more expensive, too. However, there is something that can be done to make train travel a real option. The government must invest in building a better network of train tracks across the country. Doing so would make train travel faster and less expensive. And it would be a much better experience for the traveler.

Who is the author, and what do I know about her? _____

_____

What is the author's point of view or opinion about the subject? _____

_____

Does the author provide facts, evidence, and examples to support her claims? Explain.

_____

_____

_____

_____

Where did the author get the information she uses to support her ideas?

_____

_____

Can the author's sources be trusted, or are they partial to one side or the other?

_____

Of course, not all informational articles will contain clear opinions. You must evaluate whether or not the author has backed up ideas with specific reasons and supporting evidence. Doing so will help you understand whether the author has made reasonable claims or is merely stating his or her own point of view. It will also help you understand how an author builds an argument.

Read the first part of the passage. Then answer the questions.

Henry Hudson and the River that Would Bear His Name, September 3, 1609

1   How did the Hudson River in New York and New Jersey get its name? Henry Hudson was an English explorer sailing with the Dutch in search of the Northwest Passage. Hudson was one of many explorers who were searching for a northwest passage that connected the Atlantic Ocean to the Pacific Ocean. On the morning of September 3, 1609, Hudson and his crew aboard the *Half Moon* passed the island we know today as Manhattan. They sailed into the majestic river off the Atlantic coast by chance. Strong head winds and storms forced them to abandon the northeast voyage they had been assigned.

2   Hudson was not the first European explorer to discover this river. The Florentine navigator Giovanni da Verrazano discovered the Hudson in 1524. However, Hudson traveled the river much farther than its previous explorer. After 150 miles, the *Half Moon* did not reach the Pacific, but it did reach what would later become Albany, New York. There, they turned around. As a result of Hudson's exploration, the river bears his name today.

Think About It

How does the author support the idea that the Hudson River is named after Henry Hudson because of Hudson's exploration of the river? To answer this question, look for reasons or evidence the author includes in the article that support this idea.

Read the first paragraph of the passage again.

What does the author tell you happened to cause Hudson to sail into the river?

_____

Reread the second paragraph.

Why does the author mention Giovanni da Verrazano? _____

_____

What makes Hudson's voyage more significant than da Verrazano's, according to

the author? _____

What reasons does the author give for the naming of the Hudson River?

_____

_____

_____

Do the reasons adequately support the point? _____

Continue reading the passage. Then answer the question.

3   Hudson was a headstrong but courageous commander. Though he often mismanaged his crews by playing favorites or letting morale suffer, he was a competent navigator. He undertook four dangerous voyages, and made huge contributions to geographical knowledge. His exploration of the Hudson River led to Dutch colonization of the area.

4   The Hudson River, once known to the Mohican Indians as Muhheakunnuk ("Great Waters Constantly in Motion"), was the site of key battles in the American Revolution. It also inspired an important phase of landscape painting called the Hudson River School that celebrated the natural beauty of the American landscape. Today, the Hudson is one of the nation's most important waterways. Oceangoing ships can navigate the river to Albany year-round. Pleasure boats and tugboat and barge traffic can reach the Great Lakes from May to November. Cargo such as wood pulp, steel, cocoa beans, grain, and scrap metal rely on the Hudson for deliveries. The US Military Academy at West Point overlooks the Hudson, too. What would Henry Hudson say if he saw that river today?

A CLOSER LOOK

What is the Hudson River used for today? Underline details that tell how the Hudson River is used.

What exactly would make a waterway important to an area?

How does the author support the opinion that the Hudson River is one of the nation's most important waterways?

A   by wondering what Hudson would think of the river if he saw it today

B   by providing examples of the kinds of ships that travel the Hudson

C   by pointing out that the river is the entry point for Manhattan

D   by explaining that the Hudson River inspired a school of painting

 DISCUSS IT

Think about the author's description of Henry Hudson. Turn and talk to a classmate about the kinds of sources the author could have used to support the claim that Hudson was "headstrong but courageous."

Read the passage. Then answer the questions.

Your Family Tree

1   Do you know where your family comes from? Have you ever wondered about your ancestors? Then you should think about creating a family tree. It will help you learn about yourself. It is also a fun activity to share with your family.

2   How do you begin? It's best to begin with a book, as a book will provide you with guidance. Elizabeth Shown Mills, who has written several books on tracing your ancestry, explains that a book will tell you how to find records of your ancestors and how to read the records so that you can extract important information.

3   Interviewing family members is also an important way to begin. Older family members can provide names and dates that you may not know. They can also point you to place names that may be significant in your family's history. Be careful when you interview family members, however. Some people are sensitive to their family's history. In these cases, it is important to be respectful of their feelings and their privacy.

4   Another pathway to follow in documenting your family's history is to target one or two specific stories. For example, do you remember an elderly uncle talking about coming over from Ireland? Follow up on that story. You may be able to get important names, dates, and places to help you in your search.

5   Scavenger hunts are also critical in family history research. A scavenger hunt is essentially locating various important family documents, like family albums, birth and death certificates, marriage certificates, old photographs, and diaries and journals. These pieces of information are important because they are primary sources, rather than accounts by family members who may or may not be reliable.

6   Researching family history can be confusing and cumbersome if you don't do one simple thing: begin with a narrow search of just one or two families. That means deciding whether you will trace your mother's father's family or maybe your father's mother's family. Don't be tempted to explore too many branches at a time because you will soon find yourself overwhelmed with information. Julianna Elmasri, a well-regarded genealogist, points out that failing to narrow a search in the beginning often leads researchers to abandon the project altogether.

A CLOSER LOOK

How does the author support the idea that scavenger hunts are important in researching a family tree? Underline the reasons or evidence the author gives to support this point.

> Which answer choice provides outside proof for the author's idea?

1 What evidence does the author provide to support the idea that you should begin by narrowing your search?

A The author explains that not doing so could be cumbersome and confusing.

B The author says that you should decide which branch of the family tree to trace.

C The author points to a genealogist who says people who don't narrow their search sometimes give up.

D The author insists that tracing too many branches will make you overwhelmed.

> What specific information can family members provide?

2 What are two reasons the author uses to support the claim that interviewing family members is an important place to begin research?

A Older family members may know names and dates that are important.

B Family members' privacy should be respected when they are interviewed.

C Family members may be sensitive to questions about the family history.

D Family members may know place names that are important in the family history.

E Family members may help you read important historical documents.

F Family members may want to share the activity with you.

> What kind of experience might make a source reliable?

3 Explain whether or not the author's sources for information are reliable.

_____

_____

_____

_____

Read the passage. Then answer the questions.

Ellis Island

1 Today, Ellis Island is a national park in New York Harbor near the Statue of Liberty. Here, tourists roam the grounds and look through the various exhibits. From 1892 to 1924, however, Ellis Island was a kind of gateway to this country. Many immigrants seeking a new life and those seeking to escape their homeland had to come through the island if they arrived in New York. In all, more than 12 million new immigrants were "processed" on Ellis Island. Their futures were determined right there in those halls by people they had never even met. This is the story of Ellis Island—a story that is at times heartbreaking.

2 In the late 1800s, immigrants came to the shores of the US from places like England, Ireland, Germany, Italy, and Russia. They took ships to Baltimore, Boston, and other US ports. But when they arrived in New York, most but not all were sent by ferry to Ellis Island.

3 The process for screening immigrants to the country was unfair. People who bought more expensive first- and second-class tickets on ships did not have to go through Ellis Island. They were simply asked a few questions and allowed to go ashore. The government granted the wealthier people this privilege because they said they were less likely to need the government's help. However, people who arrived in New York on cheaper tickets were sent through Ellis Island. Their experience was often humiliating.

4 The Ellis Island inspection usually lasted anywhere from three to five hours. First, the immigrants' names and ages, along with their answers to several questions, were made available to officials. Then the immigrants were examined by a doctor for signs of illness or disease.

5 The doctors' examinations were hardly what we would call thorough. Nor were they based on sound medical principals. A doctor watched immigrants file by in a line. He looked for obvious signs of physical or mental illness. If the doctor believed that a person was mentally disabled or might pose a health problem for the country, he would mark the person with chalk. Then another doctor would walk by the line and pull up each person's eyelid to check for disease. Again, if the doctor saw something indicating a person was unhealthy, he would mark the person with chalk. As Dr. Elizabeth Yew noted in her research about medical inspections at Ellis Island, "A total of six seconds was spent on each immigrant inspected on 'the line.'"

6   Detention facilities were used to house the unwell and the unwanted. As many as 20 percent of all immigrants were kept in detention centers. They were not allowed immediate entry to the country. Half of those were people marked with chalk. These included people with physical ailments that doctors attempted to treat. Some of those people had disabilities and were detained because they were not welcome in the

country. Women and children who were not accompanied by a man were also detained. So were people who were considered immoral and people who officials feared would come to depend on the government. Many of these people were deported—simply returned to their home country. As a result, some families were separated at Ellis Island. This led to the island's reputation as "the island of tears."

7   If all things went well, the immigrants went to the main registry hall. There, they were likely to wait several hours before being granted permission to stay in the country. Once granted permission, the immigrants were free to go and begin their new life in America.

1 Which of the following statements from the passage is an opinion?

   A "The Ellis Island inspection usually lasted anywhere from three to five hours."

   B "This is the story of Ellis Island—a story that is at times heartbreaking."

   C "Today, Ellis Island is a national park in New York Harbor near the Statue of Liberty."

   D "In all, more than 12 million new immigrants were 'processed' on Ellis Island."

2 Which reason from the passage supports the claim that the process for screening immigrants was unfair?

   A "The Ellis Island inspection usually lasted anywhere from three to five hours."

   B "But when they arrived in New York, most but not all were sent by ferry to Ellis Island."

   C "Then the immigrants were examined by a doctor for signs of illness or disease."

   D "People who bought more expensive first- and second-class tickets on ships did not have to go through Ellis Island."

3 Part A

How does the author support the idea that the process for checking people on Ellis Island was questionable?

A   by explaining that people who bought cheaper tickets to America were sent to Ellis Island

B   by pointing out that doctors examined people as they filed by in a line

C   by explaining that the immigrants had to answer a series of questions

D   by pointing out that Ellis Island was an entry point for many new immigrants

Part B

Which detail from the article supports the answer to Part A?

A   "In all, more than 12 million new immigrants were 'processed' on Ellis Island."

B   "Their futures were determined right there in those halls by people they had never even met."

C   "a total of six seconds was spent on each immigrant inspected on 'the line.'"

D   "First, the immigrants' names and ages, along with their answers to several questions, were made available to officials."

4 What are two reasons the author provides to support the idea that detention facilities were used to house the unwell and unwanted?

_____

_____

_____

_____

LESSON
22 Integrating Information from Multiple Sources

 **Introduction**

THEME: >>> **From Distant Shores**

Sometimes you need to use multiple texts to know enough about a subject to write about it. It is important to use more than one source so you learn as much as possible about the topic. Make sure you use reliable resources with information that is factual and up to date. To write or speak about the subject, you will need to combine the information from all the sources you used. Make sure you use facts, not opinions, unless you say a statement is an opinion.

Read the information from three texts. Then answer the questions.

"Lady Liberty"	"France's Gift"	"Facts about Liberty"
• Called "Liberty Enlightening the World" • Known as Statue of Liberty • Gift from France • Has been a welcoming symbol of freedom and independence to immigrants arriving in America	• Statue of Liberty given to US by France • Seven spikes on crown represent seven seas and continents • Holds tablet in left hand which represents knowledge • Holds flaming torch in right hand which signifies enlightenment	• Statue of Liberty is on an island in New York Harbor • Opened to the public on October 28, 1886 • Measures 151 feet high • Pedestal is 154 feet high • Symbol of freedom and independence

What information is given by more than one text? _____

_____

Write a paragraph about the Statue of Liberty using information from all three texts.

_____

_____

_____

_____

Read the first parts of two passages. Then answer the questions.

The Plymouth Colony

1 Almost 400 years ago, in September 1620, a small ship set sail from Plymouth, England. The ship was the *Mayflower*, and she was bound for Jamestown in what is now the state of Virginia. Aboard the ship were 102 passengers ready to set up a colony in the "New World." Some were people looking for a safe place to practice their religion. Today, we call them "the Pilgrims." The rest of the passengers were looking for a place to make a new home or set up a business. Some were just looking for adventure in a new land. The ocean voyage took 62 days. During that time, one person died and one baby was born.

2 A storm pushed the ship off course, and instead of landing at Jamestown, the *Mayflower* landed farther north on what is now Cape Cod in Massachusetts. When the colonists arrived, it was December and the weather was already cold. They knew it would be better to stay where they were than to journey south to Virginia. They built a few rough shelters, and some stayed on the ship. But it was a much colder winter than they expected. Illness struck many of the colonists, and by spring, only 44 of the colonists were still living.

Visiting Plimoth Plantation

by Niles Binford

1 Want to meet a Pilgrim? Care to visit the site where "the first Thanksgiving" was celebrated? You can (sort of), and you won't need a time machine to do it. You only need to spend a day at Plimoth Plantation.

2 Plimoth Plantation is located about two and a half miles from the site of the actual colonial village of the 1620s. That site lies buried under the modern town of Plymouth, Massachusetts. Plimoth Plantation is a historical theme park. It's one of several places around our country where role players in costume re-enact historical eras and events.

3 Walk through the gate of the high wooden palisade, and you're in an English village of 1627. Stroll among the houses, barns, shops, and animal pens. You'll see the men and women of the village about their daily tasks. Go ahead and talk to them. That's what they're there for. They speak in a 17th-century English dialect, but it's not hard to understand.

Think About It

How would you integrate information from these passages to write about the Pilgrims? The question asks you to think about how to combine information from each passage. When working with more than one source, it can be helpful to use a chart to list facts and details that appear in each article and in both. This can be a useful way of taking notes. Making a chart can help you identify and organize the most important information you read.

Complete the chart.

"The Plymouth Colony"	"Visiting Plimoth Plantation"	Both
• The first colonists from Plymouth, England, set sail for Jamestown on the *Mayflower*. • •	• Plimoth Plantation is located near the site of the colonial village. • • • •	• The colonists arrived in America in the 1620s. • •

Using information from both passages, explain what you know about the original Plymouth Colony. _____

_____

_____

_____

Continue reading the passages. Then answer the question.

A CLOSER LOOK
Underline information in the second part of each passage that would be useful in writing a report on the first Thanksgiving.

The Plymouth Colony *continued*

3   The colonists worked hard to build some houses from logs that first spring. They were fortunate when a Native American named Squanto visited their settlement. Squanto was able to speak English. He introduced Chief Massasoit of the Wampanoag tribe to them. The colonists and Chief Massasoit signed a peace treaty. The treaty allowed the colonists and the Wampanoag people to live together in peace for many years. The colonists helped defend the Wampanoag people from the nearby Narragansett tribe. The Wampanoag, in turn, helped the colonists by giving them food and teaching them how to plant corn, catch fish, hunt game, and collect wild fruits and nuts.

4   The people of England had a tradition known as Harvest Festival. It was held each year in the fall to celebrate the gathering of crops from the fields in preparation for winter. The colonists along with their friends from the Wampanoag tribe celebrated a Harvest Festival for several days that first fall. They feasted on deer, fish, and clams along with corn and corn bread.

5   From then on the colonists, who called their home Plimoth or Plymouth, grew in number as more people arrived from England. Over the next 50 years, 7,000 people moved to the colony. After the Revolutionary War, this colony became a part of the state of Massachusetts.

Visiting Plimoth Plantation *continued*

4   Ask them about their lives and work. Only don't call them "pilgrims." They'll look at you quizzically. The Plymouth colonists did not use that word for themselves. It only became popular in histories written 200 years later. And don't ask about "the first Thanksgiving," either. They won't know what you mean. Oh, they may tell you about the harvest festival of 1621 that they celebrated with the Indians. But don't expect them to have much good to say about the "Native Americans." (That's another term that will confuse them.) They'll express the intolerance the English settlers generally had toward native people and their ways.

5   As for the Indians, they're here, too. Just downhill from the English village, by the water's edge, is the homesite of the Wampanoag, the indigenous people of the region. You'll find traditional Wampanoag wetus, dome-shaped houses covered with bark or reeds. The native people are not actors and do not role-play. Most are actual Wampanoag, while others come from native communities across the United States. They'll talk to you about customs and demonstrate crafts native to the Wampanoag.

6   A five-minute drive away, you'll find the *Mayflower II*, a full-scale replica of the sailing ship that brought the real Plymouth colonists to Massachusetts. That's part of the exhibit, too. Walk through the ship, talk to the sailors, and observe maritime artisans at work on shipboard crafts.

7   When your touring is done, you may want to step back into the 21st century for a treat at the ice-cream parlor across the street.

> Look for the words *Thanksgiving* and *Harvest Festival.*

If you wrote a report, what might you say about why people at Plimoth Plantation would not understand what you meant by the word *Thanksgiving?*

A   They had nothing to be thankful for.

B   Thanksgiving is not an Indian word.

C   They called it *Harvest Festival.*

D   They had only corn and meat to eat.

DISCUSS IT

With a partner, make a chart that shows the similarities and differences in the second parts of both passages. Discuss how you would integrate the information from both passages to use in a report.

A CLOSER LOOK

Figuring out how to put together information from multiple sources is one goal of research. These passages include different details about similar topics. In both passages, underline details about why butterfly populations are declining.

Read the passages. Then answer the questions.

adapted from Monarch Butterflies

1   Monarch butterflies can fly as far as 3,000 miles during migration, and they are the only butterflies in the world to make this type of migration. What's more amazing is that it's not the same butterflies making this journey each year. It's their offspring!

2   The life of monarch butterflies starts as eggs on milkweed plants. The eggs hatch in about four days. Once they hatch, they are called larva or caterpillars. They stay in this stage for around two weeks, and they pretty much just eat and eat and eat. By eating the milkweed plant, they make themselves toxic to predators and thus less likely to be eaten.

3   When the caterpillar is done growing, it will attach itself to a stem or leaf and transform into a chrysalis. The next 10 days are very busy for caterpillars. This is when they are going through metamorphosis and actually changing into butterflies! When the monarch emerges, it begins feeding on flowers, laying eggs, and just enjoying the next few weeks of its life. They only live 2–6 weeks.

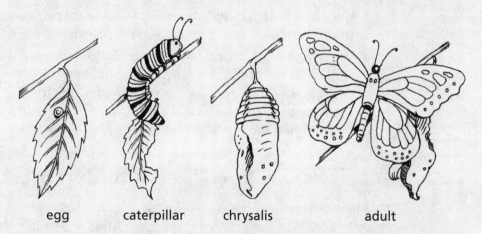

egg   caterpillar   chrysalis   adult

4   In early spring from February through March, the eggs hatched are known as first-generation monarchs. They lay the eggs of generation number two. The second generation of monarchs is born in May through June, and the third generation will be born in July through August. All of these monarchs will go through exactly the same life cycle as the first generation, dying 2–6 weeks after becoming fully grown butterflies.

5   The life cycle of fourth-generation monarchs is different than that of the first three generations. The fourth generation is born in September through October, and goes through exactly the same life cycle as the other generations except that they don't die in a few weeks. This generation of monarchs will

actually live for 6–8 months. However, they can't live through the winter in the northern United States because of the freezing weather. This fourth generation migrates south to Mexico. Remember, these butterflies have just gone through metamorphosis. They have never been anywhere other than where they emerged from the chrysalis stage, much less Mexico! Yet they find their way, and they stay there until spring. Then they migrate back north to lay eggs, and the whole process begins again.

6   As with many animals in our world today, the monarch population is in decline. The trees in the habitat they depend on in winter months are being cut down. The number of milkweed plants they need to feed on during the growing stages of their life cycle are fewer and fewer. However, there are things we can do to help:

- Plant milkweed in your garden. Even just one plant can feed several monarch caterpillars, and you'll get to watch them grow through their life cycle!
- Plant a garden specifically for butterflies. This type of garden includes flowers that bloom from spring until fall so it will help migrating and breeding monarchs. The garden can also include areas for butterflies to drink and to bask in.
- Encourage others to grow milkweed plants or not to mow down milkweed they may already have growing on their land.
- When buying lumber, look for the Forest Stewardship Certified seal. This means the lumber was harvested in an ecologically responsible way and was not harvested in the Monarch Butterfly Biosphere Reserve (a location in Mexico set aside as a wintering location for monarchs).

adapted from **Plant a Butterfly Garden**

1   Most butterflies live only a few weeks in their glamorous, winged stage of life. The majority of their lifespan is spent in other stages: egg, caterpillar, chrysalis, then adult (with wings).

2   The female lays her eggs on a plant for a good reason. The caterpillar that hatches from the egg uses the plant as food, eating almost enough for a lifetime. During the chrysalis stage, the caterpillar transforms into an adult. This transformation is called metamorphosis. Then, the adult butterfly feeds on fruits or the nectar of flowers.

Picky eaters

3   Butterflies and their caterpillars can't eat just any plant. Many are very picky. They must eat whatever plants have evolved along with them in their own neighborhoods. There are over 45,000 species of butterflies. Each species evolved eating the flowering plants that

grew in their own neighborhoods. Over tens of millions of years, the butterflies and their favorite plants have lived happily together.

4 Then people came along and mixed up the plants. They brought new plants from other parts of the world and planted them as crops or gardens or road landscaping. Some of these plants grew so well that they started to choke out the native plants. Lots of native plants got bulldozed away so people could build houses or shopping malls or ballparks. Even in the city parks and gardens, the green lawns, flowers, and trees were not natives. Trees and flowers growing in California may have evolved in Africa or Australia! Many of the native butterflies couldn't eat these foreign plants, and the plants they could eat were getting harder to find. So the butterfly populations dwindled. Actually, 90 percent of insect species can eat only the plants that are native to their own regions.

Feed the hungry butterflies

5 There is a way you can help them! You can plant a butterfly garden. It is just a matter of finding out what plants used to grow in your own backyard before people came. You may be able to find a book or website describing the native plants of your location. Then find a nursery or website that sells the seeds or the plants. You will need nectar plants for the adult butterflies and host plants for the caterpillars.

6 For example, many species of adult butterflies feed on the nectar of milkweed flowers. But only monarch caterpillars can eat the milkweed plant itself. Milkweed is common and widespread, so monarch butterflies are widespread as well.

7 Plant a garden of your local butterflies' favorite foods, and you will have a beautiful garden of flowers and butterflies. And don't cut off those flowers when they look dead. Leave them alone so they can turn into seeds or berries to feed the native birds. The plants will also reseed themselves so that they will return the next year.

8 Your butterfly garden will help the butterflies, plants, and birds continue to live happily together. You will be able to enjoy watching them interact with each other.

> **What are the stages of the butterfly life cycle?**

1 To integrate information from both passages, you could write about when the insect attaches itself to a stem or leaf and transforms to an adult. This stage of life is called _____.

   A egg

   B adult

   C chrysalis

   D caterpillar

> **Which passage talks about monarch butterfly migration?**

2 How would you describe what happens to monarch butterflies born in the fourth generation each year?

   A They freeze to death in the northern states.

   B They flock together to keep warm.

   C They lay eggs before flying to Mexico.

   D They fly to Mexico for the winter and then north in the spring to lay eggs.

> **Skim both articles, looking for information about foods that attract butterflies.**

3 If you were going to make a presentation to your class about raising a food plant for monarch butterflies, which plant would you discuss? Use details from both passages to describe why you chose this plant.

_____

_____

_____

_____

Read two passages. Then answer the questions.

Whales

1   When people describe something large, they often say it was "as big as an elephant." But if they are describing something even larger than an elephant, they might say it was "as big as a whale." In fact, blue whales are the largest living creatures on Earth. They can grow from 70–90 feet long and weigh 150 tons.

Mammals

2   Whales live in the ocean. Although they share the ocean with fish, they are not fish. Whales are marine mammals. That means they are warm-blooded animals that live in the ocean. Whales can live in some of the coldest parts of the oceans because a thick layer of fat, called blubber, protects them from the cold water.

Blowholes

3   You may recall that fish breathe through gills. Whales do not have gills. They have lungs and must breathe air just as you do. They can't get oxygen from the water as fish do. That means whales must come to the surface of the water to breathe. A round opening in the top of the whale's head allows it to take in air and blow out carbon dioxide as it breathes. This round hole is called a blowhole because sometimes the whale blows out water with the carbon dioxide and shoots a huge spout of water into the air. Some whales have one blowhole, and others have two.

Food

4   There are about 90 different species of whales. They eat many different kinds of animals found in the oceans. It is surprising that some of the largest whales, like the blue whale, have no teeth. They just swallow some of the smallest organisms like plankton. Other species of whales, such as the killer whale, have teeth. They may chase, attack, and eat

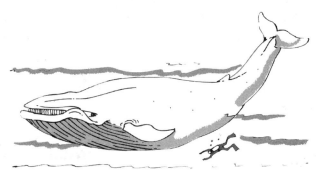

blue whale compared to a diver

other marine mammals such as seals. Fish, squid, crabs, and shrimp are also eaten by whales.

5   Whales find their prey by echolocation. They send out sounds that are clicks or buzzes. Then they listen for the sound that echoes back to them after bouncing off prey such as a school of fish or something that is not food, like a rock. The echo tells them which direction to swim and how far away the prey is. The echoes also help the whale avoid running into rocks when swimming at night or in deep, dark waters.

Hunting

6   Whales are one of the most dangerous animals to hunt, yet, for many years, they were hunted. Ships would set out with a crew of men and be gone sometimes for years as they searched the oceans for whales. Some of the meat was eaten, but mostly whales were hunted for the oil that could be made from their blubber. Whale oil was used to burn in lamps and to make soap. Other parts of the whale were used in ways we use plastic today—to make things like fishing rods and umbrella spokes.

7   Large-scale whaling—the hunting of whales—continued into the 20th century. Whales are still hunted by some countries today. All this whaling killed off so many whales that some nearly became extinct. When people began to realize that some whales, such as the giant blues, were nearly gone, many countries made it illegal to hunt whales. Today, some species of whales are recovering, and their populations are growing.

Whale Watching

8   Today, many people enjoy whale watching. Off the New England coast, boats take visitors out to see the humpback whales as they breach, or rise above the water to breathe. Sometimes they slap their tails, spraying the visitors with water. Whale watching tours are available in many areas along the coastlines. If you can't go on a whale watching tour, there are many exciting videos of whales. Check the Internet and your public library.

adapted from Right Whale

How did the right whale get its name?

1   Whalers gave the name "right" whale to this species because they thought it was the right (correct) whale to hunt. The whale was easy to kill because it swam slowly and once dead, it floated. This made it easier for the whalers to pull the whales onto ships and to shore to boil the blubber for oil. Whale oil was used in lamps and for heat until the late 1800s.

What do they look like?

2   The North Atlantic right whales do not have the dorsal fin that most great whales have. They have a broad (wide) back, paddlelike flippers, and wide triangular flukes. They are mainly black in color with varying amounts of white on their undersides.

3   The right whale is a baleen whale, meaning it has no teeth but uses baleen plates to strain its prey. The baleen plates in the mouth of a right whale are made of fingernail-like material called keratin that hangs down inside the mouth. Right whales have between 200 and 270 plates of baleen on each side of the mouth.

Where do they live?

4   The North Atlantic right whales live mostly near the coasts and the shelf waters, but they can be found offshore in deeper

Right Whale

water. They range from Nova Scotia, Canada, to the southeastern United States. In the summer, they feed in the waters off Cape Cod, Massachusetts, and in the Bay of Fundy and the Scotian Shelf. The location of most of the population during fall and winter is unknown.

What do they eat?

5   The diet of the North Atlantic right whale consists mainly of plankton (copepods), though they sometimes eat krill. They use baleen plates to filter out these tiny prey from the water. The right whale feeds by "skimming." It swims through a swarm of prey with its mouth open and its head partly above water. When it has filtered a mouthful of prey using the inner bristles of its baleen plates, it forces the water out of its mouth, dives, and swallows the food.

What are their predators?

6   The right whale has no known predators. Human activities are the main threat to the right whale's recovery.

How many North Atlantic right whales are there in the ocean?

7　Scientists estimate there are only around 300 animals left. This makes them one of the most endangered species in the world. North Atlantic right whales produce few calves to replace deceased animals.

Why are they in trouble?

8　The right whale was the first great whale to be hunted regularly by commercial whalers. Today most right whale deaths are caused by human activities. Ships hit right whales accidentally because the whales rest, socialize, and feed near the surface. They also become entangled in fishing lines stretching hundreds of feet. Entanglement can keep the whales from eating, breathing, or swimming. Lines cutting into their skin can also cause fatal infections.

What is being done to help them?

9　National Oceanic and Atmospheric Administration (NOAA) Fisheries is working to protect these animals in many ways. They set limits for when certain fishing gear can be used in areas where right whales are found. NOAA Fisheries is also working on new ways to help ships and whales avoid each other. They are also researching other things that may be harming the population, like contamination from pollution, noise in the ocean, and whether they have enough food available to them.

1 Part A

One reason both passages give for the population of whales dropping is _____.

A　whale hunting

B　they have no teeth

C　they use echolocation

D　they are mammals

Part B

What text evidence in both articles *best* supports your answer to Part A?

_____

_____

_____

_____

2 Which details from the passages would you combine to explain why whale populations are now growing larger?

    A Passage 1: "Today, many people enjoy whale watching."
       Passage 2: "They set limits for when certain fishing gear can be used."

    B Passage 1: "There are about 90 different species of whales."
       Passage 2: "The location of most of the population during fall and winter is unknown."

    C Passage 1: "Many countries made it illegal to hunt whales."
       Passage 2: "NOAA Fisheries is working to protect these animals in many ways."

    D Passage 1: "Whales are still hunted by some countries today."
       Passage 2: "Other things may be harming the population, like contamination from pollution."

3 Using information from both passages, describe how whales eat. Cite text evidence to support your answer.

_____

_____

_____

_____

_____

_____

_____

_____

4 If you were writing a report on right whales, explain why you would use both passages.

_____

_____

_____

_____

Integration of Knowledge and Ideas in Informational Text

Read the articles. Then answer the questions.

adapted from A Short History of Jamestown

1   On December 6, 1606, three ships: the *Susan Constant,* the *Godspeed,* and the *Discovery* sailed from England to North America. The ships carried 104 English men and boys to the Virginia colony. They landed in 1607 and named their settlement Jamestown after the English King, James I. Jamestown became the first permanent English settlement in North America. At the time, the land was inhabited by the Powhatan and their ruler, Chief Powhatan. Soon after the English arrived, the suffering began.

2   By June 15, 1607, the settlers had built a fort for protection from possible attacks by the Indians. A ship had been sent back to England for more supplies. Soon after the ship left, the settlers began to come down with a variety of illnesses and diseases. They were drinking water from the salty or slimy river, which was one of several things that caused the death of many. The death tolls were high. They were dying from swellings, fluxes, fevers, famine, and sometimes wars. Food was running low, but Chief Powhatan began sending gifts of food to help the English. If not for the Powhatan Indians help in the early years, the settlement would most likely have failed.

3   By late 1609, the relationship between the Powhatan Indians and the English soured because the English were demanding too much food. That winter of 1609–10 is known as the "Starving Time." During that time, the English were afraid to leave the fort for fear of Indian attacks.

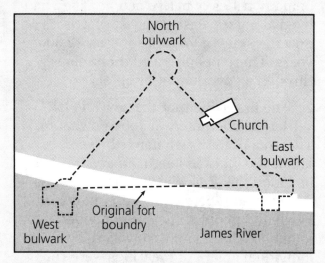

They ate anything they could, including various animals and even leather from their shoes and belts. By early 1610, 80–90% of the settlers had died due to starvation and disease.

4   In May 1610, more settlers arrived at Jamestown. They found Jamestown in shambles with parts of the fence that surrounded the fort torn down. Gates were off their hinges, and food stores were very low. They almost left, but another fleet of ships arrived from England bringing supplies, more settlers, and a new governor.

5   The newly arrived settlers helped Jamestown grow and prosper. They planted tobacco crops that were sold in England to make money for the colony.

6   Peace was established between the Powhatan Indians and the English when an Indian woman named Pocahontas was married to settler John Rolfe in 1614. But

in 1622, peace ended when the Powhatan chief became tired of the English taking over the Indian lands. He ordered an attack on the settlers in the area, and many were killed. For the next ten years, fighting continued between the English and the Powhatan tribe. During that time, more English settlers arrived and moved onto Powhatan land.

The Powhatan Indians

1   Long before 1607 when Jamestown became an English settlement in North America, the coastal lands were the home of many tribes of native people. They had lived along the eastern coast of what is now the state of Virginia for over 12,000 years. These people ruled themselves through a government by chiefs.

2   The first tribe that the new English settlers encountered was the Powhatan. The area of the Powhatan tribe was about 100 miles in length and width and included the area where Jamestown was established. There were more than 25,000 Powhatan people. They were divided into about 30 tribes, and each was ruled by an individual chief. All the tribes were ruled by the supreme Chief Wahaunsunacock.

3   The life of the Powhatan was much different from that of the English settlers. From the very beginning, this caused problems. It was the Powhatan way to be respectful and helpful to newcomers. The Powhatan men were hunters and brought gifts of wild game. The women raised gardens and gathered wild fruits and nuts. These were also given to the English settlers. The English were eager to get this help, but when they continued to expect food and made more demands, the chief told his people to no longer give help. The relationship between the Powhatan and the English became unfriendly. Without the Powhatan food gifts, the English began to go hungry. They became afraid to leave Jamestown for fear of attacks by the tribes.

4   Pocahontas was a favorite daughter of the chief. During the time of unfriendliness, she was captured by the English. While at the Jamestown settlement, she met and married an Englishman named John Rolfe. The chief gave his blessing to the marriage, and some peace was restored between the Powhatan and the English. The couple soon had a son they named Thomas. The Virginia Company that supported the Jamestown settlement sent the couple to visit England. While they were there, Pocahontas became ill and died.

5   John Rolfe returned to Jamestown where he had been experimenting with growing tobacco. The crop did well, and more settlers came from England to farm the land. The English needed more and more land for growing tobacco, and they began pushing the Powhatan from the land they had always lived on. Tensions between the English and Powhatan rose higher and higher.

6   One day in March 1622, the Powhatan attacked the English settlements. Of the 1,200 English living there, about 350–400 were killed. The Powhatan expected the English to pack up and leave, but that did not happen. Instead, a time of war began between the English and the Powhatan.

7   For more than 20 years, fighting continued. In 1644, a peace treaty was signed between the Powhatan and the English that stated the boundaries of the English land. The Powhatan were not allowed to be on English land unless it was for official business. Eventually, other treaties were signed giving the Powhatan less and less land.

8   Today about 3,400 Powhatan live in Virginia. Most have blended in with the general population. The Powhatan

language is no longer spoken, and the tribes almost disappeared. But some members of the Powhatan did not want that to happen. In the 1980s, they worked with the state of Virginia for official recognition, and seven tribes received it. Some tribal members are still working to get official recognition by the US government. That has not yet happened.

1 Part A

What did the Powhatan do when the English colonists first arrived at Jamestown? Use information from both passages to answer the question.

_____

_____

Part B

Which statement *best* supports your answer to Part A?

A   The English tried to help the Powhatan as much as possible.

B   The English expected the Powhatan to help meet their needs.

C   The coming of the English was a good thing for the Powhatan.

D   The English and Powhatan were always able to live in peace.

2 Explain what happened at Jamestown in March 1622 and why. What did the Powhatan think would happen afterward? Use information from both passages in your answer.

_____

_____

_____

_____

3 What happened in 1644 that finally ended the fighting between the English and the Powhatan? Use both passages to answer the question.

A   Pocahontas married John Rolfe.

B   The English planted more tobacco.

C   A peace treaty was signed setting land boundaries.

D   So many English came that the Powhatan left the area.

4 What information does the illustration give you that the text does not?

_____

_____

_____

_____

Read the passages. Then answer the questions.

Life Among the Plains Indians

Plains Indian Village

1 The Plains Indians lived a very different life from that of the native people in the eastern woodlands. The plains are vast grasslands in the middle of the United States. They range from west of the Mississippi River to the Rocky Mountains. They stretch from northern Mexico to southern Canada.

2 A large number of different tribes of Indians lived on the plains. They included the Sioux, the Cheyenne, the Lakota, the Arapaho, and many others. All of these people were nomadic. That means they did not live in one place for a long period of time. Usually they traveled to follow the vast herds of Buffalo that they hunted.

3 When the Plains Indians killed a buffalo, they did not waste any part of the animal. The hide was used to make tents, clothing, bags, drums, and blankets. The meat was eaten fresh, or it was dried to eat later. The bones were made into knives, tools, and sled runners. Other parts were used to make thread, ropes, and glue.

4 Men and women of the plains tribes had very different roles. Men were trained to be hunters from the time they were young boys. It was their job to supply the tribe with meat.

5 Their hunting often took them far from their camps, and they could be gone for days or weeks. The women remained in the camps, caring for the children. One of their most important jobs was to tan the buffalo hides. They used hides

Buffalo

to construct clothing and make tepee coverings. The women also prepared the meat the men brought to the camps and cooked meals. A few of the tribes did some farming, and that also was a job for the women.

6   Children of the plains tribes were well cared for by their parents. Babies were carried by their mothers on cradle boards. As they grew older, boys copied their fathers by riding play horses. Girls would make tiny tepees and play with dolls made from hide. Girls were trained by their mothers to do women's chores. Boys were expected to be strong and brave. They received a lot of training in hunting, fighting, and riding a horse. When their skills were judged good enough, they were allowed to go on their first hunting trip with the men. At about age 17, each young man went in search of his spirit by spending time alone in the wilderness. When he returned, he was allowed to join the warriors for the rest of his life.

7   When Europeans began to arrive in the lands of the plains tribes, it changed their way of life forever. Many of them now live on reservation lands, but they strive to maintain many of the tribal traditions. Many parents instruct their children in the ways of their ancestors. Schools on the reservations teach the languages and customs of the people so they can be passed on to future generations.

adapted from Plains Indians

1   The Plains Indians used different methods of communication from writing on buffalo hide to using mirrors to signal streaks of reflected light. The Plains Indians did not have a written language with letters and words. Instead they used drawings on cave walls, or smoke.

Fire Signals

2   Fire signals were used at night. During a fire signal, the person trying to communicate or get help would light the fire, and then run in front of it or around it. Indian scouts could decode this signal easily. Running around the fire meant danger was around and to "go away, get out of here!"

Smoke Signals

3   A common signal used by the Plains Indians was a smoke signal. Because the plains were flat, smoke signals could be seen for miles. They sent a message by changing puffs of smoke from short to long. Some messages were a warning, others were simpler messages such as "come home, supper's ready."

Blanket Signals

4   Blanket signals were used by warriors. These signals were used to communicate with someone who could not hear the sender but who could see them. Waving a blanket in a wild manner meant danger and to get away as fast as possible. This signal often gave the tribe a few precious extra moments to get ready for an attack.

Mirror Signs

5   The Plains Indians did not invent the mirror. A white man brought it to their camp. However, they came up with a creative way to use it as a signal. The Plains people did not trade for these mirrors to look at themselves. Instead, they used the mirror as a signal. By pointing the mirror straight at the sun, reflective rays would shoot into the sky warning people within miles that there was danger. Mirror signals were common because the mirror was portable and the signal could be sent while on horseback.

petroglyphs on rock

daily life, their heroes, and their battles. These drawings on cave walls and rocks can also be warnings.

Sign Language

7   Not all Plains people spoke the same language. To communicate with other tribes, including their own, they developed a language using hand movements. This language was and still is called "sign language." Over time the language spread and all Plains tribes used it.

8   Usually each tribe, also known as a band, had a "talker." This was a person that could translate the sign language by speaking it. The "talkers" understood over 3,000 signs! Some of the "talkers" could sign as fast as you can speak!

Picture Signal

6   Plains Indians also communicated by drawing pictures, or symbols, on cave walls, rocks, and scraps of buffalo hide. These pictographs told the stories of their

5   Which text features tell you more about the lives of the Plains Indians in each passage?

A   the final paragraph in the first passage; the photo in the second passage

B   the roles of men and women in the first passage; the role of smoke signals in the second passage

C   the list of tribes in the first passage; the caption in the second passage

D   the captions in the first passage; the headings in the second passage

6   What evidence from the first passage supports the point that the Plains Indians did not always live in peace?

A   The Plains Indians were nomadic.

B   There were many different tribes living on the plains.

C   Boys received training in hunting, fighting, and riding a horse.

D   Boys were expected to be strong and brave.

7 If you were going to write a report about warriors of the Plains Indians, what details from both passages would you include?

_____

_____

_____

_____

_____

8 How did the Plains Indians adapt to changes from their interaction with Europeans? Use details from both passages to support your answer.

_____

_____

_____

_____

_____

This unit will help you with all your writing. You will learn why it is important to edit your work. You will learn more about the different types of writing. All writers write with a purpose, and these lessons will help you understand these different types of writing. You will also learn more about the rules of English. These rules help make your writing clear for the reader.

LESSON 23 The Writing Process takes you through the five steps of the writing process. You will learn about prewriting, drafting, revising, editing, and publishing. You use this process every time you write.

LESSON 24 Argumentative Writing helps you learn more about argumentative writing. It will explain how to write a piece that persuades someone to take action or to respond. It will help you determine your argument and support it with facts and examples.

LESSON 25 Informational Writing is about the type of writing you do most in class. You will learn about the characteristics of this type of writing. You will also learn how to organize your writing so it is clear to the reader.

LESSON 26 Narrative Writing will help you write a story with a clear beginning, middle, and end.

LESSON 27 Rules of English reviews the grammar and writing conventions that help you write clear and well-thought-out sentences.

LESSON 28 Vocabulary focuses on vocabulary development. You will learn about word relationships. You will also create new words by using affixes.

LESSON 23

The Writing Process

Introduction

Writing is a process—something you do in steps. Most writers follow five steps:

Prewriting ➔ **Drafting** ➔ **Revising** ➔ **Editing** ➔ **Publishing**

An easy way to remember the writing process is to think of what you do in each step. In the **prewriting** step, you plan what you will write. You might make an outline or use a graphic organizer. The **drafting** step is when you actually write. After that, you go back for the **revising** step. This is when you make changes to what you have written. Once you are satisfied with the draft, the next step is **editing** what you have written. You fix any spelling errors, or punctuation and grammar mistakes. Finally, you **publish** your writing.

Step 1: Prewriting

In this step, you plan what you will write by thinking about:

- why you are writing (your purpose)
- what you will write about (your subject)
- what you will say (the content)
- how you will say it (your voice)
- who will read it (your audience)

Sometimes, however, you are writing for a test. Then some of these things are already decided for you. For example, read this question from a test.

Robots like C-3PO and R2-D2 in the *Star Wars* movies are very different from the robots that exist in real life today. Write an article for your school newspaper that compares and contrasts the robots of science fiction movies with real robots.

In your article, be sure to include:

- how science fiction robots and real robots are similar

- how they are different

This question tells you the purpose (to compare and contrast), the subject (robots), and the audience (the students in your school). The rest is up to you. You need to work out the content—what information you will present and how you will organize that information. Many writers begin by underlining the important words as above and jotting down notes.

Sometimes it helps to use a graphic organizer when you are planning your writing. For this assignment, you might use a comparison and contrast chart like this one.

Robots

What's Different?

Movies	Real Life
• They look and act more like humans than machines.	• They look more like machines than humans.
• They are programmed to do things like translate languages and deliver secret plans.	• They do work that is boring or dangerous.
• They can be loyal friends.	• They don't really have feelings or emotions.
• C-3PO has "creativity circuits," which allow him to tell stories.	• They have artificial intelligence, so they can do things like move around objects and pick things up.

What's the Same?

They are mechanical devices.

They are designed to do work that is usually done by humans.

They replace humans in certain kinds of jobs.

For different types of writing, other graphic organizers like these may be helpful.

- **Cluster map or web**—This organizer can help you get your ideas on paper for many kinds of writing.
- **Venn diagram**—A Venn diagram can help you organize your ideas when you want to compare and contrast two things.
- **Sequence chart**—A sequence chart is best when you are writing a narrative. It helps you map out events in the order they happen.

Step 2: Drafting

After you have planned what you will write, it's time to put your ideas into sentences and paragraphs. This step is **drafting.** Don't worry about spelling and grammar at this point. You can change things later. The important thing now is to write down your ideas.

There are two ways to draft what you want to write. One is to brainstorm or free write. This is when you just start writing, letting your ideas move forward. This works well for some writing tasks. You can write as you think about what you want to say. However, you will probably need to spend a lot of time revising what you have written.

The other way is to work from the prewriting plan you made. This is much easier because you have organized most of your ideas about what you want to write. Make sure you have a clear main idea and that you support it with details. Each paragraph should have its own main idea. Use transitions and a strong conclusion. Here is a draft that could be written based on the comparison and contrast chart on page 284. Robots in movies look and act more like humans then machines.

Real robots look more like machines then humans. R2-D2 and c-3PO, the robots in the Star Wars movies, have lots of human characteristics. They feel loyal, and form friendships. They do things like translate langauges and deliver secret plans. R2-D2 can only beep and whistle. C-3PO even has creativity circuits that enable him to make up stories.

The real robots we have today are more like smart machines. They have artificial intelligence and can do jobs in factories. They do dangerous work like handling toxic materials and defusing bombs. You can buy a robot vacuum cleaner. It's a flat oval machine that moves over the floor. It senses where dirt is and goes there to suck it up. When its done, it goes back to it's base.

The robots in sci-fi movies and real robots have some things in common They do work that is normally done by humans and can replace humans in certain kinds of jobs.

Step 3: Revising

Once you have finished your draft, the next step is **revising.** In this step, you read what you have written and make changes to improve your work. You make sure that what you have written is clear to your readers.

When you revise, you might need to change the content of your work, or you might want to rework its structure. Asking yourself these questions can help you decide what changes you should make to improve what you have written.

Content
- Does my writing have a main idea?
- Have I included enough supporting details?
- Is there any place where I should add an important detail or example?
- Have I included details that are not important and should come out?
- Does my writing have an introduction and conclusion?

Structure
- Is my writing organized in a way that fits the topic?
- Are my relationships between my ideas clear?
- Do I need to add words, phrases, or sentences to make them clearer?
- Do my sentences clearly express the point I want to make?
- Are my sentences well written?

Peer Review

Sometimes for class writing assignments the teacher might have students work in pairs to edit each other's papers according to a rubric. Then the students can review the comments and revise their work accordingly. This is known as **peer editing** or **peer review.**

When writing for a test or a classroom assignment, you may receive a rubric that lists what is expected for a range of scores. Sometimes one rubric is used for the whole writing task. Other times two rubrics are used. A score is given for topic development, ideas, organization, and use of language. Another score is given for the use of standard English—how well you observe the conventions of sentence structure, grammar, and capitalization. Rubrics for writing may differ but they should look something like the one on page 287.

SAMPLE RUBRIC

Score 3

- The writing answers all parts of the question.
- There are at least two clear comparisons and two clear contrasts.
- Transitional words and phrases connect the ideas.
- Each paragraph has a topic sentence that clearly states the subject.
- Supporting details are organized in a logical order.
- The writing is easy to read and stays on the subject.
- There are almost no mistakes in grammar, capitalization, punctuation, and spelling.

Score 2

- The writing answers almost all parts of the question.
- There are two generally clear comparisons and two contrasts.
- Transitional words and phrases connect most ideas.
- A topic sentence stating the subject is missing or unclear.
- Some supporting details are missing or are not in a logical order.
- The writing is fairly easy to read and mostly stays on the subject.
- There are some mistakes in grammar, capitalization, punctuation, and spelling.

Score 1

- The writing answers only part of the question.
- There are fewer than two comparisons or two contrasts.
- Very few transitional words and phrases are used to connect ideas.
- More than one topic sentence is missing or unclear.
- Many supporting details are missing and are not in a logical order.
- The writing is not easy to read or is off the subject in many places.
- There are several mistakes in grammar, capitalization, punctuation, and spelling.

Step 4: Editing

When you have revised your work and are happy with it, the next thing you do is **edit** your work. This means that you reread what you have written and check that everything is right. You look for mistakes in grammar and usage. You also look for mistakes in spelling, capitalization, and punctuation. You proofread to make sure that

- subjects and verbs agree
- pronoun forms are right
- punctuation marks are used correctly
- all words are spelled correctly
- names are capitalized
- titles are underlined or in quotes

When you proofread, you use some of these marks to show your changes.

Proofreading Symbols	
∧ Add letters or words.	List ideas ∧about your topic.
⊙ Add a period.	That is not true⊙
≡ Capitalize a letter.	R2-D2 and c̲-3PO are loyal.
⊂ Close up space.	They form friend⊃ships.
⋏ Add a comma.	There are robots today⋏but they are different.
/ Make a capital letter lowercase.	The R̸obots today are different.
¶ Begin a new paragraph.	¶ Real robots look like machines.
⌿ Delete letters or words.	Real robots look like ~~real~~ machines.
∿ Switch the position of letters or words.	The robots ⌐are⌐ today⌐ like machines.

Step 5: Publishing

Once you are satisfied that you have corrected any errors or problems with your work, you are ready to publish it. Publishing means to share it with others. This is the final form that your readers will see. Publishing can take many forms. You can share your work with friends or family. Or, you can post it on a bulletin board or include it in a class booklet. Another way to publish your work is to post it on the Internet in a blog or on a website. You can publish your work in a slideshow. Publishing can also mean just turning your work into your teacher or writing it on a test.

Read the revision. Look for changes. Then answer the questions.

The robots we see in movies often make us think that

robots are science fiction and that there are no robots in

real life. That is not true. There are robots today, but they

are not exactly like the robots we see in movies.

Robots in movies look and act more like humans ~~then~~ *than*

machines. ~~Real robots look more like machines then humans.~~

R2-D2 and c-3PO, the robots in the Star Wars movies, have lots

of human characteristics. They ~~feel~~ *are* loyal, and *they* form friendships.
languages
They do things like translate ~~langauges~~ and deliver secret plans.

~~R2-D2 can only beep and whistle.~~ C-3PO even has creativity

circuits that enable him to make up stories.
Real robots look more like machines than humans.
~~The real robots we have today are more like smart machines.~~
they
They have artificial intelligence and can do jobs in factories.
robots
~~They~~ do dangerous work like handling toxic materials and
There are also robots that do household chores.
defusing bombs. You can buy a robot vacuum cleaner. It's a flat

oval machine that moves over the floor. It senses where dirt is
it's   *its*
and goes there to suck it up. When ~~its~~ done, it goes back to ~~it's~~

base.
science fiction
The robots in ~~sci-fi~~ movies and real robots have some things
they
in common. They do work that is normally done by humans, and

can replace humans in certain kinds of jobs.

Think about what the reader needs to know when reading a text. What information did the new paragraph give the reader?

1 Why did the writer add the first paragraph?

_____

_____

_____

_____

Think about the structure of the text. Consider what the reader needs to know first, second, and last.

2 Why was a sentence moved from paragraph 2 to paragraph 3?

_____

_____

_____

_____

Some sentences provide important details that support the main idea. Some sentences provide details that are unnecessary or unrelated to the main idea.

3 Why was a sentence taken out of paragraph 2?

_____

_____

_____

_____

Read the question carefully. Then answer the questions.

Which is a better way to watch a movie, at home or at the theater? Write an essay that compares and contrasts the two ways to watch a movie.

When writing your essay, be sure to do the following:

- follow all the steps of the writing process
- tell how the two ways are alike
- tell how the two ways are different

1 To understand what the question is asking, look for key words and underline them. Write the key words below.

_____

_____

_____

_____

_____

2 What type of graphic organizer would you use to organize your ideas?

   A web

   B time line

   C Venn diagram

   D cause-and-effect chart

3 Now that you have thought about the topic and organized your ideas, write a draft of your essay.

_____

_____

_____

_____

_____

_____

_____

_____

_____

_____

_____

_____

_____

_____

_____

_____

Revising, Editing, and Publishing

- Revise your draft to organize your writing. Is your central idea clear? Do the facts and details support your central idea? Are your sentences well written?

- Proofread to check for correct spelling, grammar, capitalization, and punctuation. Have a peer edit your work if appropriate.

- To publish, write or type your final answer on a separate sheet of paper and turn it in to your teacher.

LESSON 24

Argumentative Writing

 Introduction

When you write an **argumentative** piece, you are trying to convince or persuade the reader of something. Usually you are trying to **persuade** the reader to agree with something or take action on an issue. You need a strong argument to do this. A strong argument is supported with facts, reasons, and examples. If you want the reader to agree with your point of view, you must support it. You should also think about the opposing point of view and offer points of your own that counter these opposing points of view.

Argumentative writing can be an essay, a letter to the editor, an email, or a column in a newspaper. Start your argument by stating your opinion. Your **opinion** is what you think or believe. You support this opinion with **facts,** or statements that can be proven. Your concluding statement should sum up your argument.

Start your argumentative writing by stating your opinion right away. Then give reasons and information to convince your readers. Your concluding sentence should sum up your ideas with a strong ending.

 Guided Practice

Read the question. Then answer the questions.

Your friends have asked you to write a short letter to convince your school principal that the lunch menu should be changed to include pizza every day. Be sure to state your opinion clearly in the opening sentence. Use facts and examples, not opinions, in your supporting sentences. Arrange your supporting points in order of importance.

Here is one student's response:

Dear Principal Arnold,

For a number of reasons, I strongly believe that pizza should be available every day on the school lunch menu. First of all, the kids at school will be happier if they like something on the menu every day. Second, because most kids love pizza, it's a great way to make sure they're eating lunch. In addition, pizza is easy and not that expensive to make. With the right ingredients, pizza can provide kids with all of the food groups!

Most important, pizza can be healthy and low in fat—if it's made using fresh, wholesome ingredients like wheat flour, low-fat cheeses and meats, and a variety of vegetables and toppings.

If pizza were on the school lunch menu every day, the student population would be happier and healthier. I really think pizza every day is the way to go.

Sincerely,

Jake Morelos

What is the main point?

1 What is Jake's topic statement?

_____

_____

How does Jake sum up his argument?

2 What is Jake's concluding statement?

_____

_____

Do you think the statement is effective?

3 Does it work well? Why or why not?

_____

_____

Read the writing prompt below. Follow the writing process in Lesson 23 to craft your writing. Write your response on a separate piece of paper.

Think about someone who you know who deserves an award. Write an argumentative essay telling the reader what award this person deserves and why he or she deserves the award. Be sure to include details and ideas that will make readers agree with your opinion.

LESSON 25
Informational Writing

Introduction

An informational piece usually answers a question or gives information. A good informational piece is well supported by facts, details, and examples. **Informational writing** is what you do when you write a report or answer a test question. It is the kind of writing you do most often. Unlike narrative writing, informational writing should be factual, not personal or creative. It should be clear and direct. The reader should know right away what you are writing about.

Informational writing needs to be well organized so that the reader can follow what you want to say. You can organize informational writing by main idea and detail, cause and effect, comparison and contrast, or a sequence of steps.

Guided Practice

Read the question. Then answer the questions.

You have been asked to write directions for younger students explaining how to use the computer to find information for a project. Write a passage with the directions you will give for searching the Web. Be sure to put the steps in order and include all the steps that you usually follow. Explain any terms you think readers won't be familiar with.

Here is one student's response:

Looking up information on the web can seem confusing at first. Sometimes it's hard to know where to begin. Here are some basic steps you can follow to find the information you are looking for.

First, choose a topic that you would like to learn more about. Next, using your computer, choose a search engine that will help you find websites about your topic. Then, pick some keywords about your topic. Try to be as specific as you can. Next, type your keywords into the search engine and press the return key. After you press the return key, you will see a list of websites about your topic. Finally, choose a website that you want to read more about and click on it. These basic steps will help you more easily located the information you are looking for on the web.

What text structure did the student use?

1 How did the student organize her directions?

_____

_____

How did the student transition from point to point?

2 What transitional words did she use?

_____

_____

Read the time line and the question. Then answer the question.

The Life of Dr. Martin Luther King Jr. (MLK)

1928

January 15 MLK is born in Atlanta, GA.

1935

September MLK begins school at an all black elementary school in Atlanta, GA.

1944

June MLK enters Morehouse College in Atlanta.

1948

February MLK is ordained a Baptist minister. He enters the Crozer Theological Seminary in Chester, PA.

1953

June MLK and Coretta Scott are married.

1954

October MLK becomes pastor of the Dexter Avenue Church in Montgomery, AL.

1955

June MLK receives his Ph.D. in theology from Boston University.
December 1 Mrs. Rosa Parks refuses to give up her bus seat to a white man in Montgomery, AL.
December 5 MLK leads a year-long boycott of the Montgomery buses.

1957

January The Southern Christian Leadership Conference is founded. Dr. King is chosen president.

1959

February MLK visits India and studies Mahatma Gandhi's methods of nonviolent protest.

1960

January MLK becomes co-pastor of the Ebenezer Baptist Church with his father.

1961

May "Freedom riders" (groups of black and white people who ride buses through the South to challenge segregation) leave Washington, DC, by bus. The bus is burned by opponents of desegregation, and the riders are beaten upon arrival in Birmingham, AL.

1963

April 12 MLK is arrested and jailed (for the thirteenth time) during a march in Birmingham, AL.
August 28 250,000 people demonstrate in Washington, DC, for civil rights. MLK meets with President Kennedy and delivers his "I Have a Dream" speech.

1964

December MLK is awarded the Nobel Peace Prize.

1965

The 1965 Voting Rights Act, which King sought, is signed by President Johnson.

1968

April 3 MLK delivers his last speech, "I've Been to the Mountaintop."
April 4 MLK is assassinated in Memphis, TN.

Read the information. Follow the writing process described in Lesson 23 to craft your writing. Write your response on a separate sheet of paper.

Your teacher has asked you to write a report for the class about the life of Dr. Martin Luther King Jr. Write three or more paragraphs about Dr. King's life based on the time line.

- Make sure your first paragraph states the main idea of your report.

- Be sure to use transitional words like *first, next,* and *finally* to connect facts and events in the order in which they happened.

LESSON
26 Narrative Writing

1 Introduction

Have you ever written a story? If you have, then you have done **narrative writing.** A narrative is a piece of writing that tells a story. Narratives can be about many different things. You can tell a fictional, or make-believe, story or a story based on real events. You can even write in story form about things that have happened to you.

Narrative writing tells a story with a clear beginning, middle, and end. A personal narrative is based on events that happened to the writer over a short period of time. A **personal narrative** might be about the first time you met a cousin or a time you were frightened. You write a personal narrative in the first person, using the pronouns *I* and *me.*

A creative narrative is a story that has been made up. Short stories and novels are creative narratives. Even though the plot is made up, writers usually use details and information from real life to make their stories come alive for readers. The details of a narrative should usually be presented in the order in which they happened. A narrative should also be set in a particular time and place, called the **setting.** The time might be "yesterday" or "once upon a time." The place could by your classroom or outer space. The last sentences of a narrative should pull the story together.

2 Guided Practice

Read the question. Then answer the questions.

Write a story for your class about a time you had to go to the doctor. Choose a visit when something interesting happened. Arrange your details in time order. Be sure to include clues to the setting.

This is what one student, Tasha, wrote:

My last visit to the doctor's office happened when I broke my finger while chasing after Nipper. Nipper was my puppy, and she had gotten out of the backyard that morning. I had no idea that my visit to Dr. Smith's office would be such an interesting one.

On the way to Dr. Smith's office, I was feeling scared because I didn't know what was going to happen to my finger. I was also very sad about losing Nipper that morning. She was such a special member of the family.

When my mother and I walked into the doctor's office, I heard a yelping sound, like a dog howling. The strange sound made me forget about my finger. All I wanted to do was to get up and check out the room from which the sound was coming. My mother told me to just sit quietly and wait for the doctor, but I couldn't. The yelping was loud, so I ran across the office toward the sound. There was Nipper!

A man had brought her to Dr. Smith's because he had found her nearby. Her paw was hurt. I threw my arms around Nipper and sat beside her as Dr. Smith put a splint on my finger, I had no idea that my visit to Dr. Smith's office would end up reuniting me with Nipper.

What is the topic sentence?

1 What specific event did Tasha focus on?

_____

_____

What text structure did she use?

2 List the words or phrases Tasha used to show time order.

_____

_____

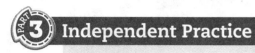

Read the prompt. Follow the writing process described in Lesson 23 to craft your writing. Write your response on a separate sheet of paper.

Write a narrative that tells about a time when you were excited about an upcoming event. Describe the event and why you were excited about it. In your narrative, be sure to include a beginning, middle, and ending.

LESSON 27 Rules of English

 Introduction

Good writing starts with good sentences. Choosing the right word is important in writing. Correctly using punctuation and possessives is also important to creating good sentences. Knowing and using the rules of grammar and usage will help you in your writing.

Comma

A **comma** is used to separate the speaker and verbs such as *said, asked, answered,* and *exclaimed.* If the speaker comes before the quotation, a comma follows the verb.

> Kmiko said, "I want to be an engineer."

If the speaker comes after the quotation, and there is no question mark or exclamation point, a comma is used before the quotation mark.

> "This backpack is very heavy," said Steven.

A comma is used to separate the name of a person being spoken to from the rest of the sentence.

> Jessie, are you going home now?
> I'll be leaving in a minute, Ben.

A comma is used after words that introduce a sentence or connect it back to the sentence that came before. Sometimes these are single words like *yes, no, well, indeed, however,* and *therefore.*

> Yes, I'd like to see the basketball game.
> However, I may have to clean my room on Saturday.

A comma is also used to separate another question that is part of a sentence.

> That's you calling me, isn't it, Jared?

A comma is used to separate an introductory element from the rest of a sentence.

> Today, I will be leaving for vacation.

A comma is used to separate items in a series.

> The United States flag is red, white, and blue.

Quotation Marks

Quotation marks are used before and after the titles of short works such as stories, poems, magazine articles, chapters in a book, songs, or TV shows.

> STORY: "The Necklace"
> POEM: "Chicago"

CHAPTER: "After the Revolution"
SONG: "America the Beautiful"
TV SHOW: "American Idol"

The titles of longer works such as books, magazines, movies, and plays are underlined or put in italics.

BOOK: *Ramona the Pest*
MAGAZINE: *Smithsonian*
NEWSPAPER: *The New York Times*
MOVIE: *Charlie and the Chocolate Factory*
PLAY: *Wicked*

Possessives

A possessive noun shows ownership. A noun can be made to show ownership by changing its form.

A picture of my **family** is on the desk. (noun)
My **family's** picture is on the desk. (possessive noun)

To make a singular noun possessive add an apostrophe and an -*s* as you did to family. A singular noun that ends in *s* still has an apostrophe and an -*s* added.

Hilda's gloves are on the table.
Mrs. **Kass's** tulips are blooming.

To make a plural noun that ends in s possessive add an apostrophe only.

The **students'** reports were on display.
The **Smiths'** house was being painted.

To make a plural noun that does not end in *s* a possessive noun, add an apostrophe and an -*s*.

The **children's** notebooks were collected for review.
The **mice's** footsteps could be heard.

Sometimes it is hard to tell if a word is a possessive noun or a plural noun just by hearing the word spoken. For example, *teachers, teacher's,* and *teachers'* all sound the same. However, by looking at the spelling of the word and the way the word is used in a sentence, you can determine what it is.

The **teachers** are meeting today. (plural noun)
The **teacher's** meeting is today. (singular possessive noun)
The **teachers'** meeting is today. (plural possessive noun)

Possessive Pronouns

Possessive pronouns are pronouns that show possession or ownership of something. Just as subject pronouns replace nouns as subjects, so possessive pronouns replace nouns that show possession.

Miranda washed **Miranda's** dishes. (possessive noun)
Miranda washed **her** dishes. (possessive pronoun)

Singular possessive nouns are *my, mine, your, yours, his, her, hers, its.*
Plural possessive nouns are *our, ours, your, yours, their, theirs.*

Some of these possessive pronouns are always used with nouns. These include *my, your, his, her, its, our, their.*

Other possessive pronouns always stand alone, which means nouns do not follow them. These include *mine, yours, his, hers, its, ours, theirs.*

I think that notebook is **mine.**
This is my blue jacket. **Hers** is on the chair.

Sentences

Sentences are the building blocks of writing. A sentence is a group of words that expresses a complete thought.

Every sentence has two parts: a subject and a complete predicate. The subject tells the person, place, thing, or idea that a sentence is about. It also tells who or what is doing the action in a sentence. The predicate tells something about the subject. It identifies what the subject does, is, has, or feels.

Our teacher <u>wants us to turn in a permission form.</u>

The subject in the sentence above is Our teacher.
The predicate is <u>wants us to turn in a permission form.</u>

A complete subject can be one word or several words. The key word in the complete subject is the simple subject. It identifies what the subject is about. The simple subject is often a **noun,** although sometimes the subject is a pronoun.

Subject Pronouns

Singular	Plural	
I	we	<u>She</u> filled out the permission form.
you	you	<u>It</u> was easy to fill out
he, she, it	they	<u>We</u> will turn it in tomorrow.

A complete predicate, like a complete subject, can be one word or several words. The key word in the complete predicate is the simple predicate, or verb. The verb may be a single word, or it may have a helping verb.

Birds sing.   The birds <u>are singing</u>.

Verbs such as *sing* are called **action verbs.** Action verbs are sometimes followed by an object. An object, like a subject, is often a noun and can be one word or several words. The object receives the action of the verb. Look at the object nouns underlined in these sentences.

I play the <u>piano</u>.

We sing <u>"The Star-Spangled Banner"</u> during assembly.

An object can also be a pronoun. Look at the object pronouns underlined in these sentences.

Object Pronouns

Singular	Plural	
me	us	We sing <u>it</u> every day.
you	you	Jared heard <u>them</u> outside.
him, her, it	them	

Verbs such as *is, were,* and *seem* are called **linking verbs.** The verb "links" the subject and the noun after the verb. Here each linking verb is in bold type, and the noun it connects to the subject is underlined.

　　Those books **are** <u>novels</u>.　　　Lara **is** a <u>heroine</u> in that novel.

Subject and Verb Agreement

For a sentence to be correct, the subject and the verb must agree in number. That means that if the subject is singular, the verb must be singular. If the subject is plural, the verb must be plural. Remember, singular means one; plural means more than one. In the following examples, the subject is underlined once, and each verb is underlined twice.

　　The <u>horse</u> <u>pulls</u> the wagon. (singular)
　　Two <u>horses</u> <u>pull</u> the plow. (plural)

Generally, singular verbs in the present tense end in *s* or *es.*

　　The <u>student</u> <u>finishes</u> her homework. (singular)

Plural verbs in the present tense do not end in *s* or *es.*

　　The <u>students</u> <u>finish</u> their homework. (plural)

However, if the singular subject is *I* or *you,* this rule does not apply. The verb does not end in *s* or *es.*

　　<u>I</u> <u>finish</u> my homework. (singular)

A compound subject is two or more simple subjects joined by and or or. A compound subject and its verb must also agree in number. When the subjects are joined by *and,* the verb is plural. This is true whether the subjects themselves are singular or plural.

　　<u>Los Angeles</u> *and* <u>San Francisco</u> <u>are</u> in California. (two singular subjects)
　　<u>Apples</u> *and* <u>oranges</u> <u>are</u> popular fruits. (two plural subjects)

A compound predicate is two or more simple predicates joined by and or or. The verbs in a compound predicate must agree in number with the subject.

　　The <u>airplane</u> <u>makes</u> a loud roar *and* <u>rises</u> off the ground. (singular)
　　The freshly baked <u>cookies</u> <u>smell</u> great *and* <u>taste</u> good. (plural)

Fragments

A sentence needs both a subject and a predicate to express a complete thought. If one or both of these is missing, the sentence is incomplete. An incomplete sentence is called a sentence fragment.

Although a fragment may begin with a capital letter and end with a punctuation mark, it is not a sentence. A fragment may lack a subject, a predicate, or both.

> The dog in the house.

Run-on Sentence

A run-on sentence is two or more sentences that run together with commas or without any punctuation. This creates confusion because a reader does not know where one thought ends and the next thought begins.

> We will have to hurry now, we will be late. (comma)
> We will have to hurry now we will be late. (no punctuation)

There are two ways to correct a run-on sentence. One way is to write a complete thought as a separate sentence.

> We will have to hurry now. We will be late.

Another way is to use a conjunction to combine each complete thought to create a compound sentence. A compound sentence is made up of two simple sentences that are joined by a comma and a conjunction such as *and, or, but,* or *so.*

> We will have to hurry now, or we will be late.

Shifts in Verb Tense

Verb tense has to do with time. They help the reader know when something took place. Verb tense can reveal the time when something occurred or the sequence in which events happened. They also reveal the state or condition when used with linking verbs. Avoid changing verb tenses when you write.

There are three main divisions: the past, the present, and the future. The progressive verb tense shows an action in progress.

> I was walking to school when I saw Tim. (past progressive)
> I am walking to school today. (present progressive)
> I will be walking to school in the next half hour. (future progressive)

The perfect verb tense shows actions that occurred in the past.

> I had walked to school last week with Tim. (past perfect)
> I have walked to school with Tim before. (present perfect)
> I will have walked to school for three months. (future perfect)

The present perfect is a past action that occurred at some point in the past. Or, it is an action that began in that past and continues in the present. This is formed with either the verb *has* or *have* and the past participle that ends in *-ed*.

I have walked past his house twice.

The past perfect is an action that was completed before another past action. This is formed by using the verb *had* and the past participle of the verb.

I had walked by his house last night before he called.

The future perfect tense is an action completed before a set future time. An action needs to occur before another action. This tense is formed with the verb *will have* and the past participle of the verb.

I will have walked around the block twice before supper.

Conjunctions

Conjunctions are connecting words. They can join two subjects. Or, they can join two complete sentences to create a compound subject. Some conjunctions include *and, or, but,* or *so.* Correlative conjunctions like *either/or, neither/nor, not only/but also* are used in pairs. The elements that follow them should be parallel.

Karen is **not only** kind **but also** helpful.
Do you want to get **either** Chinese food **or** Italian food for dinner?

Prepositional Phrases

A prepositional phrase is a group of words that begins with a preposition (*of, in, on, to, into, for, at, from, with,* and *by*) and ends with its object, which is a noun. A prepositional phrase may also include words that describe its object.

Compare the following prepositional phrases. In each phrase the preposition is in bold type and its object is underlined. Notice the words used to describe the object in the second example for each phrase.

in the <u>park</u>   **in** the city's new <u>park</u>
up a <u>tree</u>   **up** a large oak <u>tree</u>

Sometimes you can combine two sentences by changing one of them into a prepositional phrase. Then you can add the phrase to the sentence that comes either before or after it.

The troop camped out overnight. They camped **in the park.**
The troop camped out overnight **in the park.**

**Edit the paragraph to correct all mistakes in punctuation and grammar.
Use standard proofreading marks to make your corrections.**

1

Early forms of transportation included wagon trains,

Thousands of people traveled across the plains and over

the mountains in canvas covered wagons. most of the

passengers were heading west because of the California

Gold Rush. Everyone wanted to get rich quickly? Many did

not make it and the trails became littered with broken

wagons dead animals and human skeletons. Do you think

you would have enjoyed traveling by wagon trains.

Replace each underlined group of words with a possessive noun.

2   the chalk belonging <u>to the teacher</u> _____

3   the whistles belonging <u>to the coaches</u> _____

Underline each action verb and its object.

4   The founding fathers of the United States adopted a system of
    government similar to that of the ancient Greeks.

5   They wanted a democracy.

Edit the paragraph to correct all mistakes in punctuation and grammar.
Use standard proofreading marks to make your corrections.

6

Beth knows that ants is fascinating to watch, so he decided to build an ant farm. Beths' friends wants to help. They ask she what materials to use. Beth tells they to gather the things on hers list. Her will supervise the building of the ant farm with the friend's materials. Beth and her friends researches ants to learn more about it. The friends or Beth plan to make a poster about ants. The girl's research has taught them that ants live in colonies, and different kinds of ants has different jobs. The queen lays eggs. She is larger than the other ants. Worker ants take care of hers. Soldier ants protect the colony. Beth and her friends also learn that some ants bite. Beth tells her friends, "Me and you will have to be careful! Us don't want to get bitten!"

Use specific adjectives to complete each sentence.

7 The _____ horses grazed on the prairie beneath the

_____ sky.

8 Visiting the _____ building was a(n)

_____ adventure for the whole family.

9 The _____ drizzle kept the _____ children
in the house all day.

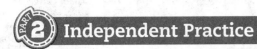

Read each sentence. Then circle the correct verb in parentheses.

10 A plumber (fix, fixes) a water leak.

11 Word games and video games (is, are) fun to play on the computer.

Read the sentence. Then circle the correct subject in parentheses.

12 The (rock, rocks) are sometimes slippery.

13 My (leg, legs) has a bruise from the last time I fell in the water.

14 My (friend, friends) were worried that I would drown.

Edit the paragraph to correct all mistakes in punctuation and grammar. Use standard proofreading marks to make your corrections.

15

Trains are an important part. Of the transportation

network. Across American and around the world. They

move both people and things from place to place. Carry

freight to major centers. The freight is then moved to

trucks. Take it to specific destinations.

Some people prefer traveling in trains. Train travel

is slower than flying most riders don't mind because

trains are more comfortable train travel is cheaper.

LESSON 28 Vocabulary

1 Introduction

Many words are made up of different parts. They include **prefixes, suffixes,** and **roots.** If you know what some or all of the word parts mean, you can usually figure out the meaning of the word.

Correct is the root word.

in-   correct   -ly

The prefix *in-* means "in" or "not."   The suffix *-ly* means "like" or "in that way."

So, the word *incorrectly* means "not in a correct way."

Prefixes

A **prefix** is a word part added to the beginning of a root. A prefix changes the meaning of a root to make a new word. The prefix *un-* means "not." If you add the prefix *un-* to the word *expected,* you have a new word that means "not expected."

Most prefixes come from Latin or Greek words. For example, the prefix *auto-* is from the Greek word that means "self."

Prefix Chart

Prefix	Meaning	Example
ambi-	both	ambidextrous
arch-	chief, main	archenemy
auto-	self	automobile
bene-	good, well	benefactor
bi-	two, between	bipartisan
bio-	life	biology
contra-	against	contradict
de-	do the opposite of, take away or off	deform, defrost
di-	separate, double	divide
dis-	not, do the opposite of	disunite
ex-	out of, separate from	extract, expatriot
fore-	before, in front of	foretell, forearm
mal-	bad	maladjusted
multi-	many	multipurpose
sub-	under, below	subzero
sym-, syn-, sys-	with, together	synchronized
ultra-	very much, overly, more than	ultramodern

Match a prefix with each of these roots to make a word that fits the new meaning.

Prefix	Root Word	New Meaning	New Word
	tell	to tell in advance	
	appear	stop being seen	
	modern	very modern	
	polar	involving two poles	

Suffixes

A suffix is a word part added to the end of the word. A suffix also changes the meaning of a word.

> Eric was *fearless* as he and his friends explored the hidden cave.

You know that the verb *fear* means "the feeling of being afraid." The suffix *-less* means "without," so you can figure out that Eric was not afraid when he was exploring the cave with his friends.

Many suffixes change words to different parts of speech.

WORD		SUFFIX		NEW WORD
fright *noun*	+	*-en*	=	frighten *verb*
cloud *noun*	+	*-y*	=	cloudy *adjective*
perish *verb*	+	*-able*	=	perishable *adjective*
soft *adjective*	+	*-ly*	=	softly *adverb*

Suffix Chart

Suffix	Meaning	Example	New Part of Speech
-able, -ible	able to be, tending to be	responsible	adjective
-ance, -ence	state of, condition of	resistance, reference	noun
-ation, -ion, -tion	act of, process of	cancellation, distribution	noun
-ful	full of, tending to	beautiful	adjective
-ism	action, process, practice	racism	noun
-ize	to make	familiarize	verb
-less	without	priceless	adjective
-ly	like, in the manner of	weakly	adverb
-ment	act of, result of	shipment	noun
-ness	quality of, condition of	goodness	noun
-ship	state of, condition of	relationship	noun

Match a suffix with each of these roots to make a word that fits the new meaning.

Root	Suffix	New Meaning	New Word
breath		without breath	
adjust		act of adjusting	
member		state of being a member	
public		make public	
enjoy		able to be enjoyed	

Roots and Word Origins

Prefixes and suffixes must be added to **roots** to make new words. The root is often a word that can stand on its own, but the root also can be a word part that cannot stand on its own. Roots may come from other languages, usually Greek or Latin. If you know what the root means and you know what different prefixes and suffixes mean, you can usually figure out the meaning of words.

> The senator had to stop his speech because of an *interruption* from the audience.

The word *interruption* has a prefix, a root, and a suffix. The Latin root *rupt* means "break" or "burst." The prefix *inter-* means "between" or "among." The suffix *-ion* means "the act of" or "the process of." So, you can conclude that an *interruption* means the act of breaking the flow of something, in this case a speech given to a group of people.

Root Chart

Root	Meaning	Example
aud	hear	audible
amphi	both sides	amphibian
aqua	water	aquarium
chron	time	chronograph
cycle	wheel, circle	bicycle
demo	people	democratic
duct	lead	conductor
graph	write	autograph
logos	study of	biology
min	small	minute
phono	sound	phonograph
port	carry	portable
temp	time	temporary
terr	earth	territory
tract	pull	retraction
vit	life	vitamin

Understanding **word origins** can also help you determine the meaning of unfamiliar words. In Greek mythology, Hercules was famous for his great strength and for performing twelve seemingly impossible tasks for his king. The word *herculean* comes from the word *Hercules* and means "laboring long and tirelessly." Narcissus was another figure in Greek mythology. He saw his reflection in a still pool of water and fell in love with his own image. The word *narcissistic* means "someone who admires himself excessively"—just like Narcissus did in the Greek myth.

Synonyms and Antonyms

Synonyms are words that mean the same, or almost the same, like the words above. They are all synonyms you can use to describe something very special. Knowing synonyms can help you be a better reader and writer.

Look for a pair of synonyms in these sentences:

Benjamin's cousins reside in Indianapolis. My cousins live there, too.

If you did not know the word *reside,* you could figure it out from the synonym *live* in the second sentence. Both sentences tell about the same thing—cousins in Indianapolis—and the word *too* is a clue that they are alike. You could exchange the synonyms and both sentences would mean the same thing.

Antonyms are words that mean the opposite of one another. Look for a pair of antonyms in this sentence.

> Randal has a severe case of flu, but Rachel has only a mild cold.

The words *severe* and *mild* are antonyms. The words *but* and *only* tell you that Rachel's illness is the opposite of Randal's.

Words with Multiple Meanings

Some words have multiple, or many, meanings. Although the words with multiple meanings may not be pronounced the same, they are spelled the same. A dictionary lists each meaning separately, usually with a number in front. Here are some of the meanings of the word *present:*

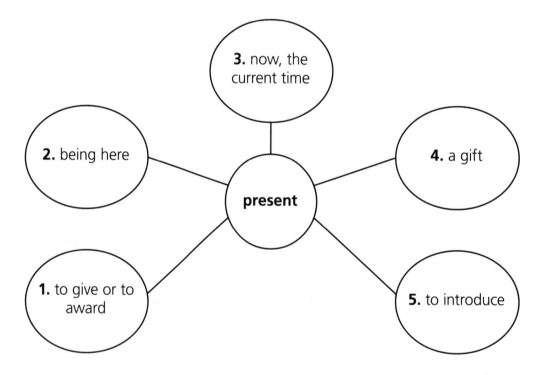

With so many meanings for one word, how can you know which meaning is correct? Sometimes reading is like being a detective. You need clues to find out what a word means. When you read a sentence, you can usually find clues to the meaning of a new word. Notice how a word is used in a sentence. Is it a verb (an action word), a noun (a person, place, or thing), or an adjective (a word that describes)?

> The head of the studio *presented* the television actors with expensive cars.

You can tell that the word *presented* is a verb in this sentence. The letters *-ed* at the end tell you that the action happened in the past.

Next, try to substitute the meaning for the word in the sentence. Here are two meanings of *present* that are verbs:

1. introduce

2. give

If you replace the word *present* with these meanings, only "give" makes sense.

Write the correct meaning of *present* for each sentence. Use the meanings in the word web.

Sentence	Meaning
William received a **present** for his birthday.	
Mrs. Garrett, let me **present** my neighbor, Mr. Tran.	
When the teacher took attendance, all the students were **present.**	
At **present** she is on the city council, but she would like to run for mayor.	

Context Clues

Your vocabulary is made up of all the words you know. You use many words when you speak and write, but you know even more words than the ones you use. Those are the words you understand when you listen or read.

Even if you don't know a word, you can often figure out its meaning from other words in the sentence or paragraph. These words are **context clues.**

Read this sentence from *The Phantom Tollbooth,* by Norton Juster:

> "What did they all do?" the Humbug *inquired*, suddenly taking an interest in things.

You may know that the word *inquired* means "asked." If you didn't know the word, you could figure out its meaning from the other words and ideas in the sentence. You have two context clues: the word *what* and the question mark. These clues tell you that the Humbug is asking a question, so *inquired* must mean "asked."

Punctuation, such as the question mark in the sentence above, may not always give you a clue. Usually, the context clues will be in the form of **synonyms, antonyms, examples, definitions,** or **descriptions.**

Type of context clue	Synonyms	Antonyms	Examples	Definitions	Descriptions
What they do	have nearly the same meaning	have opposite meanings	show what a word means	tell what a word means	tell more about a word

Synonyms

You learned about synonyms and antonyms on pages 315–316. A sentence or paragraph might use two **synonyms,** or words that have meanings that are nearly the same. If you know the meaning of one word, you can figure out the meaning of the other.

> Matt and Ryan *raced* for the finish line, but Ryan *sprinted* ahead and broke the ribbon.

The words *raced* and *sprinted* both tell about people running a race. Even if you didn't know the meaning of *sprinted,* you could figure it out from the context. Ryan went ahead of Matt and broke the ribbon, so he must have run very fast. In this sentence, *sprinted* means the same as *raced* or "ran very fast."

Antonyms

Antonyms are words that mean the opposite of each other. Look for a pair of antonyms in this sentence.

> Mom forbids us from playing football in the street, but she allows us to play in the parking lot.

The words *forbids* and *allows* are antonyms. The word *but* tells you that forbidding something is the opposite of allowing it.

Examples

Some sentences or paragraphs give **examples** that help show what a word means. Look at the word *communal* in the first sentence below. Can you figure out what it means from the paragraph?

> Getting ready for a picnic is a communal effort. Mom makes the sandwiches and salads; Dad puts the drinks in an ice chest; I pack the paper plates and napkins; and Rory collects the games.

What does *communal* mean? The examples show that everyone is helping to get ready for the picnic. You can figure out that *communal* means "involving all members of a group."

Definitions

Definitions are another kind of context clue. Look for a definition in these sentences:

> The sky over the bay was cerulean, the kind of blue that you see only on a clear, sunny day. It was the kind of blue that fills the sky and makes you think it must go on forever.

Cerulean [suh•ROO•lee•uhn] is a word that you may not see or hear very often. But you can still figure out what it means because the sentence gives you a definition: "the kind of blue you see only on a clear, sunny day." You can tell that *cerulean* means "sky-blue."

Descriptions

Sometimes a sentence will contain a **description** to tell you what a word means. Do you see the description in this sentence?

> Mr. Cory is proud of his authentic Civil War rifle that had been carried by a soldier in the Battle of Antietam.

The word *authentic* means "real." The sentence gives you a description of the history of the rifle. Because the weapon had been carried by a soldier, you know that it is not a fake.

Read this article about an inspiring teacher. Then answer the questions.

1 What would life be like without music? To Roberta Guaspari, it would be <u>unimaginable</u>. She loved playing the violin and wanted to share her love with others. She decided to become a teacher and teach New York City students how to play the violin.

2 Even though Guaspari was motivated to become a teacher, at first it was almost impossible for her to find a job. She was inexperienced. Most of the schools were underfunded. They did not have enough money to hire music teachers, especially one that had never taught before. Guaspari kept trying, and she was finally successful. A school in East Harlem hired her to teach music.

3 At first, the parents and children were doubtful about the program. Then Guaspari's determination won them over. The families soon learned that music had the power to transport them. Guaspari taught music for ten years. Then the program was cut because of lack of money. Guaspari decided to fight back.

4 Guaspari planned a concert. She needed everyone she knew to <u>cooperate</u>. She enlisted friends, students, parents, and other teachers to help. She held the concert at Carnegie Hall, a well-known concert hall. She even convinced famous violinists to perform.

5 When the concert was over, Guaspari had raised enough money to keep school music programs alive throughout New York City. Her story attracted national attention and inspired the 1999 movie *Music of the Heart.* Guaspari went on to become the cofounder of the music program Opus 118. This music program in East Harlem continues to support the artistic <u>development</u> of New York schoolchildren.

1 In paragraph 1, the word *unimaginable* means _____.

   A easy to imagine

   B possible to imagine

   C difficult to imagine

   D not possible to imagine

2 Read this sentence from the article.

"The families soon learned that music had the power to transport them."

This means that music had the power to _____.

A change people

B take people places

C make people athletic

D make people unhappy

3 When people *cooperate,* they _____.

A work apart

B work together

C disagree

D perform surgery

4 What is the meaning of the word *development?*

A able to develop

B to develop before

C the act of developing

D the state of being developed

5 Raising money for the music program was a task that could be described as _____.

A herculean

B narcissistic

C titanic

D siren

Read the passage. Then answer the questions.

1   Storytelling may be <u>entertaining</u>, but for the Navajo people, it is also a way to <u>preserve</u> their history and traditions. The Navajo are an ancient people who live in the deserts of the Southwest. They live <u>simply</u>, guided by the principles and beliefs of their ancestors. These American Indians pass down their history by telling stories. By listening to stories of the traditional ways, young people learn about the <u>values</u>, culture, and history of their people.

6   The word *entertaining* means _____.

A   fun

B   cute

C   grand

D   cheerful

7   To live *simply* is to live in a way that is _____.

A   busy

B   noble

C   plain

D   noisy

8   To *preserve* is to _____.

A   keep

B   praise

C   measure

D   command

9   The word *values* means _____.

A   facts

B   habits

C   victories

D   principles

Read the article. Then answer the questions.

A Day at the Fair
by Macy Noble

1   Many people are sad when August comes because it means the end of summer. Not me! I am excited when August rolls around because that means it's time for the Indiana State <u>Fair</u>. I love visiting the exhibits and seeing all the different animals and people. The fair is quite a <u>spectacle</u>!

2   One of my favorite exhibitions is the All the King's Horses show. You might not think of horses as athletes, but the Royal Lipizzaner Stallions will change your mind. These elegant <u>equines</u> dance to music and leap high into the air. The performance is fit for kings and queens. The stallions are truly <u>regal</u>.

3   The Jungle High Dive presentation is another show I never miss. Every time I see the daring dives, I have to catch my breath. The performers do a triple high dive and a fire dive. There are even some funny parts of the show to allow the audience to recover from the excitement of the death-defying stunts.

4   One of my favorite things to do with my younger sister is to take her to the Little Hands on the Farm exhibit. Agriculture is an important part of life in Indiana, and this exhibit shows her how food products travel from the farm to the table. She can feed chickens, milk a cow, and even <u>haul</u> hay for the animals. After she has been through the different barns, she can sell the products she collected at a mini farmer's market. Then she can use the money she earns to buy products at a grocery store. I especially enjoyed this exhibit when I was younger, so I'm glad I can share the experience with her.

5   This year, the fair will have added suspense for me. I am entering a peach pie in the baked goods category. We have many peach trees in our yard, so I have a lot of practice making pies with the sweet, juicy fruit from our trees. Hopefully the judges will agree with my family and friends that I make delicious pies. Every year, I bring home prizes from the <u>midway</u>, but this year I hope to bring home a shiny blue ribbon for my pie.

10   What is the meaning of the word *fair* as it is used in paragraph 1?

  A   an event with exhibits and rides

  B   neither excellent nor poor

  C   free from injustice

  D   attractive

11 A *spectacle* is _____.

   A an impressive sight

   B something that helps you see better

   C a person who watches an event

   D a dull event

12 *Equines* is another word for _____.

   A athletes

   B kings

   C exhibitions

   D horses

13 What is a synonym for the word *regal* in paragraph 2?

   A stallion

   B royal

   C elegant

   D athletic

14 What is the meaning of the word *haul* in paragraph 4?

   A carry

   B a load

   C a narrow passageway

   D a room for public gatherings

15 In paragraph 5, *midway* means _____.

   A part of the way home

   B the entrance to the fair

   C the exit to the fair

   D a path down the center of the fair with food and games

Write answers to the following questions on separate sheets of paper. For each question, take a few minutes to plan what you are going to write. Use notes, outlines, and other prewriting ideas from the writing process. Write the best first draft you can. Then allow yourself one revision. Each final draft should be about two pages long.

QUESTION 1

People often have hobbies or other activities that they enjoy and would like to share with others.

Think of an activity or hobby that you would like others to consider doing. Write a personal narrative that tells how you became involved in the hobby or activity, describe what it is, and explain why it is important to you.

QUESTION 2

Your teacher would like to create a class list of favorite books. Write an essay about a favorite book you would recommend. Write your opinion of the book and provide reasons why you think others should read this book.

In your argumentative writing, be sure to

- include a topic sentence that clearly states your opinion
- support your opinion with a least three good resaons

GLOSSARY

A

Acts: the divisions of a play

Anecdotes: personal stories

Antonyms: words with an opposite meaning

Autobiography: a biography written by the subject

B

Biography: a story that tells about a person's life

C

Cast: the characters in a play

Cause: the reason something happens or what made it happen

Characters: who a story is about

Chronological order: the order in which things happen

Comparison: how two things, actions, or ideas are alike

Conclusions: details figured out by putting together information from a story

Conflict: a problem or struggle in a story

Connotation: a suggested idea or feeling toward a word

Contrast: how two things, actions, or ideas are different

Convince: to make someone feel sure

D

Definition: words that tell what another word means

Dialogue: the words characters speak in a play

E

Effect: the result or thing that happens

Evidence: proof

Example: word description that helps show what a word means

F

Fable: a story, usually involving animals, that teaches a lesson

Fact: a statement or information that can be proven true or false

Fairy tale: a story with imaginary qualities and qualities of magic

Fantasy: a story in an unreal setting with talking animals and unreal creatures

Fiction: a made-up story

Figurative Language: language that is not meant literally

Folktale: a story that teaches a lesson or explains how something came about

---

G

Genre: the type of literature

H

Historical fiction: realistic fiction that takes place in a past time period

Hyperbole: an exaggeration

I

Imagery: visually descriptive language

Inferences: information figured out with details from the story and what you know

---

J

Judgments: personal opinions

L

Legend: a story from the past about people, places, and events

---

M

Main idea: the most important idea of a paragraph or story

Metaphor: the comparison of two like things without using the words *like* or *as*

Moral: concerned with principles of right and wrong

Myth: a story that explains something about nature or a people's customs or beliefs

---

N

Narrator: the person who tells the story or describes the events to the audience in a play

Nonfiction: a true story with facts

O

Opinion: something that someone believes or thinks

P

Personification: giving human characteristics to a concept or object

Play: a story performed by actors on a stage

Plot: the events or actions of a story

Poetry: a story full of musical language with rhyming or rhythm

Point of view: who is telling the story

> **First-person:** the main character is telling the story; uses first-person pronouns *I* and *we*

> **Second-person:** the author is narrator; uses second-person pronoun *you*

> **Third-person:** narrator is limited to knowledge of the thoughts and feeling of only one of the characters; uses third-person pronouns *he, she,* and *they*

Prefix: part of a word added to the beginning of another word that changes the meaning of the word

Prior knowledge: what you already know about a topic before reading

Props: objects used by characters in a play

R

Realistic fiction: a made-up story that could have happened

S

Scene: a division of an act in a play

Scenery: backgrounds and larger objects that create the setting of the play

Science fiction: a story that takes place in an unreal setting with some science facts for the background story

Sequence: the order in which things happen

Setting: where and when a story happens

Simile: a type of figurative language that compares two unlike things using the words *like* and *as*

Stage directions: how actors should move and speak on stage

Stanza: a group of lines within a poem, similar to a chapter in a book

Suffix: part of a word added to the end of another word that changes the meaning of the word

Summary: a few sentences that tell the main idea and most important details of a story

Symbolism: a symbol that stands for something else

Synonyms: words that have a similar meaning

T

Theme: the topic or subject or main idea of a story

Tone: the mood or feeling of a story